ISBN 978-1-330-60428-1
PIBN 10081317

PREFACE

TO

THE BUDDHIST TRACTS.

THE Mahávansi, Rájá Ratnácari, and Rájávali, although containing the train of national history, and recording the events most materially connected therewith, attach such an absorbing importance to the doctrine of Guadma, as renders it highly desirable, and indeed necessary, to give that extension to this work which the following original tracts supply. Collected in Ceylon by Sir Alexander Johnston, from the same sources as those which supplied the histories, and thereby stamped with a species of official guarantee for their authenticity, it may be confidently hoped that their contents will contribute to enlarge our means of examining the dogmas of the Buddhist faith, as prevailing in this beautiful portion of our Indian empire.

The collection commences with three series of *Seventeen Questions* each, and one tract of *Ninety Questions*, proposed by the Dutch governor to the most distinguished Buddhist priests on the island, on the chief points of their doctrine; and although some of the questions do not evince much acumen on the part of the propounder, yet, as the exoteric or popular sense of the system may be fully gathered from the import of the answers, their acquisition, in our present state of comparative ignorance of Buddhist literature, may be deemed both interesting and instructive. Although the dogmas of Guadma fall far beneath the kindred writings of Nipal for ethical refinement, yet these replies demonstrate their growth from the same root. One example may suffice to illustrate this assertion. Mr. Hodgson was justly struck with surprise at the Nipalese statement respecting the creation of man; his remarks thereon are contained in the 2d volume of the "Transactions of the Royal Asiatic Society," page 234, and the ninth note in the Appendix to that paper. The reader who will take the pains of comparing these passages with the details in pages 16 and 157 of this volume, will perceive their perfect conformity.

If again we examine the reply made in the shorter tracts to Query 5, "*How sin entered into the world?*" *avarice and anger* are stated in each answer. The fatal effects of anger, by introducing death into the visible creation, we know from higher authority; and the enlarged sense given to the expression "*avarice,*" in the reply of the Mahábadda priests, namely, "*the love of riches,*" is sufficiently indicative of that base passion of the heart which he who read its inmost recesses terms the root of all evil. The true meaning of the answer, rendered "*stupidity and thoughtlessness,*" must be deemed very ambiguous; but the probable meaning may be drawn from the *Ninety Questions*, page 157, *which refers sin to the corrupted and mischievous temper of man.*

The list of manuscripts contained in the chief Viháris, although it merely presents the titles of these literary stores, yet exhibits extensive classes, on various subjects, which would probably yield much important information; and therefore it may be deemed a step to acquire a knowledge of the titles of Buddhist collections of tracts, especially when, as in the present instance, they are accompanied by comments or notices on their contents, however scanty.

The Pittakas, Winne Sútras, and Abidharma, contain a classification of some of the most important doctrines of Guadma; the Mahávansi regularly referring to them as the treatises which are most in request.

The tract on the transport of the Bogaha-tree to Ceylon, is rendered valuable from its connexion with the account of the lakes, those great and stupendous national works, which are so honourably mentioned and eulogised in the report made by command of the British Government on the present state of the island of Ceylon. The same official paper makes mention of a curious exhibition of the dátú of the Buddha, so often named in the histories, taking place in 1828, before a vast concourse of Singhalese resorting for that purpose to Kandy: the deep-rooted influence of the doctrine cannot be more strongly exemplified than by quoting this fact.

The *Jutakas* may probably appear to many of our readers as flat and insipid. Three of the most esteemed by the Singhalese, namely, Bombadat Rájá, Useratenam Rájá, and Wessantara, were, in fact, so characterised in a French review of " The Doctrine of Budbism," which appeared in the "Journal Asiatique" of Paris, January 1830. It may be deemed sufficient in justification of their publication, simply to state the rank which these books always occupy in Buddhist literature; which fact may be safely rested on Note I, conveying so clearly the sentiments of a Buddhist Œnanse on these tales; the influence also which their doctrine of individualism exclusively illustrates, being the main hinge of the metempsychosis, the manifestations of the thoughts and words of Guadma, as embodied in these tales, are eagerly consulted for moral guidance when in similar circumstances. This point was not deemed either trivial or unimportant by avowedly the best-informed individual on Buddhist literature which France possessed, the deeply regretted M. Abel Rémusat; and his remarks are also subjoined, that this point may rest on its true merits.

In discussing the dogmas which influence and exercise the belief of millions of our race, entertainment is not so much the object of our efforts as the knowledge of facts: it is probable that these translations may express somewhat obscurely their scope and sense; but no alteration has been made in the original words, lest their real meaning might be perverted: matters of narration may be often successfully corrected by the context, but matters involving ethical points are rarely made clearer by emendations.

The minor treatises, such as the Púja to the Buddha, the question of the lawfulness of taking oaths, and the remarks on the priests' dresses, &c., having been so often referred to in the histories, were thought entitled to insertion.

Although every effort has been made by the Editor to render this collection available for the elucidation of the Buddhist faith and its literature, he is well aware that much remains undone; but it may be hoped that future research will present us with histories that blend with Indian epochs, and thus enlarge our knowledge of essential facts. The dialectics of Buddhism may amuse, but they rarely instruct us; while every relic of really authentic history we can rescue from the oblivious cloud which at present enshrouds all Indian records of the past, must be deemed alike interesting to the public, and highly useful as illustrative of the character of our species.

NOTE I.

"There is a tradition among the Cingalese, that one of the kings of Hindostanee, immediately after Budhu's death, collected together 500 learned ascetics, and persuaded them to write down on palmyra leaves, from the mouth of one of Budhu's principal disciples, all the doctrines taught by Budhu in his life-time. The Cingalese admit that they received their religion from the hands of a stranger; and it is probable that it was propagated in the Burman empire soon after its reception in Ceylon, that is, about 450 years after Budhu's death. The Burmans believe, that 650 years after that event, in the reign of Muhumoone, Booddhughoskû, a brahmin, was deputed to Ceylon to copy the work Vishooddhimargu, which includes all the jutakas, or histories of the incarnations of Budhu; and it is fabled, that the iron style with which he copied this work was given him by a heavenly messenger, though others will have it that Budhu-Sutwu gave it to him.

"These jutakas are said to have amounted to 550 books,

some of which are, however, lost. A work called the Ten Jutakas is now the best known, and is held in the highest veneration. The names of these jutakas are Timee, Junishu, Sooburmu-ramu, Nenee, Muhoshutla, Bhoouduttu, Chuda, Koomaru, Nardu, and Wessantara. Since the above period, many Burmans have translated and commented on those writings. In a work entitled "The great History of the Burman and Pegu Kings," it is recorded, that during the I'hiooru-Kshutriya dynasty, not fewer than fifty-five translations were made, and as many comments written on these books. But the Burmans are believed to possess works of greater antiquity than these jutakas, on history, poetry, medicine, astronomy, grammar, &c., borrowed from the Sungskulu, or the productions of the Budhu sect: time must disclose.

"It is a singular circumstance, that the Budhus should have chosen for their hero, like the Hindoos for Vishnu, ten incarnations; and still more singular, that they should have designated the histories of these incarnations by the names of ten Hindoo sages."

NOTE II.

Yin-youan. Ce mot exprime la relation qui lie l'effet à la cause, et marque la destinée, la fatalité, l'enchaînement qui existe entre tous les actes dont la succession constitue l'individualité. On dit que, par l'effet du *Yin-youan*, l'âme d'un homme passe dans le corps d'un autre homme; par exemple, une pauvre femme qui vivait, il y a des milliers des siècles, au temps du Bouddha Vipasyi, ayant fourni un peu d'or et une perle pour réparer une défectuosité qui déparait le visage d'une statue de ce Bouddha, forma la vœu d'être par la suite l'épouse du doreur qui fit cette réparation; ce vœu se réalisa; elle renaquit durant quatre-vingt-onze kalpa, ou périodes du monde, avec une face de couleur d'or; ensuite elle renaquit encore comme dieu Brahma; sa vie comme dieu étant épuisée, elle devint brahmane dans le pays de *Mágadha*, et ce fut dans sa famille que naquit *Mahá-káya*, le premier disciple de Shakia; de-là lui vint le nom de *Kin-se* (couleur d'or). C'est un exemple de ces *Yin-youan* ou dispositions individuelles.—*Observations sur quelques Points de la Doctrine Samanéene*, par M. Abel Rémusat, *Nouv. Journ. Asiat.* tom. vii. p. 291.

NOTE III.

Fo (Shakia mouni) racontait à ses disciples comment, dans des existences antérieures et prodigieusement anciennes, il avait mérité, par d'assez mauvaises actions, de souffrir des peines graves; et comment alors même qu'il était parvenu à la dignité de Bouddha, il lui restait encore à endurer un reste de ces justes punitions pour d'antiques méfaits; ce qui expliquait comment un être actuellement si parfait pouvait être soumis à de si rudes épreuves. Une femme nommée Sun-tho-li avait accablé d'injures Shakia Bouddha; celui-ci en apprit la raison à ses auditeurs en ces termes: " Il y avait autrefois, dans la ville de Bénares, un comédien nommé *Tching-yan* (l'œil pur). Dans le même temps vivait une courtisane nommée *Lou-siang*. Le comédien emmena cette femme avec lui dans son char, et la conduisit hors de la ville dans un jardin planté d'arbres, où ils se divertirent ensemble. Dans ce jardin un Pratyeka bouddha se livrait à la pratique des œuvres pieuses. Le comédien attendit que ce saint personnage fût entré dans la ville pour y mendier sa nourriture, et ayant tué la courtisane, il l'enterra dans la chaumière du Pratyeka bouddha, et mit sur son compte le crime que lui-même avait commis. Cependant, au moment où le saint allait être mis à mort, il éprouva des remords, se fit connaître pour la véritable coupable, et fut livré au supplice par ordre du roi. Ce comédien," ajouta Shakia, " c'etait moi-même ; la courtisane c'était *Sun-tho-li.* Voilà pourquoi, pendant une longue durée de siècles, j'ai souffert, en conséquence de mon crime, des peines infinies ; et quoique je sois maintenant devenu Bouddha, il me restait encore à endurer, comme reste de châtiment, les injures et les calomnies de la femme Sun-tho-li." Beaucoup d'anecdotes du même genre attestent, dans la personne même de Shakia, l'inévitable influence de ces Yin-youan, ou destinées individuelles; mais outre ces cas particuliers, on distingue douze dégrés ou chaînons de fatalités communes à tous les hommes, et c'est ce qu'on nomme en Sanscrit les douze *Nidânas*, en Chinois *Yin-youan.* M. Deguignes, qui avait à sa disposition le Vocabulaire pentaglotte, y aurait pu lire les noms Sanscrits des douze termes de cette catégorie: *Avidya*, l'ignorance ; *Sanskâra*, l'action ou la passion; *Vidjúânam*, la perception ; *Námaroûpam*, le nom et la forme (l'individualité), &c. On peut voir, dans les extraits des livres bouddhiques de l'Inde, quel est le nœud qui s'établit, dans l'opinion des moralistes ou psychologistes de l'Inde, entre ces actes successifs, supposés enchaînés les uns aux autres, comme l'effet à la cause. L'âme y est assujettie ; elle est comme enfermée dans le cercle qu'ils constituent, tant qu'elle n'a pas pu parvenir à s'affranchir de ses rapports avec les êtres qui composent le monde extérieur.—*Page* 292.

FIVE SERIES OF SEVENTEEN QUESTIONS

ON

THE PRINCIPAL TENETS

OF THE

BUDHIST FAITH,

ADDRESSED TO

THE CHIEF PRIESTS OF THE PRINCIPAL VIHARIS IN CEYLON;

ALSO,

TO THE MAHA MODLIAR RAJAPAXE,

BY THE DUTCH GOVERNOR.

---

1. Mulgirri Galle, Chief Priest Karatotta Oenanse.
2. The Galle Priests.
3. Mahagodda Oenanse.
4. The Mahabadda Priests.
5. A Doctrinal Tract, communicated by Rajapaxe.

BUDHIST TRACTS.

Karatotta Oenanse's Answers.

Query 1. What views have you of the Supreme Being? or are there more gods than one?

Answer. Maha-Brachma-Rajeya is the Supreme Being when Budhu is not in the world, but when he comes to be born in the world then he is the Supreme Being, for Maha-Brachma-R. ministers to him. According to the doctrine of Budhu there are an immense number of gods, as well in the sixteen heavens called Brachma-Lōka, and six called Dewa-Lōka, as in the trees, rocks, rivers, &c.

2. How do you account for the creation of the world?

The creation of the world is not to be ascribed to any person: its rising and perishing is by nature itself.

3. How long since it was created, and by whom was it created?

The time of its rising does not appear in the doctrine of Budhu: its rising is by nature.

4. How do you account for the creation of the first man and woman? for there must have

been a first man and woman from whom we have all proceeded.

According to the belief of the Budhists there was no such thing as that of the creation of the first man and woman; we all have proceeded from those who, having ended their lives in the heaven called Bambelowā, have been transmigrated to this world in the first calpa.

5. How did sin enter into the world?

Sin did not enter into the world by any other means than by the three principal means, as that of avarice, covetousness, and anger: the heart which is given up to one, two, or all three of these vices, is called a sinful heart, and what we say, do, or think, with such a heart, is sin.

6. Have men souls, or some principle or spirit that lives after the body dies?

All men have some principle called Winyanaskandaya, that lives after the body dies, in order to be born (by transmigration) in some place according to their merits or bad actions.

7. Are there further rewards and punishments after this life, or do all men go to the same place?

Surely there are rewards and punishments after this life, as every one deserves, for their good or bad acts, but there is no such thing as that of all men going to the same place.

8. What are your views of heaven or a place of happiness?

There is a place of happiness called Nirwanā-pooraya, where is neither misery nor death, but they enjoy happiness for ever and ever.

9. What are your views of hell or a place of misery?

There are 136 places of misery where the sinners suffer great misery.

10. How is the place of misery to be shunned?

The place of misery is to be shunned by doing charities, and by avoiding all sorts of sins.

11. How is the place of happiness to be secured?

The place of happiness is to be secured by a true belief in the doctrine of Budhu, and by fulfilling the same.

12. What are your views of moral good and evil?

That moral good and evil make men happy and miserable.

13. What laws or commandments have you?

There are many commandments of Budhu, all which dictate to do good and avoid evil, and purify the conscience.

14. Is there any such thing in man as con-

science, whereby he feels uneasy when he breaks the law or does wrong?

There is such a thing in man as conscience, which makes a man uneasy when he breaks the law or does wrong, and also makes him happy when he does good and performs charities.

15. In what does your worship consist?

It consists in a true faith, remembering always virtue.

16. What are the perfections of your god or gods?

The perfections of the supreme beings, that is to say of the Budhus, consist in thirty-two great accomplishments, and eighty joint accomplishments, and more other virtues, wisdom, &c.

17. Have you any books or ancient writings to direct you?

Yes; there are many books in the Palee language containing the doctrines of Budhu.

The Answers of the Galle Priests.

Query 1. What views have you of the Supreme Being? or are there more gods than one?

Answer. Yes; it appears that there are. It further appears in the law of Budhu, that there are a great number of beings who go under the name of gods, but, when it is translated into Cingalese, it signifies "those who enjoy happiness:" besides those there is a supreme and chief god over them all.

2. How do you account for the creation of the world?

The creation of the world (which is called in Cingalese Lōka, that is, "existing it existeth not,") appears to have been self-created, as it was natural at all times that the world should be self-created and perish by itself, and likewise by means of the power of gods and the fortune of the animals who are on it. It further appears, that there is in the midst of the ocean a large rock called Mēroo, eighty-four yoduns* high, only the part above the surface of the water having four sides of four different colours, and around which are seven circles of rocks, which are successively diminishing in height, as much as a half from one to the other, having different seas in the intervals from one to the other, at such a breadth as equal to the height of each of them successively. At each of the four sides of the above-mentioned Mēroo, on the sea, there are

* One yodun is equal to sixteen English miles, or thereabout.

500 countries and one large country, cousequently there are, at the said four sides, 2000 small and four large countries. There is one Chakkra-Vāttah (a circle of rock) surrounding the whole, together with the sea, which' forms the limit of the world; and the said Chakkra-Vāttah is 82,000 yoduns high, and in circumference, 36 lacses 10,350 yoduns. And there are under this earth 136 hells, and above this earth there are in the sky 26 heavens, each over the other in due order. That enclosed within the said Chakkra-Vāttah (the circle of rock), when every thing above stated, as well above as below, &c. are complete, makes one world; besides which, from without the said Chakkra-Vāttah there are innumerable worlds like this world.

3. How long since it was created, and by whom was it created?

It is not possible to fix the number of years, or say how long the world had been created; however, the already created world has four paritchādes, namely, the self-creation of the world, its existency, the gradual destruction, and the time of its being in destruction. Within these four paritchādes, some anthag-calpas revolve, that is to say: of time if the world should grow one inch high in the space of every thousand years, it would grow seven and a half gau* high before one of the said anthag-calpas is passed; four such anthag-calpas have passed. Gau is reckoned, as it is mentioned in the law of Budhu, as follows: about twenty measures from a seven cubits pole is called one ismbah, and eighty ismbahs make one gau. It does not appear that this world has been created by any one.

4. How do you account for the creation of the first man and woman? for there must have been a first man and woman from whom we have all proceeded.

On the destruction of the former world, which also was self-created before this present world, the animals who were on it being born by transmigration in the heaven or Brahma-Lōka, came to the world again on its self-revival, and became acquainted with the worldly pleasure as men and women, and it appears that we are descended from them; but it does not appear to have been multiplied by one man and one woman only.

5. How did sin enter into the world?

It appears that when those the above-mentioned first came to the world, sin appeared not to have been in them, as covetousness, anger,

* Gau is about four English miles.

and stupidity; afterwards those things gradually increased in them, in consequence of which they began to commit sinful acts; so the happiness of the world passed away and sin entered.

6. Have men souls, or some principle or spirit that lives after the body dies?

It appears that none of the following four things do live after the death of the person, namely: the earth or flesh, the water, the fire, and the winds, such as breath, &c. which are in the body. It further appears, that there are in the body fifty things that are not visible but nominal, which also do not exist; and twelve others, like the above, but distinct from them, and twenty-two more, which are also resembling the above, but distinct from them; besides which there are a great number of others, all of which do not appear to have any existence. There is also one principal thing that does live, concerning which what appears in the law of Budhu will inform.

7. Are there further rewards and punishments after life, or do all men go to the same place?

It appears that after this life, in futurity, there are abodes of fortune and misfortune, and that all will go to one or the other place, and obtain the same, but they acquire them by means of their virtue or sin accordingly.

8. What are your views of heaven, or a place of happiness?

For the enjoyment of the happiness of the blessed it appears that there are twenty-six heavens.

9. What are your views of hell, or a place of misery?

It appears that there are 136 hells, but they all are contained in one hell.

10. How is the place of misery to be shunned?

He who has gone to the place of misery, after he has suffered enough for his miserable deeds or sins, it appears that he can become free of it.

11. How is the place of happiness to be secured?

It appears that the securing of the place of happiness is the securing of the body and mind without entering into the wrongful deeds of sin, and the securing of the faith towards the glorious Omnipotent Being by behaving according to his law.

12. What are your views of moral good and evil?

As to moral good and evil, or doing good

actions and leaving sinful deeds, there are commandments, or many preachings of the Omnipotent Master of all the worlds.

13. What laws or commandments have you?

The commandments are ten: — 1st, Do not kill; 2d, Do not steal; 3d, Do not commit adultery; 4th, Do not lie; 5th, Do not slander; 6th, Do not call ill-names; 7th, Do not speak words which are to no purpose but harm; 8th, Do not covet others property; 9th, Do not envy; 10th, Do not err in the true faith, or think it to be false.

14. Is there any such thing in man as conscience, whereby he feels uneasy when he breaks the law, or does wrong?

Yes; besides the above-mentioned commandments, there are five kinds of heavy, or more mortal sins, namely, the killing of parents, &c. It appears natural, that whosoever commits any such sin shall go to hell; for he cannot be comforted either by doing any other act of charity, or by any faith.

15. In what does your worship consist?

The true faith, which is like a precious stone that cleareth the troubled water, must be kept in mind.

16. What are the perfections of your god or gods?

There appears in the law of Budhu only one Omnipotent Being. I give here a short answer as to his perfections, as appears in the law. As difficult as it would be to chop a ship's mast into a handle of a chisel, so difficult will it also be to state the same. But all these are perfections that he has:—heavenly wisdom, heavenly eyes and ears, such as could perceive, see, and hear every thing throughout all the different worlds, in present, past, and future times; and also he has Sariră-Irddy and Chittă-Irddy, &c.

17. Have you any book or ancient writings to direct you?

Yes; there are books to direct. Those are the books of Toonpittăkă, which contain 84,000 chapters of sermons how to direct these three things, namely,—the body and mind; good and evil deeds, which are produced by means of them; and how to purify the body and mind from evil deeds.

Mahagodda Oenanse's Answers.

Query 1. What views have you of the Supreme Being, or are there more gods than one?

Answer. That he is a Supreme Being above all others; and, although there are many gods, yet there is a supreme one, who is god of the gods.

2. How do you account for the creation of the world?

The creation of the world, or rather the rising of the world, is a natural case.

3. How long since it was created, and by whom was it created?

Since the commencement of the rising of the world there having been an immense time, it is not to be reckoned, therefore it is infinite.

4. How do you account for the creation of the first man and woman? for there must have been a first man and woman from whom we have all proceeded.

As it is always the case, in the beginning of this calpa some Brahma-rajas came from the heaven called Ahbassara Bambelowa to this world, from whom we have all proceeded.

5. How did sin enter into the world?

By means of avarice, covetousness, and anger.

6. Have men souls, or some principle that lives after the body dies?

They have souls, or some principle that lives after the body dies.

7. Are there further rewards and punishments after this life, or do all men go to the same place?

Surely there are rewards and punishments after this life; but all men do not go to the same place.

8. What are your views of heaven, or a place of happiness?

The heaven is an empty place, but there is a residence of happiness in it.

9. What are your views of hell, or a place of misery?

There is a hell, or a place of misery.

10. How is the place of misery to be shunned?

The place of misery is to be shunned by avoiding the sins.

11. How is the place of happiness to be secured?

The place of happiness is to be secured by charity, with pure heart.

12. What are your views of moral good and evil?

Moral good makes man happy, and evil makes him miserable.

13. What laws and commandments have you?

The five commandments, and also the ten commandments, and many others.

14. Is there any such thing in man as conscience, whereby he feels uneasy when he breaks the law or does wrong?

There is such a thing in man.

15. In what does your worship consist?

It consists in a true faith, according to the doctrine.

16. What are the perfections of your god or gods?

The perfections of the gods appear in the religious books.

17. Have you any books or ancient writings to direct you?

There are many books and ancient writings.

Mahabadda Priests' Answers.

Query 1. What views have you of the Supreme Being? or are there more gods than one?

Answer. That he is a being above all others. There are many gods; the god called Sahanpati-maha-brahmayo is above all others; so that it does not appear in our religion that there is only one god.

2. How do you account for the creation of the world?

The creation of the world is to be ascribed to nature, as having risen on account of the good and bad deeds of all the souls.

3. How long since it was created, and by whom was it created?

It was created as above-said, about 1756 coties, 15 lacses, 97,357 years since. It was not created by any person, as appears in the second answer.

4. How do you account for the creation of the first man and woman? for there must have been a first man and woman from whom we have all proceeded.

We do account for the creation of the man and woman as follows:—After the rising of the world, some souls, called Brahmayo, who had ended their lives in the heaven called Brahma-Lowa, having been transmigrated into this world, lost all their perfections and happiness (which they formerly enjoyed), on account of their covetousness, and by eating* of all sorts of food which lust effected in them. Thus they became man and woman, according to their fate, from whom we have all proceeded.

5. How did sin enter into the world?

Sin entered into the world on account of the riches, consisting in gold, silver, pearls, precious stones, &c.

6. Have men souls, or some principle or spirit that lives after the body dies?

* See "Sketch of Budhism," by H. B. Hodgson, Esq. in the Transactions of the Royal Asiatic Society, vol. ii. page 234, query 2; also note 9.

They have souls, which are transmigrated from one place to the other, after the body dies, till the same shall obtain the happiness of Moksaya, which is the important one to mankind.

7. Are there further rewards and punishments after this life? or do all men go to the same place?

After this life, those who have done good are transmigrated, as well in this world as in the heavens called Dewá-Lōka and Brahma-Lōka, where there is happiness, and they enjoy all sorts of blessedness; those who have done evil transmigrate into the four great hells called Ahpahya, and suffer all sorts of miseries: but at the perishing of the worlds all go to the same place, except those who have denied this and the next world, their father and mother, the god and the Budhu, the doctrine and the priests, &c.

8. What are your views of heaven, or a place of happiness?

The heavens are places of happiness, and they are called Dewa-Lōka and Brahma-Lōka.

9. What are your views of hell, or a place of misery?

According to our views there are several

hells, or places of misery, where sinners suffer for their sins.

10. How is the place of misery to be shunned?

The place of misery is to be shunned by doing good. The wicked will be transmigrated to the places of misery, where they shall remain till they have suffered for their guilt.

11. How is the place of happiness to be secured?

The doctrine dictates that it is to be secured by doing good.

12. What are your views of moral good and evil?

Moral good is the doing all sorts of charities, being virtuous and perfect in the ten sorts of good called Dassa-coosala; the moral evil is the doing all sorts of wickedness, being vicious, and subject to Dassa-acoosal-carmaya (ten sorts of sins).

13. What laws or commandments have you?

The laws or commandments are numerous; all which dictate to do good and avoid evil.

14. Is there any such thing in man as conscience, whereby he feels uneasy when he breaks the law, or does wrong?

There is such a thing in man.

15. In what does your worship consist?

Our worship consists in the laws and commandments.

16. What are the perfections of your god or gods?

Our God has seen and known all things of the three sorts of worlds. He is perfect in every thing above all others. The perfections of our god or gods cannot be stated in few words; according to our faith they are the supreme beings, above all others.

17. Have you any books or ancient writings to direct you?

We have thousands of religious books, called Sootrabe-darma-Wenaya and Sankayata-tri-pitakayee; besides which, many other books or ancient writings, called Attoowah, Teekah, Get-tapahda, Yojanahprakarana, &c.

Translation of a Doctrinal Tract replying to the Queries made by order of the Dutch Governor.

1. What views have you of the Supreme Being? or are there more gods than one?

There are, according to the religion of Budhu, innumerable gods, namely: Uppa-Pādooka gods and Utpatty gods, who are born, and who shall be born, by transmigration, in the following places, to wit: Aroopaboomy, that is, a place where there is no body, but soul: these gods shall be born in this place by means of four affections, called Aroopa-Wāchera Koosela-Wipākas; secondly, Solos-Rootalla, that is, the sixteen places where gods are born, and shall be born, by transmigration, having bodies, by means of five different passions, called Roopā-Watchara-Kooselawipākas; thirdly, Camah-Boomiah, that is, where the gods are born, and shall be born by transmigration, with bodies where they enjoy the pleasures of the five senses, and they shall be born by means of eight different passions, called Cāma-Wātchera-Kooselawipākas. This world belongs to the said Cāmah-Boomiah, where there are born and shall be born gods, by transmigration, on the trees, rocks, seas, rivers, and lakes, &c.

2. How do you account for the creation of the world?

This sackwalla (this world) is in circumference 36 lacses 10,350 yoduns. Together with this sackwalla there are other different sackwallas, in number kella lacses, each of them of the same bigness with this. When the time of their destruction comes, they all naturally perish at once; when the time of their growth comes, they all rise at once. This is the way of the destruction and the rising of the world, even in the former times, and as it will be in future; but it does not appear to have been made, or caused to be made, by any body.

3. How long since it was created? and by whom was it created?

Now the time is thus: four calpas called asanka, make one maha-calpa; one asanka-calpa makes twenty anthag-calpas. Out of the above-mentioned four asanka-calpas, three asanka-calpas are passed: they are called Sanwarta, Sanwarttastayis, and Wiwarta. The present asanka-calpa is called Sanwarttastayi, out of which three autbag-calpas are passed: the fourth is the present anthag-calpa. There remain sixteen anthag-calpas more to come, and then will be the end. An answer to the question "Who created the same?" is given in the second answer.

4. How do you account for the creation of the first man and woman? for there must have been a first man and woman, from whom we all proceeded.

Wiwartha-Sagarah (the flood) abating by degrees, the world was self-created, as it was before, on the same place where it had been. After which, some of the brachmas who were in the heaven called Abaswartaiah dying, came and were born in this world, in Soonnaih-Brahma-Wemans; and by their multiplying in this world they lost the light of their bodies; and when they had begun to eat the rice called Soyanjahta-El, there were produced within them excrement and urine, and, in order to discharge them, there were produced the different orifices, as had been natural from the former time. And further, there were produced the sexes of men and women; and by the constant looking of the men and women at each other came lust, from which they had been free from long time, by means of Diānayah. After that, by means of the carnal enjoyment of the men and women, they began to conceive children, &c., up to this time, and it will be so till the end of the calpa.

5. How did sin enter into the world?

The three principal causes of all sin are covetousness, anger, and thoughtlessness; these three things cleave to a man always. Such men, when they are born by transmigration in any place, those three things, namely, the said covetousness, &c., will go with them, in the same manner as a shadow goes with the substance, and give root to many different sins.

6. Have men souls, or some principle or spirit that lives after the body dies?

The five parts of a man are, the body, feeling, imagination, thinking, and mind; these are called in general a person. When the mind is gone, the aspiration and respiration of the breath, and the passing and repassing, laughing and speaking, &c., and the different other acts, together with the aforesaid feeling, imagination, and thinking, all these will perish, and the body will only remain as a wooden image, but nothing else.

7. Are there further rewards and punishments after this life? or do all men go to the same place?

Had a man done charity before his death, when he is dead he shall be born in heaven, and enjoy happiness; had he committed sin, he shall be born in the six apayas (hells or places of misery), and be subject to different sufferings and punishments. Men who had done charity in their former life shall be born in the following seven places, namely, the six lowermost heavens, and the world, by transmigration. Men who had committed sins, shall be born in one or other of the 136 hells, in the form of beasts, pretah, and in the Asoora-Nikayah, according to their sins. On that account there is not a fixed place where they must be born.

8. What are your views of heaven, or a place of happiness?

Nirwāna (place of happiness) is the highest and best place, which destroys all sorrow, and acquires all happiness. Wise men will obtain Nirwāna, and fools will lose it; and the same must be obtained by doing good.

9. What are your views of hell, or a place of misery?

There are four apayas (places of misery); namely, eight great hells, having sixteen osoopats (hells) on the four sides of each of them; altogether 136 hells: all these are one apaya. One pretah-nikayah (a life), one asoorah-nikayah (a life), and the other is Tirisan-apayah (the life of beasts): these four apayas are designed for the wretched, or sinners. Wise men, who perform charities, avoiding bad deeds, and who do not allow themselves to be possessed of sins by means of the following three doors, namely, body, word, and the mind, they shall not be subjected to any sufferings of the said apayas. Men who do not so, are subjected to sufferings in those apayas.

10. How is the place of misery to be shunned?

He who becomes righteous himself, getting free from the following sins, viz. killing animals, lying, covetousness, &c., which proceed from the body, word, and mind; and who becomes himself kind and good towards mankind, and does other charities, shall be saved from the four apayas designed for the wretched, or sinners.

11. How is the place of happiness to be secured?

By all means getting free from sins, and by keeping, or by the assistance of the law, doing good, by behaving himself well; minding these three things, viz. anittayah (not lasting for ever), dook-kayah (sorrow), anātmayah (not a body), thus may be obtained Mōksayah.

12. What are your views of moral good and evil?

What is good? That is the getting rid of sin, and the having a mind to do charity. What is evil? That is the neglect of charity, and the having a mind to sin. So the man who does charity shall obtain every good, even in this world, and heavenly happiness, &c. in the next world. The bad man shall be subject to every misfortune and evil in this world, and likewise, in the next life he shall be born in one of the four apayas, according to his sins, and be subjected to sufferings and punishments.

13. What laws or commandments have you?

The commandments are: the not delaying agriculture and trade, &c.; the doing charity; the not doing all the sin that proceeds from the inlets above mentioned, such as body, &c.; the acquiring of blessings by means of alms; keeping commandments; thoughtfulness with regard to religion; the faculty of the mind in destroying the different sinful senses; and the joy, &c. When the mind is blotted by covetousness, &c., he surely takes the bad journey which goes to hell. So the mind must be made pure by avoiding covetousness, thoughtlessness, &c., which are the causes of evil. The casting away shame and fear from the mind is the origin of all sin; and retaining of shame and fear is favourable to every good; and as thoughtlessness is a cause of many evils, one must always be thoughtful.

14. Is there any such thing in man as conscience, whereby he feels uneasy when he breaks the law or does wrong?

Those who break the law, and commit heavy crimes, shall have no comfort nor pardon in the Budhu's law; but there is no killing, binding, punishing, &c., in the law of Budhu: a man who commits such crimes shall merely be put away from his priesthood. If it be not a heavy crime, such as anantariah (matricide or parricide), &c., he may become again a layman; and if he does charities, as alms, and keeps commandments, &c., and behave himself as a righteous man, it is possible for him to obtain happiness in the next world.

15. In what does your worship consist?

As a man who is desirous of fruits, leaving the unfruitful trees goes in search of a fruitful one, even so those who search for the happiness of heaven and Nirwāna, must believe the man who shall be so kind and able as to accomplish their desire. These kind persons are Budhu, his words, and priests. Budhu is void of lust, and every other sinful desire; void of every sort of passions; void of every thoughtlessness; his words are a conveyance to heaven: the priests are those who properly keep the commandments. Those who know for certainty that such good and kind persons are able to accomplish their desires, as above stated, shall believe in those three things. These three things, which are precious, ought to be believed. The believing is a matter of the thought, that is, a part of Sangiskaras-Kandayah. This Sangiskaras-Kandayah is one of the five parts mentioned in the sixth answer. On that account, know hence that belief is within one's mind.

16. What are the perfections of your god or gods?

The pure god, Budhu, has a body possessed or composed of the accomplishments called

Roopa-kayah, that is, thirty-two manly great accomplishments, called Detismahāpoorsalah-senah, and eighty manly accomplishments, lesser than the above: they are called Anoowenjanah-laksenah; and he is likewise composed of the accomplishments called Darma-kayah, that is, ten bodily powers, ten powerful wisdoms, four daring wisdoms, called Warsaraddatnanah; six piercing minds or sensibilities, called Satabitna-nah; and fourteen other wisdoms, called Bood-datnanah; eighteen Awenika-darmas, that is, certain virtues or qualities belonging to a Budhu; seventy-seven sorts of wisdoms called Satsatte-tynana-wastoo; twenty-four kella lacses of palah, that is, certain rewards a Budhu has got already, by means of his good deeds in the former life; and he is thus accomplished with all these Mahawatjaratnana (piercing wisdom), namely, the above said Roopa-kayah and Darma-kayah. Know hence, that many other innumerable Budhus were possessed of the like accomplishments, namely, of endless dispositions, wisdoms, charities, glories, &c. Besides which, in answer to the question made about the Utpatty gods, the following are given:—The palace in which the god Sakkraia Rajah resides, is in the heaven called Tawootisabawanah, is 10,000 yoduns in length, and the same in circumference, and

700 yoduns high. His seat, called Pawndoo-kambela-Saylasanah, is 60 yoduns; his state elephant is 150 yoduns high; his coach is drawn by 1000 horses, called Sayindawa; his gardens are called Nandawnan-wannah, Chitter-lata-wannah, and Misserkā-wannah; he has two kellas and 50 lacses of heavenly women, together with his queen Soojātāh: he is king over two heavens. This is the glory of one god only.

17. Have you any books or ancient writings to direct you?

The doings or acts for the acquirement of the following blessings, namely, worldly happiness, heavenly happiness, and the happiness of Nirwāna, and the instructions given for obtaining relief, or escaping from the sorrows, are composed in 12 lacses 37,000 grantas (verses); and there are books in which these verses are fully contained.

When these books are used, it will appear in them what one ought to do or accept, and what one ought to avoid; in the same manner as when lamps are lighted in a dark house, every thing in the house may be seen. Each of the above-said verses contain thirty-two letters.

A SERIES

OF NINETY QUESTIONS AND ANSWERS

ON POINTS OF THE

BUDHIST DOCTRINE,

ADDRESSED TO, AND ANSWERED BY,

THE CHIEF PRIEST OF MULGIRI GALLE VIHARI.

A Series of Ninety Queries proposed by the Dutch Governor on Points of Budhist Doctrine; also, the Answers thereto, by the Chief Priest of Mulgiri-galle Vihari.

Query 1. What signifies Mulgiri-galle? and why is it so called?

Answer. Mulgiri-galle signifies a rock lying in the country of Giriepawda-ratta, and that has a subterranean cavity, in the centre of which rock there has been constructed a statue of Budhu; and, as a series of offerings are made at the place, and as the rock is in size superior to any other in that quarter, it is therefore called the Mulgiri-galle, or chief rock.

2. What is implied by Nayka Oenanse?

Nayka Oenanse (chief priest) is to express a principal of many others; and, in consequence of his working for the good of many, he is named the Nayka Oenanse.

3. What is called Samenaira? and what does it signify?

Samenaira signifies one who studies to obtain that chief priesthood called the Oepasampala, and although a disciple only, is considered as a son by the principal priests.

4. What is meant by the term Swamy? Is he who has that name a sacred person?

Swamy (lord) means a person bearing a superiority over a body of men, whom being treated both good and bad by that superior, they must consequently acknowledge him their swamy. Amongst such swamies there will be many who are pure and impure: but the religion allows that Budhu is the only swamy free from impurities of all kinds. And, in short, the word swamy implies one who provides for the good of many people, &c., favouring, instructing, and protecting them.

5. Are the two deities, namely, Satagiry and Assoory, those supreme gods who protect the universe? and do they govern the heaven too?

The first-mentioned, Satagerenam-Dewatawa, is a chief over the multitude of devils, subject to the king of devils, named Wayes-Srawanam, who it does not appear governs the heaven, but who commands the devils under him. And as to the Assoory, there appears no deity by that name; but, on the contrary, a celebrated god, as Assoora, who is the sovereign of the world Assoora-Lōka, lying beneath the Mahameroo-Parkwatte (world stone), and consequently he is called the Assoora Rajah, or Assoora King.

6. Who is Ṡakkraia? Is he the chief of the heavens?

Sakkraia is an inhabitant of the heaven called Tawateinzaia, and is only chief of the heavens Dewa-Lōka, and the next lower heaven, Chatoork-maha-rajikai; but not over all the sixteen heavens.

7. Who is Maha Brahma, and what are his attributes? Has he the power of illuminating and obscuring the world?

Maha Brahma is the very King Sahampatinam-Maha-Brahma-Rajah, inhabiting the sixteenth highest heaven, and is twelve yoduns high, and exhibits the four virtues, namely, affability, munificence, meekness, and kindness, towards every one. He has the power of illuminating one world through the brightness which issues from wherever his finger is pointed, and transmits down to the world every blessing* but the hall of glory, and possesses a supremacy above every other, excepting the Budhu, and is blessed with an age of 84,000 years.

8. How are the above-mentioned four gods called in the Palee language?

They are termed, in the Palee language, Sathagiria, Assuriadaia, Sakkraia, and Maha-Brahmaia.

* This passage manifests the pertinacity of the Budhist doctrine in ascribing the acquirement of Nirwana solely to moral deeds.

9. Are there four gods who govern this world? If so, how are these described? What are their attributes, and how are they termed in the Palee language?

There are no four appointed gods for governing this world; but from the region of Sakkraia down to this human world it is all under the government of Sakkraia, who hath devolved the several quarters of this world to the superintendence of the subordinate deities, namely, Iswara, Maheswara, and those who protect the earth.

10. How many worlds are said to have existence in the religious books of the Cingalese?

There will be within a universe many places inhabited by men, such as the Brahma world, the world of gods, and the Naga-Lōka, or world of cobra capiles, which all being thus divided into three, it appears by the religion they are termed the worlds Kame-Lōka, Roopa-Lōka, and Aroopa-Lōka.

11. There were a great many Budhus; but of whom did the gods ask for advice, and hear the sermons?

An infinite number of Budhus have descended into the world, from all of whom gods did solicit advice, and attend to the sermons.

12. Could a human being himself attain to

the dignity of Budhu? And could such a one give advice and instruction to God?

It is appointed to become Budhu by being born a human soul; but for a deity, Brahma, &c., it is not possible; neither for every man, nor for a brute so much as to think of it, for it is attainable only by means of exercising all kinds of difficult, wonderful, and innumerable works of charity, and amongst them ten grand deeds in particular, and incessant bestowing of alms during a space of four sanké caplaxé, or eight sanké caplaxé, or twelve sanké caplaxé; but it is not possible for every other human being to obtain it.

13. Would an accomplished scholar (if there be any) in every science oppose Budhu?

Such a learned person would not oppose Budhu.

14. What are the three worlds respectively, and the histories thereof?

The three worlds are Kame-Lōka, Roopa-Lōka, and Aroopa-Lōka; and of them, wherever there exist the five senses, namely, hearing, smelling, seeing, &c., there is the first-mentioned world, Kame-Lōka, which contains the four hells, the world Naga-Lōka, the human world, and the world Assura-Lōka, and the six lower heavens.

The sixteen higher heavens of Brahmas (which are free from the sensual indulgence), namely, Bramah-parie-Sadjaia, Brahma-Parohietaia, Maha-brahmaia, Paritta-baia, Ap-pamana-baia, Ahassaraia, Paretta-Subaia, Ap-pamana-Subaia, Suba-Kiranaia, Wehat-talaia, Assainje-tallaia, Awenjaia, Attap-paia, Sudassaia, Sud-dhssaia, and Aka-nitta-Kaia, are the second-mentioned Roopa-lōka.

The place where prevails the delightful sentiments (which exist by means of rendering acts of difficult charities), is invariably called the last-mentioned Aroopa-Lōka, which comprises Akasa-Nanchaia-tanaia, Wignia-Nanchaia-tanaia, Akinja-tanaia, and Nirwasanjanai-Sanjaia-tanaia.

15. In the time of Bramah-Dewanam Budhu, Maha-bodie-Satwaio having exhausted all the riches in the exercise of charity, as well as the soul itself, hoped to become Budhu. What are the circumstances of that Brahma-Dewanam Budhu?

That Brahma-Dewanam Budhu having witnessed the former Budhus, and, like unto our Maha-bodie-Satwaio, being far advanced in acts of various charities, at a distance of time of one calpa-laxé and twenty asanka-calpas to the present Mahabaddra calpa, and in the time of the Nandanam-asankai, and at the solicitation of the

Siranam-dewoo-Bauboom (both gods and brahmas) having made his exit from the region of Tosita-pooaia, was, in honour of the King Jhanadepanam, conceived in the womb of the Queen Marigulanam, at the city of Yasa-watie-nuwara, in Maddie-desay, of Jambu-dwipa, and at the expiration of a space of ten months was delivered into the golden sein, held by Maha-Brahma, and standing on the flower, emerged from the earth, looked up and down into the ten directions. And intending not to expect any to excel or equal him, and pronouncing " I will be the most high and the supreme," gave a loud, yet unterrifying noise; and thenceforth was, by the care and protection of gods and brahmas, gradually brought up, and, like unto our Budhu Gautama, attained the Budhuhood, and wrought for the good of the world.

16. Does there appear an explanation of the powers and attributes of the Budhu Gautama? If so, relate it?

After the long train of Budhus who (from the period of the Budhu Brahma-Devanam) had existed in the course of one caplaxé and seven asanka-calpas, and at a distance of one caplaxé and teles asanka-calpas to the present Maha-baddra calpa, and in the time of the Sarkwe-baddranam-Assankai, the said Poorana Gautama

Budhu did, after the manner of the preceding Budhus, make his exit at the heaven Tosita Dewa-Lōka, and, in honour of the King Yasa-niewasa, was conceived in the womb of the Queen Wiemaba-Maha-dewie, in the city of Yasamewasa-Nuwara in Jambu-dwipa, and being delivered into the golden sein, and held up by Maha-Brahma, he was elevated as the Budhu Gautama.

17. Describe the powers and attributes of Diepan-kare Budhu?

After the train of Budhus who (since the period of the aforesaid Poorana-Gautama Budhu) had become elevated in the course of one cap-laxé and nine asanka-calpas, and at the distance of one caplaxé and four asanka-calpas to the present Mahabaddra calpa, and in the calpa of Saranandanam, Diepan-kare Budhu, like unto the preceding Budhu, being far advanced in deeds of charities, attained unto the heaven Tosita Dewa-Lōka, from whence making his exit, he was, in honour of the King Sudewanam, conceived in the womb of the principal Queen Sumedanam, at the city of Rammawatie, in Jambu-dwipa, and was born and treated after the manner of the former Budhus, having an age of seka lacse, and being eighty cubits high.

18. To whom did the Prince Sumeda Pau-

detanam-Brahma-Kumaraia offer his wealth in charity? in what manner was it, and what became of himself afterwards?

That Sumedanam-Brahma-Kumara-Teina, or Prince, having exerted himself in such works of charity as were necessary for becoming Budhu during a course of one calpa lacse, and twelve asanka-calpas, and at a distance of one lacse of calpas and four asanka-calpas to the present Maha-baddra calpa, was born a Prince Sammedanam, in the nation of Maha-Brahma, and in the city of Ammarawatie Nuwara, and having grown up, and seeing the plentiful riches and treasures which had been amassed by his ancestors for seven generations together, and reasoning within himself that his relatives had departed this life and gone to the other world, leaving behind them the said riches, he resolved that he would disperse those riches in charities and almsgivings; and for that purpose having obtained the sanction of the king, he, by beating of tom-tom, caused every beggar in Jambu-dwipa to be assembled; but not being able to exhaust those immense riches in deeds of charity, at last he retired into the wilderness called Himalawane, and betook himself into the monastery which Sakkraia had created for him, in the vicinity of the rock Dharmieka-Parkwatai; and there being invested with the priesthood, and being, in the course of seven days, animated with the power of flying in the air (which is called the Tatsanaia), and thus spending his days in that felicity, he was one day flying in the air over and above the city of Rammawatie Nuwara, when he understood that Deipankara Budhu, who had in this interval arrived to the state of Budhu, was coming into the city of Rammawatie Nuwara. He then descended from the above element, and extended himself on the road through which Budhu was to pass, with his face downwards, and with his head towards Budhu; and at the same time prostrating and hoping for Budhuhood, he obtained the final and solemn ratification of it from the said Budhu.

19. Where is the city called Rammawatie Nuwara situated?

It is impossible to point out or speak as to the site where thàt city Rammawatie stood, because one lacse of calpas and four asankacalpas have been extinguished and created again; and more particularly when a calpa is expired, the earth also is destroyed, so that it would be impossible to speak accurately as to the above.

20. What was the cause of the pair of

ear-rings of Sakkraia, called Cundala-barana, which have a constant wavering and a shining lustre?

There may be gods throughout the heavens who are both superior and inferior to Sakkraia, and each of whom will have their ear ornaments; and as to the Cundala-baranaia of Sakkraia, there is no other particular explanation to be drawn from it than the bright lustre which it emits when in the act of trilling.

21. In what place did Sumeda-Tapasaio die at, what was his country, where was he born afterwards, and who were his parents?

Sumeda-Tapasaio, or hermit, made his exit in the very monastery created for him by Sakkraia, and was born in the heaven of glory; and as it is said that gods in their heavens spontaneously come into vision, and as it is considered they then are as mere apparitions, there appears to be no parents for a god.

22. What was the country that King Wessantera was born in, and what were the names of his parents?

The King Wessantera was born in the city of Jaya-turanam Nuwara; his father was the King Sanjaianam, and his mother the Queen Tusatienam Deiwie.

23. Where is situated the kingdom of the

King Suddodana, and what were his attributes?

The city of the King Suddodana was the province Kapilawastoo - Pooraia, lying to the south of the banian-tree standing in the middle of the continent of Jambudwipa; and from among the train of princes who reigned in succession since the period of the King Maha-summata, in the former calpa, there were 22,010 kings in number, all of whom reigned in the country of Kapilawastoo - Pooraia; and of them the King Sinhabanoo, son to the King Jaiasena, was the last who reigned: the King Suddodana, father to our Budhu, was the son of the said King Sinhabanoo. The attributes of this King Suddodana cannot be fully illustrated by a succinct detail. He having been full of hopes, during a period of one caplacse, to be made himself father to a Budhu, at last attained his ends by being father to our Budhu; and having experienced favours and assistance both from deities and Brahmas, when arrived at the age of 120 years, he, from his seat on the throne, vanished and attained the hall of glory.

24. Describe all the strange things or wonders that took place on the birth-day of the Budhu Gautama.

At the moment of the birth of our Budhu,

Maha-Brahma received him in a golden net, and feasting his eyes with his beauty, he addressed the queen: "I congratulate thee on the birth of a son from your womb, who is supreme over the whole three worlds;" and soon after two bodies of water, similar to a large bar of silver, having come from above, and washing the mother and the child, it instantaneously vanished; then from the hands of the Maha Brahma the child was received in a soft and convenient hide of a tiger, by the kings called Weeran-Rajas, and by the priests in a superfine linen cloth, from whose hands the child wanting to descend, pointed its feet towards the earth, and instantly a large flower emerged forth and received the child's feet, who then standing on the flower, looked up and down into the ten directions (according to the Cingalese calculation), when all the gods, the Brahmas, and the human beings, with offers of fragrant flowers, lifting up their hands unto their forehead, addressed him: "Lord there is no one either to equal or excel you; you are the most high." And thereupon he went seven steps towards the north, when step by step sprung forth flowers; then stopping, and saying, "I will be the highest; I will be the chief and the superior over all the worlds," he set up a loud but not terrifying noise, which noise, piercing into the 10,000 worlds, the 10,000 Brahmas in those worlds, holding white umbrellas each three leagues in height, offered the same; the 10,000 Sakkraias made offerings of blowing of 10,000 conch-shells, all wreathed to the right, and each were 120 cubits in length, and which when blown support an unremitted and unslackened echo for a space of four months and two pooyas (full moon days); 10,000 rajas, or kings of the third heaven, made offerings of display of fire-works called chamarra, each of which was three yoduns in height; 10,000 Sootusita kings made offerings of 10,000 diamond fans; 10,000 musicians played on the violin, each of which was three leagues in length; and the rest of the subaltern deities, such as Sienerinita and Parenerinita, made offerings of golden caranduas, or cases, rubied caranduas, golden sandals, rubied sandals, diamond crowns, head-bands, royal sabres, divine perfumes in heaps, and other solemn works; and, at the moment of the above-said birth, the world experienced thirty-two unprecedented acts of bounty; namely, 1st, the earth of the 10,000 worlds quaked; 2d, every world paid homage unto one; 3d, all born blind obtained sight; 4th, the deaf obtained their hearing; 5th, the dumb the power of speech; 6th, the lame the power of walking;

7th, the humpbacked and the bowed were straightened; 8th, the confined had their release; 9th, the hell fire suffered a momentary extinguishment; 10th, the demons had their hunger satisfied; 11th, the brutes banished their dread;* 12th, the infirm were made whole; 13th, the world was established by parental words; 14th, horses neighed; 15th, the elephants yawled; 16th, the lions roared; 17th, all the rest of the quadrupeds made a melodious howling; 18th, every jeweller's utensils made a sound; 19th, a body of light dispersed throughout every ten directions; 20th, the air was agitated with gentle winds; 21st, the heavens rained; 22d, a body of water emerged up, penetrating the earth; 23d, all kinds of poultry descended into the earth, without flying in the air; 24th, the streams of the river stopped; 25th, the salt water of the ocean became fresh; 26th, the sea was adorned with flowers; 27th, the flowers were blown on the surface of both the land and sea; 28th, every tree was bent down with flowers; 29th, flowers emerged up by penetrating through the ground, stones, and trunks of trees; 30th, the heaven was canopied with the flower canopy;

* Does this import, lost their fear of man? If this be its true meaning, it is a curious and important allusion respecting the gift to Adam of supremacy and rule over the creation.

31st, the whole world rained upon throughout with flowers; 32d, the whole world was filled with banners: and beside all these thirty-two things, a variety of other miracles reached the world, both at the moment the Budhu was conceived in his mother's womb, and at the moment he was born, and therefore it is too tedious to describe by a concise enumeration.

25. Whose daughter was the Queen Yasodara-dewie?

She was the daughter of the Queen Amitawnan, who was the youngest sister to the eldest brothers of the Queen Maha-maia-dewie; namely, the kings Suprabadda and Suddodana.

26. What is the description of the place called Maddye-Mandelai, and are there any other countries also in it?

It is the very village known by the name of Kanjagalanam-Mamgame of the east, in which there is situated a sal-tree, at the very extreme length of the village, and is bounded to the east by the river Salalawake Ganga, to the south by the village Setakarnakanam Niangamme, to the west by the village Toonanam Bahmoonu-gamme, and to the north by the rock Badjanam Parkuataia. This place, which is 1200 leagues in length, 1000 in breadth, and 3600 leagues in circumference, is called the Madde-desaia; and to the east of the above Madde-desaia are situated the six cities, namely,* Hastipooraia, Matangaia, Ganwieraia, Gaiekastraia, Poondariekaia; to the west the six cities called Sawatty, Jetuttara, Sagala, Kusawatie, Rajaegaha, and Mitilaia; to the south are the eight cities Assapura, Kulasawoo, Ay-yodja, Kosasie, Pawtaliputta, Kauria, Gauda, and Daddapooraia; and to the north are the eight cities Oettara, Pauchalai, Roja, Wassana, Takkasiela, Kusinara, Tamba-Pannie, and Goudadesaia: all these are within the aforesaid Madde-desai.

27. What were the symptoms observed on the journey to the orchard, or oeyana?

Making three journeys, and having met a wretched figure, with teeth worn out, gray-haired, corrugated skin, bowed down, and standing trembling with a staff in the hand; also an infirm figure, with a body infected and badly formed; also a withered shape, with a body swelled and wan, worms issuing from it, with a mouth wide opened. Having thus witnessed these three shapes at three several periods, and having never seen the like before, he inquired of the waggoner about the same, and being satisfied of the whole, he deferred his journey to the orchard, and returned to the city with an

* Only five cities are here enumerated.

agitated heart. On his fourth journey he beheld a figure of a priest, and having questioned and learnt the same, he was delighted that eternity should be unto him who had assumed this sedate metempsychosis, and he resolved to continue his way to the orchard, and be himself introduced into the priesthood. The said four exhibitions were wrought by God.

28. Who is he that calls himself Wisme-karmaia?

Wisme-karmaia, properly Wisme-karmanam Deewya Pootraia, is an inhabitant of the heaven of Sakkria-poorai, and is the chief artisan of Sakkraia; and as he is famous for, and eminently skilled in, works of architecture in a manner not to be excelled nor paralleled by any one else, he is called the Wisme-karmaia, or wonderful artist.

29. Give a detail of the war of the Assuraia with Sakkraia, if it is to be found among the good histories.

This Assuraia was born in the heaven called Tawootissa-Dewa-Lōka; and when living there, Sakkraia* having seen the birth of Assuraia, proposed going there with a company of other

* Another portion of the doctrine asserts that it was Guadma, in an anterior stage of his existence, on whom this deceit was attempted to be practised.

deities, in order to attend the festival of the birth of Assuraia, which the Assuraia being acquainted with, had prepared a jiapané (toast) to be drunken, which Sakkraia having understood, charged his divine company not to drink that toast; but the Assuraia having mistaken, and taken the toast himself, became inebriated, and lay exposed from place to place. At last, Sakkraia, aided by his other deities, took the Assuraia by the feet, and flung him into the ocean; and having overcome the above-said heaven, he made himself king of the gods thereof. Now when the paloll-tree, of the height of 100 yoduns, which had been given for Assuraia, through the merits of his charitable deeds, and which had thrived to a distance of 10,000 yoduns throughout the Treekootta, beneath the Mahameru, puts forth flowers, the Assuraia, contemplating that the flowers of their parasatoo-tree were not like these, he and the whole body of Assuraias, wanting to regain their native heaven, took arms and marched off, and climbing up to the Mahameru, went forward, without halting at the four guard places called Koombanda-budaia,* Yakhsa-hudaia, Garoonda-hudaia,

* These are the regions immediately above the earth, inhabited by the inferior guardian deities of Sakkraia.

and Naga-hudaia, when the Assuraias saw the chakkra-walalla* (a very sharp and circular weapon invented by Wismekarma) in the hands of Sakkraia and his followers, armed also with offensive weapons, upon this the Assuraias were greatly terrified and took to flight; but Sakkraia being aided by other deities, repulsed the Assuraias. This expedition of the Assuraias was to make themselves masters of the kingdom of Sakkraia.

30. Give a perfect detail of the circumstances of Kissa-Gautamie.

Amongst the 80,000 queens, wives to the Budhu Gautama when he was in a lay state, the Queen Kissa-Gautamie was a woman who, in point of beauty, might be compared to the Queen Yasodarawau, who was born of the maternal aunt of the Queen Parabnamwoe-Yasodara-Dewie, youngest sister to the King Suddodana, and her (the said Kissa-Gautamie) father was the King of Weggre-pooraia.

31. What is the history of the minister Jananam-Amaptaia?

This Jananam-Amaptaia having, during a period of one lacse of calpas, exercised acts of

* The walalla is described in similar terms as the thunderbolt of Jove, or the shackra of Vishnu, are described in the Grecian and Braminical myths.

charity, with sanguine hopes of aiding at the induction into the priesthood of one who was to become Budhu, was, on the very day of the birth of our Budhu, born in a ministerial family, and endowed with the strength of 1000 men, and in his infant state playing and amusing himself with Budhu all the time, and regarding him (Budhu) with due deference; at last, on the journey of Guatama to become Budhu, he attended the Budhu, and after Budhu was so become, he, Jananam-Amaptaia, was made priest, and soon after vanished, and obtained the hall of glory.

32. Describe the particular circumstances of Kantakanam Aswa-rajah.

Kantakanam Awsa-rajah, hoping to be formed for a conveyance of a person going to become Budhu, exerted himself in acts of charity for a space of one caplaxé, and being born on the very birth-day of our Budhu, and having safely grown up in length to eighteen cubits, and in proportion thereto in height, and as white as a polished conch-shell; so that the Budhu was carried upon the Kantakanam Aswa rajah, being fixed to a superb chariot, (which could in fifteen hours drive round the universe, which is 36 lacse 1,000,350 yoduns in circumference, and return to the spot whence it set off,) when, with Budhu upon his back, he leaped over the river called Anoomanam, which is 800 cubits in width; and there the Budhu, having professed himself priest, gave charge of the horse to the care of his grooms, and sent him up to the city; but at the spot where the said Kantakanam Aswa-rajah lost the sight of Budhu, through mere grief he died of a broken heart, and was born in the heaven of glory; and there having attended to the sermon preached by Budhu, he from thence obtained the hall of glory.

33. In what kingdom was the door which had been made only to shut with the aid of a thousand men?

It was the door made by the King Suddodana for the east gate of the city Capilawastoo.

34. The Cingalese deny that the sun and moon are eclipsed, and infer that they are taken away by devils: if so, state the names of those devils.

According to the Cingalese religious books, the eclipse of the sun and moon denotes an attack of Rahu (one of the nine planets), but not by a devil; much less the religion allows (except in some astrological books) that the same is an attack of both Rahu and the planet called Kehetty,* whose body below the head resembles the trunk of the snake cobra capile.†

35. Where runs the river called Annomanam Ganga?

It lies to the south of the banian-tree, at 120 miles distance from the city Kapilawastoo.

36. Where is the city called Rajegaha-Nuwara? and where is the kingdom of the King Bimsaré?

This city Rajegaha-Nuwara is situated at a distance of thirty yoduns (a yodun is four miles) from the said river Annomanam, and is the city of the King Bimsaré, who is the

* Such is the representation made of Kehettoo in the Bali, or Incantations. Vide Plates in "Doctrines of Budhism."

† The following amusing legend is given of this subject in "Le Pancha Tantra," translated by the Abbé Dubois:—

"In former times, when the gods and the giants resolved to churn the ocean of milk, and to extract the amritta, which would confer immortality, two giants, enemies of the gods, mixed themselves by stratagem in their assembly without being detected, and thus drank of the amritta, which made them immortal. The sun and the moon having observed them, discovered them to Vishnu, who, enraged at the fraudulent introduction of these impious beings, and of their deceit, sought to slay them by striking them with his terrible shackra; but it was in vain, as the amritta rendered them immortal.

sovereign over the two kingdoms Ango and Magahdah.

37. It is said that the milken rice was received on the full-moon day of the month of May, under the tree called Ajapawlanam-Niggroda-Mooleaiah: calculate in what year was it.

From the reception-day of the milken rice to the Saturday of the 20th November, of the year of Christ 1813, it makes 2400 years and 27 days.

38. Who was Sujatawoo?

She is that virtuous woman who wrought many good works during 1,000,000 calpas, hoping to be so beneficent as to make an offer of milken rice to a Budhu on the very day of his

"Vishnu then, in order to punish them in some degree, changed them into two planets;* and these two giants henceforth became transformed, the one into the planet Rahu and the other into the planet Ketty. From that time these planets have preserved an implacable hatred against the sun and the moon, the cause of their disgrace; and although *by far more* feeble than these luminaries, they cease not to wage war with them, and often make them suffer from their enmity, by obscuring their brightness in consequence of the eclipse which they occasion."—"Pancha Tantra," p. 160.

* Rahu and Ketty are the two fixed stars which form the head and the tail of the constellation of the dragon, of which the Indians have made two planets.

promotion, which she at last fulfilled by being born daughter to a sitawno (a rich man), of the country Senananam Neangame, and as wife to the chief sitawno of the Bareness,* she having offered a golden bowl to the worth of 1,000,000 gold massa full of milken rice to the Budhu on the day of his promotion; and after his promotion, having attended the sermon of his preaching, she obtained moksé, or hall of glory.

39. Where runs the river called Neranjanam Ganga?

This river runs through the city of Bareness, which is situated to the south of the banian-tree, the water of which is sacred.

40. What are the trees that are called salgas?†

They are not produced in any of the petty islands, but in Jambu-dwipa, even where the same are excellent species of trees, and to be had only in orchards or botanic gardens of great princes.

41. What is Kusatana?

Kusatana is a very salubrious and superior species of grass, which affords wholesome feelings to a man when he sits upon it, and has a

* Benares.

† The salgas, or sal-trees, named in a former tract.

fragrant smell, which grass is produced no where else but in Jambu-dwipa.

42. Who is Wasawarty-Dewa Rajah?

The deity Wasawarty-Dewa Rajah is a powerful but bad deity, who sins against the commandments of the Wasawarty-Dewa-Maha Rajah, or the supreme being of the sixth heaven, or more properly the kingdom of Wasawarty, being inclined unto sinful deeds, refractory and disobedient towards the said Wasawarty-Dewa-Maha Rajah, and living in a part of the said kingdom with a great company of wicked, turbulent, and diabolical deities.

43. What was the conduct of Mahabody-Satwaio after he had obtained the sanction from Brahma-dewanam Budhu?

Our Body-Satwaio, or the expectant of Budship, is he who, through a variety of his good and meritorious works, has acquired the happiness of promotion to Budhuship, which he at last accomplished in the following manner, to wit: he entertained the wished-for purpose *in heart,* by making a regular appearance to 125,000 Budhus, who were successors to each other, regularly descended down from age to age, namely, from the Budhu Brahma-nadeweh to the Budhu called Pooranné. After the completion of which, he wished the intended purpose by *word*, by making his appearance again to 30,887 Budhus, of whom he obtained the sanction for his promotion, but the time not specified, till at last it was limited by the Budhu called Diepankara, and afterwards by twenty-four Budhus, who were promoted to Budhuship successively, in the space of 10,000,000 calpas and 4 asanka-calpas, and at last he was made a Budhu.

44. Give an explanation of the circumstances of the priests Aja-Kondanjan after they were made priests.

Those Paswaga Mahanoo-nanses, or the five priests, are brahmins, who, far advanced in knowledge of all sorts of arts, and among them that of soothsaying, having seen the characteristic marks of his person, namely, twenty-three symptoms called Assoolakoonoo, and 216 ditto called Magool-lakoonoo, had borne a foreknowledge of the certainty of his promotion as Budhu, they forsook their families, and became themselves priests, and followed him and ministered to him during six years before he became Budhu; and after having attended his sermon, which he preached in the first instance, from thence they attained the hall of glory.

45. Give a description of the temple Issapatana-ramaia.

It is a temple which is situated on a very pleasant spot of land, to the south of the banian-tree, at a distance of eighteen yoduns, in which all the Budhus have performed their first preaching after being promoted to Budhu-ship; and the same is frequented by a great number of magis, or wise men, who are able to fly in the air; in consequence of which, this temple is named by those who have seen it Issa-patana-ramaia.

46. Did Budhu treat the gods in the right way, by preaching forth his religion to them? or how is it to be understood? and if so, did these gods at any time afterwards deviate from the right path?

By virtue of a sermon, which was preached on that day, called Damma-Chakka Sootray, a number of eighteen kelas of brahmas, three asankas of deities, and one of the men, named Anja-Kondanja Teroonancy, who was a priest, have attained the Nirwāna; the state of which is so good, that none of those can be again changed; but it is impossible to give a description thereof to those who have little knowledge of the Budhu's faith, but to those only who are skilled therein. There may be thousands and millions of reasons of every kind whereby to understand the above.

47. Did Budhu, on the 15th day of the month of January, and in the ninth month of his succession to that situation, arrive at Ceylon and extirpate the devils? if so, what are the histories thereof?

Budhu resorted to Ceylon purposely to propagate his religion here, by dispelling the devils Kuwaraia, Jayasainia, Manebaddraia, Tambradatiea, Wierasainea, &c., all of whom were then divided into two parties against each other, and were ready to make war.

48. Where is situated the place called Mahiyangania, and by what name is it now known?

It is situated in the country called Bintenne, which is on the east of the city Seukada Sayla, or Kandy, and the cupola, which is in the temple called Mihingoo-Vihare, or Kauke-Chatize, is the one that was built upon the very spot of ground on which he was sitting on the day the devils were expelled.

49. To whom belonged the palace which was twelve miles in length and six in breadth?

As Ceylon was then void of people, there were no cities nor palaces, except a garden of naw (iron-wood) trees, which contained in its length twelve miles and breadth eight miles; and the same was the habitation of the devils till the time of Wijayia, who invaded Ceylon from

Jambu-dwipa with a great multitude of people, and set forth to reign, after which the same was turned to use for the population.

50. Who is Saman-dewie Rajah?

The deity Saman-dewie Rajah is the chief of a number of other subaltern deities, who having attended the preaching of Budhu at his first arrival at Mayhangamy, and having denounced all wickedness, is now living, with his said deities, upon the top of Samanalagalle (Adam's Peak), with power over Ceylon.

51. Where is situated the Oeruwel-Danawoowa?

Oeruwel-Danawoowa is a country which is situated at Madde-Mandaley, in Jambu-dwipa, between the great banian-tree and the river Neranjanai.

52 What did Budhu do at Ceylon on his first journey there?

In his first voyage to Ceylon he went to Mayhangany; then terrified all the devils, who were ready to war, and sent them out to an isle called Yakgirie-dewainna. And having afterwards preached to Saman-dewie, and other deities, and having delivered them to Nirwāna, he remained a moment on the spot where now stands the cupola Mijoogoona-Vihari, making supplications, as it was customary, to all Budhus;

and then on the same day he returned to Jambu-dwipa.

53. Where and in what kingdom is Jetawana Ramaia situated?

Jetawana Ramaia is situated towards the south-east of the banian-tree, in a garden of Prince Jatch, which is in the city called Srawarty, in the country called Kosalek.

54. Explain the animosity that subsisted between the two kingly snakes, cobra capiles, namely, Choolodera and Mahodera?

Those two kingly snakes had found a precious stone (the Minnypalange) among their haunts, and a consequent altercation ensued between them; saying each to the other, "It is mine," "It is mine." But being unable to gain it one from the other, they began to make war with their great hosts of snakes.

55. Where is the place called Wadunna-galle situated?

Wadunna-galle is situated at Wannia, which is to the south of Naga-Diepé (the isle of snakes).

56. What tree is that called Kiripaloogaha? and what is the cause of it?

The Kiripaloogaha-tree is a species of tree called Kirre-naga, also called Rajaiatenah.

57. Where is lying the rock called Samanta-Koota-Parkwate?

Samanta-Koota (Adam's Peak) is situated in the country called Saffergam, in the wilderness of Sree-pawde Adawisa, which being a mountain of five miles high, is called Samanta-Koota; so that no other mountain in Ceylon will be found superior to this, either in height or size.

58. Who is Wibiesana-Dewie Rajah?* and what are his properties?

Wibiesana-Dewe Rajah is he who protects the temple of Calany, and is a mighty chief over a certain number of deities, equal to Samana-Dewe Rajah.

59. Who is Wisme? and what are his attributes?

It appears in the ancient story-books called Pooranerawme, &c., that Wisme is a powerful deity, having great influence, and living in the mountain of Waykooté, which is in the wilderness of Jambu-dwipa, called Himmalawanne, to whose charge Ceylon has been committed by

* The deities of Adam's Peak, Calany, &c., namely, Sumana Dewe, Wiebesenne, and Wisme, are the Pattina gods, and are intermixed with the ancient demonolatry of Ceylon.

Sakkraia, and is consequently protecting the religion of Budhu there.

60. What became of the precious stone Minnypalange, and the tree Kirepaloo afterwards?

It appears by the religion that the stony seat Minnypalange has been buried below the tree Kiri-naga Rooka, which is in the isle Minni-naga Dewe-inne, the same being left, by the charge of the deity called Samana-dewe Rajah, for the purpose of offering and making supplication thereon by the heavenly snakes, that they may thereby obtain blessedness, as the same is the stony seat which was placed below the said tree, which is in the said island, whereupon the Budhu sat down, leaning himself towards the said tree, and preached; and the feelings of his body were conferred upon that seat.

61. After that where did the god go to?

The answer to this question will be the same as appears in the paragraph 60.

62. Give an explanation of the attributes of the kingly snake Naga Rajah, by whom the Budhu was requested to come to Ceylon for the third time?

Dewe Naga's haunt is in the rocks called Ganga-parweta, having illuminative apartments at divers places, and they are equal in other felicities to other deities. They are capable of becoming transformed into divers shapes, as they please, at all times, except in four cases, namely, resting in sleep, becoming liable to death, eating food, and enjoying the carnal pleasure; they have also mighty power, even so far as to destroy the country, by breathing out venomous fumes, rain, fire, and winds; independently of all happiness and long life, they have equally with others celestial bliss; and the divine snakes who invited Budhu at the third time, called Mani-Okkeké, and who live in the river of Calany, have also the same power and happiness.

63. Where is the place called Deganakaia situated?

The monument called Deganakaia is situate at Battecolo, which is also called Naka-wehera.

64. Where is the situation of the hells? what is their description?

The hells called Sanjeewe, Cawle-soottraia, Sangawtas, Sanjataia, Rourawaia, Maha-Rawraia, Thawpaia, Prethawpaia, and Awiechia, are situated below the earth, gradually each upon the other, in the form of a case of pots, and each of which eight great hells are accompanied by sixteen petty hells, called Oossadeho, all of which amount to 130; in which hells the wicked souls of men who have committed the five sins, namely, murder (meaning both of man and beast), thefts, adultery, lying, and drunkenness, and various other sins, are smarting beneath pungent miseries, according to the nature of their deeds; which miseries are indescribable by a brief detail.

65. Where is to be found the state of the Dewa-Lōka, or heavens of glory, in the Cingalese books?

The first heaven, called Chawtoor-Maha-Rajakai, is situated upon the rock called Sakwallagala (this, according to the European calculation, is supposed to be the pole), which is in form of a circle, and which is in circumference 3,610,350 yoduns, and in height it reaches to the rock called Yugandara-Parwatte, which is 42,000 yoduns high from the earth, and is parallel to the rim of the said Sakwallagala. In the four corners of the said heaven, the four guardians, or divine kings, subject to Sakkraia, namely, Satawaran Rajah Dradarasta, Wiroodah, Wieroopaxé, and Wayssrauana, reigned. Above the said heaven, to the same height from thence, is situated the second heaven, called Tawatensaya, upon the rock called Mahameru-Parwatte (world stone), extending to the abovesaid Sakwallagala throughout; in which heaven

Sakkraia, who is the sovereign king of the foregoing two heavens, reigned; so that the heavens called Yawmey, Tosite, Nummane-rata, Paranermite, and Wasawatty, are regularly situated, each above the other, and the divine kings, called Soojame, Santosite, Sonemmite, and Wasawattie, reigned each in his respective heaven, ascending by degrees.

66. In what manner is denoted, in the religion of Budhu, the end of life, or moksé? and what was the will of the Budhu on that point?

The salvation of men is the moksé, in which neither the birth nor the death is renewed: and the same is therefore called Amanta-maha Nirwāna, or the eternal happiness; the moral of which imports the blotting out, or the death of both the body and soul for ever, and which moksé is obtained only by those who are advanced in good works, &c. The intention of Budhu was to lead men to moksé, the state of which it is not possible to explain at large, but I will relate in a concise manner, so as every man of penetration may form an idea, that is to say, that this moksé is obtained only by all those who have abstained from every sensual indulgence.

67. Give an explanation about the people of the kingdom called Sewet Nuwara, who pur-

posely arrived at the kingdom called Jetawana-Ramaia, to see, worship, and offer things for Budhu; and on their not finding him there, they returned home with grieved hearts, leaving there the offerings they had carried with them.

Budhu, while he dwelt in the temple of Dewooran-Vihari, understood, through his omnisciences whether there were any benefit, with regard both to this and the other worlds, to the multitude who dwell in the regions thereabout, which they may gain by beholding him; and if so, he used to go either in a public manner, in company with thousands of priests, and displaying great miracles, or privately, by himself, either through the sky, or by diving through the earth, or by his usual walk, displaying himself to every one, that they may obtain mercy by seeing him. And when he had paid such a visit once to the city, some of the 7,000,000,000,000,000 devout people called Oepasakayas, who were unacquainted of his arrival, came as usual, offering odoriferous flowers and lamps; but finding him not there, nor a person suitable to whom to offer those things, as the same are not applicable to their own use, they were thrown by them within the fence of the temple.

68. What is Jetawana? and by whom was it offered?

As appears in the answer 53, the Sitano, called Anede-Pandike, who had longed to offer a temple to Budhu, during one lacse of calpas, having purchased a garden, by paying in gold spread out on the ground, built thereon a temple, by expending fifty-four kelas, and offered the same to the Budhu.

69. When Budhu had arrived at Jetawana Ramaia, the citizens waited on him, and with reverence begged permission to have his portrait taken, which he granted. Relate it particularly.

The offerings which, as appears in the answer 67, were thrown within the fence of the temple, having been seen by the King Kosal, the Sitano Anepedoo, and Wisakawo, and other virtuous women, having combined themselves together, they repaired to Budhu on the day on which he was to come to the temple, saying that they wished to make an image in the likeness of Budhu, that they might gratefully worship the same, in his stead, during his absence; whereupon he permitted them to do so, saying, that their proposal was eminently laudable, as the four cases, namely, the making and offering of such images, the offering of things to his banian-tree, his cups, and his clothing, into which the feelings of his body were conveyed, and the offerings to his remains after his demise, would lead them to the Brachma-Lōka and moksé. And he further permitted them to take a branch from the banian-tree called Sree-maha-bodie, and plant the same in the temple, and worship it. And they accordingly, rejoicing with great delight, took a piece of red sandal-wood, to the worth of one lacse, of which they shaped an image of Budhu, and planted a banian-tree; and they worshipped it in his absence, and obtained thereby great mercies.

70. Who was Annanda-Maha-Teroonancy? Give an account of him.

Each of all the Budhus has got a high-priest, who will infallibly know their thoughts, which priests are called Aggre-oopastayekes;* and thus the Aggre-oopastayeke of our Budhu was he who is also called Annanda-Maha-Teroonancy, who, with the same hopes to become Budhu, has wrought many good works, during one lacse of calpas, and who is the son of the Budhu's uncle, or the younger brother of his father, and is a king called Dowtrowdene Sackje Maha Raja, who was so capable as to learn by heart all the doctrines of 84,000 heaps of books,

* The Aggre of the Budhu is a perfect example of the Ferwer of Mithras. See Porter's "Travels in Persia," vol. i. p. 657.

when the same are only once preached by Budhu in very high Palee language: and the said king is mightier than the five following skilful people; namely, those who have sound memory, those who bear knowledge so às to understand many things, those who are experienced by questioning upon many things, those who are skilled in the tenets of Budhu, and those who are called oopastayeke.

71. There is said to be a variety of worlds: in those worlds does the human race exist?

In the Sackwalla, or world, is contained a number of gods, Maha-Bambas; so men, &c. in the same manner are contained in divers innumerable Sackwallas, Budhus and Sakwity Rajas, or the kings who solely reign over the whole world; all of whom are produced here.

72. In heaven, also, does adultery prevail; and if so, what is the origin thereof?

Because gods in their celestial habitations are satisfied by only seeing divine meats, but taste not: they have no urethra, in consequence of which, though they indulge not in libidinous intercourse with the other sex as well as men, yet they desire it; and they indulge, to their extreme satisfaction, in the divine desire they enjoy by hugging bodies one with the other; and as their origin is said to be of mere spontaneous appearance, and of coming into vision, their ranks and qualities are thus discriminated: if a goddess, on the conjugal seat or throne; if a son, on the lap; if inferior beings, in divers apartments in the divine palace.

73. What are the blessings and the happiness in the heavens? describe the state thereof.

It is not possible to relate particularly the nature of the happiness in heaven in a summary way, but I will mention it so briefly as the wise may comprehend; namely, every thing that is in colour grateful to the eye, or in music melodious to the ear, a smell grateful to the nose, a taste delicate to the palate, a convenience wholesome to the body, a proposal pleasant to the heart, are spontaneously brought about, according to the wishes formed. Another enjoyment of the divine felicities is, by indulging in the pleasure of feasting the eye on the charms of the goddesses dancing in the beautiful and divine palaces, which are constantly illuminated by the rays of every kind of invaluable diamonds.

74. Who is the King Dharma-Soka-Raja-juwo? what is his condition? and how many years after the death of Budhu was he born?

The King Dharma-Soka* was the son of the King Bindusaré, and who, putting the circle of order in force in the land of Jambu-dwipa, up to a distance of two yoduns, one from the sky and the other from the land, exacted services from the snaky demons; and doing charities at the expense of three lacses out of his riches, and causing the number of 84,000 of both convents and monasteries to be erected throughout Jambu-dwipa, he, in a most laudable and praiseworthy manner, accommodated and satisfied the mansion of Budhu; in short, he was a most excellent king, of great virtues, might, power, and influence; and it was 218 years after the extinction of Budhu that he was elevated king.

75. How many years after the decline of Budhu was the King Dootoogameny born, and what were his attributes?

It was a year after the extinction of Budhu that the King Dootoogameny was crowned king, and he was the brave son of the King Kakawaine Tissa. Dootoogameny having invaded thirty-two cities, taken captive ten lacse and thirty-four thousand Malabars that inhabited them, and put their king, Ellala, to the sword,

* The particulars of the reign of Dharma-Soka, also of Dootoogameny, the subject of the next query, are fully given in the histories of the two preceding volumes.

and established the region Lacdiva; and also caused to be constructed ninety-nine high and eminent temples, and, at the expense of twenty kelas of his riches, caused the monument Meresawetty, and another temple roofed with nine stages, with 1000 auxiliary buildings, to be constructed at the charges of thirty kelas; also another monument, or cupola, known by the name of Ruanwelly, where he entertained ninety-six kelas of priests with alms; he celebrated a festival bý expending eighty-four of his precious jewels and 1000 kelas; also by various other deeds of charities then done by him, at the charge of immense wealth.

76. Is the state of Mulgiri-galle the same as when the King Moottusiwe reigned?

Yes, it is now in the very same state.

77. Explain what is to be inferred from the term Budhu.

The full interpretation of the word Budhu cannot be enlarged upon by a short detail, but will be hereafter stated so briefly as the wise may understand, that is to say, in consequence of the knowledge of every event belonging to the times past, present, and future, he was called by the name Budhu.

78. Who are termed Attapiris?

They are the eight persons, namely, the four

gods Brahma, Mawra, Tawatinsaia, Chatoork-Maha-Rajikaia; and the four human beings, namely, Xestriea, Brahmana, Grahapatrea, and Sramana-Sanketa.

79. What is the knowledge that is called Astawedsawe?

It is the eight omnisciences:* of foreknowing the death and birth of the creation in the time to come; of seeing any distant place, when wished for, near at hand; of increasing the little and decreasing the much; drawing close the distant, and lengthening that which is the nearest; the power of hearing any noise or sound that goes on in any part of the world; the power of seeing every thing in the world; the wisdom of knowing the hearts of others; the penetration of knowing the shape lived in in the past transmigrations; and the prudence of suppressing every lustful desire.

80. Who was the King Malla-Rassooroowo? and what was his kingdom?

He was a descendant of the family Mahasammata, and a prince of great virtues, influence, might, and power; his city was Kusina

* This definition fully illustrates the Budhist term of Omniscience, viz. knowing the past, the present, and the future; which clearly defines itself to be the knowledge of the transmigrations of the existing calpe only.

Nuwara, lying to the north of the banian-tree, and it was in this very city that our Budhu made his exit.

81. It is said that there are 2000 islands (excepting the one called Satara-Mahadiwe); describe how they are situated.

There are situated 500 petty islands circumjacent to each of the superior ones, so that there are 500 petty islands (which are appropriated to the superior island Jambu-dwipa) round about Jambu-dwipa, and the three other islands are situated in the very same manner.

82. Is Sakkraia the protector of Ceylon?

Since Sakkraia has been charged by Budhu with the protection of his religion in Ceylon, it is the fact that he (Sakkraia) preserves the island.

83. Has Sakkraia any pagodas devoted to him in Ceylon?

As no pagodas have been consecrated on this nether world for those gods who inhabit the heavens (except to those earthly deities who are begotten for the sake of trees and rocks), so the deity Sakkraia Diwerajaia has no pagoda dedicated to him in Ceylon.

84. What is the shape of the deity Sakkraia?

The deities that inhabit the heavens are of bright shining bodies, similar to the light of a lamp, and are three leagues in height, wearing diamond crowns of one league height each, their bodies being constantly bathed with perfumes, clothed with divine raiments, and ornaments emitting rays from their apparel; and as the god Sakkraia also presides over them as king, he has a superiority in point of every thing stated above.

85. In what year was it that Sakkraia delivered the charge of Ceylon to Wisnoo?*

From the day of the delivery to the 29th of November, of the year of Christ 1813, it makes 2,355 years, eight months, and seven days.

86. It is said that there are many Sakkraias; state how and what are they.

The regions or sackwallas are numerous, each of which has a god Sakkraia; consequently, their numbers also are numerous, but from amongst them only 10,000 Sakkraias, belonging to 10,000 regions or sackwallas, can assemble to the festival of Budhu.

87. There are many worlds: what are their names?

There are three worlds; the first of them constitutes the twenty regions of Brahmas, four hells, human region, &c., so that within a world

* Wisnoo, or Wismekarma.

there are thirty-one regions that are inhabited by creation; of which, from the world of snakes unto the sixteen heavenly kingdoms, all the regions that are inhabited by creation are known by Kamelōkaia, from the heaven Brahma-parisadjaia Bambalowa, unto the utmost heaven Bambalowa; the eight regions between them which are inhabited by creation are called Roopelokaia; and the other four regions, also inhabited by creation, namely, Akasanan-chacatena, Wigniananchaia-tenai, Akinjaia-tanaia, and Niwesansaia-tanaia, are called the Aroopalokaia; so that there appear three several worlds in the religion; and all the future worlds will contain as those already stated.

88. Is it a sin in the Cingalese to take their night's repast?

It is no sin for every Cingalese (except to those who are consecrated by being admitted to fulfil the ten commandments of Budhu, called Dahasil, also another eight commandments, called Atasil) to receive their night's repast; and as the same has been so strictly forbidden by Budhu to the priests, unto those in the above hallowed state, it would be a sin of high degree for a person so forbidden to take the night repast.

89. It is mentioned that Budhu was raised in

consequence of his having abstained from all the sins; if so, explain how it was.

It is true that Budhu was so promoted on account of his having avoided many sinful deeds: such a brief statement as this will not admit of the whole particulars thereof, wherefore it will be related in such a short manner as the wise may understand, namely, as the desires are the chief aptitude of all sins, the Budhu abstained from all sensual indulgence, and by that means attained his end.

90. Why are the priests excluded from receiving goats, sheep, oxen, &c.?

In former ages the priests, like unto all sensualists in the secular state, were accustomed to deal in goats, sheep, oxen, and hogs, and subsisted thereby, but the people beginning to murmur, remonstrating that no distinction was thereby to be made between the sensualists and the priests, it came to the knowledge of Budhu, who thereupon strictly forbade the same to the priests; in consequence of which, woe be unto him who now presumes to sin in the like manner!

TRANSLATION

OF

A CINGALESE COMPENDIOUS DESCRIPTION

OF THE

BÚDHIST DOCTRINE,

AND OF THE EDIFICATION OF THE FAMOUS PAGODA UPON ADAM'S PEAK, DENOMINATED

MULGIRRI-GALLE;

Sent, on the 3d of December, 1766, to His Excellency the Honourable Iman Willem Falck, Doctor of Law, Governor and Director of the Island of Ceylon and its Dependencies, in compliance with his Excellency's desire (when in the Pagoda Mulgirri-galle), by the High Priest residing there, named Sue Bandare Metankere Samenere Samewahanse.

BUDHIST DOCTRINE,

ETC. ETC.

The powerful gods Satagierre and Assoere, the four gods who are the supreme rulers and protectors of all the worlds, the god Sakkraia who governs six heavens, and Maha-Brahma who illuminates all the worlds, have, with several other gods, proceeded to the Budhu, and, stooping down before him, prayed him to make a sermon out of love to them.

The said Budhu, who is a king in making such sermon, and a lord in governing the three worlds, Brahma-Lōka, Dewe-Lōka, and Maneispe-Lōka;—the first, a world above the Dewe-Lōka heavens; the second, one that is in heaven itself; and the third, which is inhabited by men—is also a person who removes the evil from the inhabitants of all the three worlds, and is very great and beautiful; and when the other gods and inhabitants of worlds approach him, all their beauties, power, and other qualities, are impaired, and in him alone are so transparent, that the others rejoice at it. Before he came to the state of Budhu, he had, as he wished, abandoned all his riches and shewed all possible mercifulness, after which he died often, and being born again, he met first the Budhu named Bragmedewe, and then wishing to become also Budhu, fell at his feet. Since that, walking during innumerable years, with a sincere intention of his heart, he met a second Budhu called Gauteme, and worshipped him also with such desire.

Afterwards, flattering himself with that hope during immemorial years, he remained under the government of the Budhu Diepankerenan, who, like a shining light, was the highest ruler of the said three worlds in the city of Ammerawetie. Born from the high parentage of bramins, and called the Prince Soomedenam, as he grew up there, he had an aversion to all temporal riches, and, on the other hand, conceived a desire to go over to the priesthood; whereupon he proceeded to the king of that country, and informed him of all the treasures of his ancestors as far as seven generations, and that he wanted to distribute the same among the poor. The king was very glad of it, and praised his intention, causing the poor to be gathered by beat of tom-tom, amongst whom the prince caused his treasures to be distributed; after which he proceeded to the woods, and, deep in the same, discovered a rock with a building upon it like a palace, called Parne, which, with whatever was to be found in it, by order of the god Sakkraia, was produced by his favourite, named Wismekarma, in the twinkling of an eye. The garment, which was also to be found in it, was put on by him, and then he appeared like a pilgrim; and, walking in the air, and seeing that the roads in the city of Ram-Jenam were beaten and decorated by the inhabitants, asked them for what purpose it was done? They said for the arrival of the Budhu Diepankerenan, who, with 400,000 rahatoons, signifying spirits in the air, were expected there, asking him whether he did not hear of it? As he who was in the air heard it, he stepped with such a trembling noise upon earth as if an ear-ring of the god Sakkraia had fallen down, and asked them whether they could not give him also a spot to clear? They gave him thereupon a valley to fill up. He then thought he should be able to cause the necessary earth to be brought from heaven; but it being a knowledge by his faith that it would be better to do it by his own labour, he therefore took a basket, in which he himself conveyed the necessary quantity of earth, and filled up that valley. In the middle of his work, it happened that the said Budhu Diepankerenan, with several gods more, and the said

400,000 rahatoons, came to the said place with much splendour and pomp; and when the valley was not perfectly filled, the pilgrim thought that it was not good to make such illustrious persons go through that half-filled valley, the more so as he who could do so much had undertaken that work; on which account he laid a sheet over it, and went and lay himself forward upon the same, in order to serve as a bridge when those great people should pass by. The Budhu came then and stood near his head, and being inspired, said to his people, "O! happy men, look at this happy pilgrim, Soomedenam, who, after innumerable years, shall also attain to the state of Budhu like me, and procure to all the gift of Nirwāna;" and predicted further in which city he would again be born as Budhu, who would be his parents, and who his wife and children, what would be his support, and the consequence of him, and also that he would be called Guadma Budhu; after which he, having walked with joy around him three times, and having offered eight handsful of flowers, went away from there with those who were with him, who also, together with several gods, brahmins, and other people of the earth, did so: whereupon the said pilgrim went and sat upon a heap of flowers brought there to be offered; and recollecting very well that he did not neglect to give all his treasures to the poor, and to be charitable, satisfied, courageous, true, hoping, just, industrious, and to have knowledge of the birth after this life, upon that assurance he lived and died. He was again born anew, with the name of the King Wesantara, gave all his wealth to the poor, and died; but afterwards, being born again in the fifth heaven, called Tosite, all the gods that were in that heaven requested him, when he was in the glory of his life, to come in the world of men, and to accept of the dignity of Budhu; and thus he, having been conceived in the womb of the lawful wife of the King Suddodarna, called Mahamaarie, was born of her after ten months.

He was then growing like the increasing moon, and became the king of the four parts of the world; afterwards, he having lived in carnal conversation with the princess named Jasodera and 40,000 concubines, during thirty-one years, upon the three signs which he saw he proceeded to his country house, and being in the middle of it, there appeared before him Wismekarme, by order of 1000 gods, in the shape of one who always adhered to him, and dressed him in clothes in which 1000 points were hanging, adorned him with several jewels, tied his head with 1000 heavenly head-dresses, and crowned him with a crown of precious stones; whereupon being informed that a son was born for him, he called him Rahulla, and went out as cheerful as Sakkraia returning after having conquered his enemies the Assuras. On the road he met a woman called Kisagooteme, who, in a song, represented to him the good and evil which befal men during life: he rejoiced at it so much, that he took off a chain which he had about his neck and gave it to his followers, desiring it to be given to her, and afterwards came into his palace, which was as bright as that of Sakkraia, where, he having sat in his apartment upon his chair, some women came to divert him; but he not liking it, and coming near the door, he thought if he entered his house, and saw his wife and children, that they would not allow him to become Budhu. He therefore returned, and went to his courtier named Tjannenam, who was asleep, whom he awoke, and ordered to saddle the horse called Kantekenan, which was eighteen cubits long, and high in proportion, and to bring the same, which having also been done, he got on horseback, and rode on as a ruler of the aforesaid three worlds, when the large gate which was opened and shut by 1000 men went open of itself by the management of God; and in consideration of his having formerly always kept an open door for the poor, he, like the moon which escapes the swallowing of the eclipse, and being also freed from all worldly things, came on the border of the river Anomanam, and alighted from his horse, after having ridden 120 miles. Afterwards he with his right hand, laying hold of his hair, took his gold sword with the left, and cut off a good part and threw it towards heaven, where it was taken up by Sakkraia, and having put it in a gold box, took it to his habitation.

Hereupon Maha Brahma Rajah brought a garment of a priest and delivered it to him, which he also took and put on, and afterwards, out of joy, remained there during seven days; then he crossed the river, and having arrived in the city called Rayegahanoewere, begged of every one for a handful of rice, and sitting near a stone, ate it.

Thence he came into the city of King Binsere, who having asked him why he begged, as he was the son of King Suddodarna, and was a king himself? he said he did so to become Budhu, and intended also to come ere long as such in the city. Afterwards he spent his days during seven years in many difficulties, and, on the 15th of May, having come near a devil-tree, there he got an offering, from a virgin called Soeyata, of rice boiled with cocoa-nut milk, which he brought near a river named Neranjene, and having made of it forty-nine balls, ate the same; sitting on the border upon the sand, he afterwards threw the gold basin in which he got the rice (of the value of 100,000 larins) in the river, thinking, should he become Budhu, that it ought to float against the stream, which happened also. After that he proceeded into an adjoining wood of certain sort of trees called sal, and having rested there the whole day, he went at night on a road which was cleared by the gods to another devil-tree. On the road he met a brahmin, who gave him eight handsful of grain called Kusatane, which having been strewed by him near that tree, the earth was split open, and out of it came a seat of the height of fourteen cubits; upon which he went and sat, leaning against that devil-tree, which was like a silver pillar, when all the gods appeared there, and having praised him, a great light appeared there. Then came also, upon an elephant, of the extent of a large mountain, in a frightful shape, a deity called Wassewarti-mara, with innumerable followers, armed with pikes and swords, and he himself had a sword in his hand wherewith heaven could be hewn, in order to frighten the Budhu and other gods, and to take away the seat; for which purpose he also caused it to rain nine times, but nothing could prejudice the Budhu; he, on the contrary, having recollected himself the ten virtuous deeds done by him, they were all driven away, as it were, by ten giants; whereupon he, on account of the good which he did since the time of the Budhu Bragme-dewe until he ascended the seat, obtained forgiveness of his sins, and became Budhu, with the name of Guadma, being of a high birth, where he remained during seven weeks. Afterwards, at the request of Maha Brahma Rajah, having gone to the city Barennas (Benares), he made his introductory sermon there, in the large hall called Issipattene, whereby a high priest called Anjakendanje, and innumerable people, were converted, and many blind were made to see, and many miracles occurred; and the gods and others were by his doctrine brought to a clear state and in the right path. Nine months afterwards, or on the 15th January, he came to this island of Ceylon, and went to the devil who was on Mayjanginne, in the palace of Nangewenodenneje, twelve miles long and four miles broad, where he, hovering in the air, produced a thick darkness over the whole earth, and thereby frightened the devils so much that they all retired; and he got thereby an opportunity to tread upon the earth, and to go and sit upon a seat which came forth of itself, and to cause fire to issue forth from the four corners, whereby the devils were more frightened; but he comforted them, and caused afterwards a wood called Jakgierrie, through his power, to come there from the place where it was situated, where he having banished the devils, sent the said wood again to the place where it was formerly situated. Afterwards he edified the gods who were assembled at Mayjanginne aforesaid with his sermon, and liberated them from hell; and having given to Samandiwe Rajah a handful of his hair, pointed out this island for the habitation of men, and afterwards proceeded to Oerroewieldanauwe. Whereupon the said Samandiwe Rajah, having put the handfull of hair received in a chest with precious stones, kept the same at the aforesaid place, Mayjanginne.

This is what our Budhu did the first time he came to Ceylon. Five years afterwards he came forth from the pagoda Telewanne, and put a stop to the battle of the two gods in the shape of snakes, by name Tchulodere and Magodere, the first whereof was at Waddoenagelle, and the other at Calany, who kept themselves under the earth, and were at war on account of the seat of precious stones, and he edified them with his doctrine; whose innumerable followers were also converted by him. Then both the snake-gods, saying, that if either of them had retained the seat a contest would have arisen again, offered to the Budhu the same, as well as some victuals which they brought forth through their power, who then, having sat upon the seat and having eaten the victuals, delivered afterwards a tree called Keriepalloe, which, when he came from the said pagoda, was used by the god Samman-dewa as an umbrella to protect himself from the sun, and also the said seat, which were both used in his service, to the god Wiebiesinne, in order that the snakes, by worshipping the same, might obtain Nirwāna; and afterwards he returned again to the pagoda. When he came again to this island on the 15th of May, in the eighth year, at the request of the snake Mannierkeyeram, he sat on that very beautiful seat; then he also ate the meat brought there by the said snake, and converted many persons by his sermon; and having also remained for some time in the pagoda Balance, with 500 rahatoons, appeared, at the request of the god Samman-dewa Rajah, as the moon which comes from the east, on the rock called Sammantekoete; where he, having attended, the gods, out of joy, rained down flowers and precious stones; and he afterwards left the impression of his foot upon that rock. Subsequently, having remained with his suite, and other priests who were with him, for some time, he departed with great joy to a place called Dieganekeye, and thence to the city Anurahde-pura, where he visited the places Srimahabode-distaen, Ratnemales-taene, Toepa-ramettame, and Wonnissakenani Barroewattes-taene; and having remained a little time upon each of the said places, and having preached before the gods who were there, he returned to the said pagoda, and remained there forty-five years, preaching and shewing his good works. Afterwards he proceeded to the court of the King Mallele, and there went and lay, according to his own pleasure, on one of the cots which were decorated in the two halls, and considered in which quarter of the world his divinity and laws would be best acknowledged and adopted, which is the extent of thirty-six hundred times hundred thousand ten thousand three hundred and fifty yoduns, and whereof the one part of the world, called Poerewewideeseje, is 7000 yoduns; the second, called Jambu-dwipa, 10,000 yoduns; the third, called Apperego-jancge, 7000 yoduns; and the fourth, called Oetoeroekoeroe-diweine, 8000 yoduns; besides 2000 small islands more;

and knowing, through his omniscience, what would happen in this quarter during 5000 years, whereupon he called from amongst the gods that were there, one named Sakkraia, and said to him whilst on Ceylon, which he had visited three times, and had driven the devils from it, that his laws would be better followed there, and directed him to protect Ceylon and its inhabitants well; which order Sakkraia took also upon his head, bowing down, and afterwards devolved the protection on his assistant god Wisnu. Budhu Guadma died blessed, on a Tuesday, the 15th of May, after he had edified all the gods and inhabitants of the highest heaven by his sermons; whose corpse afterwards being put in a golden coffin, was burned by the assembled Sakkraias, Brahmas, and others, who came from 10,000 worlds, with sandal-wood, which was heaped up to the height of 120 cubits; after which they made sacrifices during three weeks.

Of the good works of the said Budhu, which are as great as the ground of the world is large, the sea is deep, the heaven is high, or the air is full, something more is mentioned here: he was guiltless of slaying any thing which enjoyed life, of the commission of theft, and of fornication, of telling lies, of speaking evil, and of speaking indecent words, of eating at nights, of dancing, singing, playing, smelling flowers and other smelling things, of sitting at higher places than the height of a carpenter's measure, of being covetous of gold and silver, of desiring all sorts of paddy, slaves, goats, lambs, fowls, pigs, elephants, horses, cows, buffaloes, gardens, and fields, of delivering any writings or presents, of taking or giving away treasures, of keeping false measures and weights, of disinheriting any heirs of gifts or presents, of deceit in falsifying gold and precious stones, and of taking villages and other possessions; besides all those things, he was moreover free from all indecency, and, on the other hand, performing every thing which is good, like the priests who keep the laws of Budhu, and commit also no crime, namely, killing, or other such deeds, but live according to their honour.

Now is described the high doctrine of the Budhu, who is the lord of the three worlds, who several times, leaving his magnificence, proceeded to the world as a beggar, and being moved with mercy over men, and having suffered many oppressions, has attained to the said state.

Of whatever the people in the world were instructed, each in his own language in an intelligible manner, the good and evil being at the same time represented to them, but so little is spoken here as a drop of water taken from the sea.

1st. That whoever kills, or causes such to be done, must undergo, even in this life, many oppressions, and hereafter be born again in hell; and although he, after having made amends there, may again be born in the world from a good family, he will not however have the least benefit, but be subject to wretchedness.

2d. That whoever steals is punished in this life, his hands and feet are cut off, and other castigation is undergone, and hereafter he goes to hell; and although he, having suffered there much, may again be born in the world, he however would be obliged to beg, without being allowed to have any thing to fill his stomach with, or to cover his nakedness, or to find a dwelling for shelter.

3d. That whoever desires women shall be obliged to suffer many oppressions in this world itself, and hereafter be born again in hell; and although he, after having lingered there long, may be born in this world as a girl 100 times, no man however will look at her, as such woman will only have the figure of a human being, without being created either as man or woman, and consequently will undergo many difficulties and vexations.

4th. That whoever speaks lies shall die in this life itself in his sins, and be again born in hell; and although he, having suffered there long, may again at any time be born in this world, he shall have no fine figure or good voice, but a stinking breath, and shall have two tongues like the snakes, and, speaking the truth, shall not be believed, and in any thoughts, words, or works, although innocent, shall be considered as guilty.

5th. That he who drinks himself drunk loses his understanding, and is detested by every one. That a drunkard, moreover, treats his parents and masters unjustly, and, in his journey to heaven, shall be surrounded by impediments like a jungle in the road; that his bad thoughts shall tend to his own destruction, and be more and more augmented: the killing of cattle, committing robbery and adultery, and speaking lies, backbiting, speaking unnecessary and idle words, coveting the wealth of his neighbour, and envying the works of his neighbour, imagining himself that there is no sin or eternal salvation; all these things, which happen through drunkenness, are prohibited by the Budhu; so that whoever dies in such sins shall be born again in hell, and suffer there much; and at some future time being born in this world, shall be delirious, and be subject to incurable diseases. That he who seeks dirty treasure, by selling liquor, beef, living cattle, arrows and bows, firelocks, or such arms wherewith birds are shot, ought to leave it off; and, on the other hand, to mind such things as these, viz. good riches obtained by one's own labour, by sowing and reaping, and by carrying on good trade, to give to the poor with joy, to think of Budhu, to maintain his good doctrine, to assist his adherents, to keep his institutions, to be equally charitable to all men, to honour parents, masters, Budhu, and his followers, and do them good according to his ability, to teach the doctrine to others as far as he knows it, to listen attentively to the instruction thereof, and to place a constant faith upon it. He who is and remains so, shall, after this life, go to Braḥma-Lōka, and, enjoying every thing good there, inherit Nirwāna.

Whoever does good works in this world on behalf of Budhu, as well during his presence as afterwards, and persists in it, shall have the force of the sun; whoever esteems his doctrine shall obtain so much wisdom as the ground of the world is large; whoever honours his adherents shall obtain gold, silver, precious stones, villages, and lands, according to the promise of Budhu; so that whoever leaves off evil as aforesaid, and observes good deeds, shall share Nirwāna.

When the said Budhu remained in a certain city called Sewas, in the pagoda situated there, called Jetewanemaha-Vihari, he perceived at once, by the spirit of omniscience, the whole world, and seeing that there were many blessed people, he, to make them happy, went to them from that pagoda; and exactly on that day the king of that place, called Kosol, came there, together with several other people, but not meeting the Budhu, he thought to himself and said, that that pagoda was abandoned, and that he who was so favourable to men was now lost; at which he became very sorrowful, and laid in the hall all the treasures which he brought with him, and returned to his city; but the Budhu came there shortly after.

The next day the said King Kosol appeared, taking with him many people and much treasure, in the said pagoda, and seeing the Budhu sit there, he said to him, falling at his feet, that he came there the preceding day with his people, but not seeing him, returned with great grief: therefore he asked for leave to cause an image to be made like him, for the comfort of mankind. The Budhu being very glad at it, said that his intention was very good, and permitted him to get such an image made; whereupon the king, on account of the affection of the Budhu, fell at his feet and worshipped, asking how that image was best to be made? He answered thereupon and said, it could be made, according to his pleasure, of wood, stone, earth, metal, iron, copper, silver, gold, or precious stones, long or short, large or small, saying, at the same time, that although any person had the ability to fill this part of the world (which is to the extent of 10,000 yoduns) with small grains, and afterwards to count the same one by one, yet the happiness of those who make such images cannot be estimated: which exhortation respecting the making of images the king very gladly heard, and, upon permission obtained, going again with his suite to his palace, caused a piece of red sandal-wood to be brought out of his treasury, and an image to be made thereof according to the likeness of Budhu; after which he dressed the same with a yellow garment, and kept it at a secure place: all those who saw it were very glad. Hereafter the said King Kosol went again from him with a numerous retinue, provided with flowers and burning lamps, to the said pagoda to Budhu, and worshipped him, saying, that the image was finished, and was pleasing to be seen; at which he became very glad. The king returned to his palace, and caused there to be made a hall, with gold and all sorts of precious stones, which was covered with gold tiles, and fine cloth and curtains; and decorating the same in this costly manner, caused an altar to be erected towards the south side thereof, and placed the image there, causing also the roads to be cleaned thence to the pagoda, and all high places to be levelled, white sand to be strewn, and fine cloth to be spread thereupon, and on both sides to be decorated with bows of honour and painted cloth, and the lamps to burn with fragrant oil; then he, taking his people with him, and all sorts of music and sacrifices, proceeded to the said pagoda, and prayed Budhu to go with him. The Budhu thereupon immediately dressed himself in a yellow garment, and covered himself therewith, when he shined like the sun, and, like it, attended by 500 rahatoons, and treading upon flowers, which through the force of his happiness and providence came spontaneously from earth, and enjoying the honour which all the gods shewed him, proceeded to the said hall, to the great joy of every one. Having arrived there, the image which was made by the king and his people was devoted to Budhu and his rahatoons. But when Budhu went into the said hall, the image of red sandal-wood made some motions upon the altar, as if it thought that it was not proper, when the Budhu arrived, to sit on such high places, and on that account wished to come down; but the Budhu perceiving it, said, pointing with his right hand towards it, that as he intended within a short time to go to Nirwāna, his name would be thought of 5000 years on account of that image, and therefore did not allow that image to come down: and in order that thus long all gods and men should make sacrifices to the same with love, he took eight handsful of flowers and offered himself; which the rahatoons having perceived, did the same with all kinds of flowers, as well as all the Brahmin princes, and about 4000 wives of the king; and all the inhabitants of the town came with flowers and treasure; on account of which high sacrifices, the king treated, out of joy, the Budhu, in the said gold hall, upon a throne made expressly for that purpose; and placing the said rahatoons in the same, treated them during seven days with nice sweetmeats. After which he, informing the Budhu of his ignorance, and of the Budhu's great abilities in making images, prayed to know what benefit a person who makes images can expect in this world, how he would proceed to heaven from this life, and what he would enjoy there; and he said he wished much to hear it, and to keep it in his heart. The Budhu replied, that he asked it rightly, and promised that he would fully explain it, in order that he might keep it in his heart. His servant, the priest Annedemahateroewahanse, interrupted him in the meantime, and asked what good a person who writes his sermon can expect? He then said he was glad at that question also, and answered upon these points in the manner following:—

1. That he, who according to his ability, makes an image or writes sermons, shall never be born in either hell.

2. That such shall not be born out of the circumference of the world, but in the same.

3. That he will not be born from the womb of any one's slave, but from a respectable family, and shall faithfully maintain the laws of Budhu.

4. That he will not be born as a girl, or be subject to the falling sickness, frenzy, want of speech, deafness, deformity; nor be subject to any eruption or other complaints; but, on the contrary, shall be made like a gold image with tiger's teeth.

5. That he will not be frightened by tigers, bears, &c., nor undergo any injustice at any time, but be born from a respectable family, and obtain wealth every where, which also shall be augmented like as the moon increases after its

appearance; and that the family from which such a one shall be born shall receive no affront.

6. That he shall become rich in pearls, precious stones, paddy, rice, fine clothes, slaves, faithful subjects, elephants, horses, coaches, palenkeens, cows, and buffaloes.

7. That he shall be born in heaven, and with 1000 heavenly wives live in an unspeakably shining habitation, and in every thing obtain his wish, and enter the glory moksé.

In this manner the Budhu having stated the happiness of those who make his image and write his sermon-book, it was heard with joy by the King Kosol and the high priest Annedemahateroe-wahanse, and kept in their hearts; and since that time the making of images and writing of sermons were introduced into the world, and by the king of this quarter of the world called Dharma-Soka, under whom 84,000 other kings were subject; as many pagodas were erected in which sacrifices of joy were made, according to the lesson of Budhu, happiness was to be derived therefrom; also, the king of this island, called Dootoogameny, caused for that purpose ninety-nine pagodas to be erected, and great sacrifices to be made therein; and his followers therefore caused also hundreds of houses for sacrifices to be erected, and, in consequence thereof, inherited the Brahma heaven. Another king of this island, called Dieweni-patisse, who resided in the city Anuradhe-pura, caused, in the 809th year after the birth of Roedoo, in consequence of the happiness which consisted in his doctrine, this pagoda, called Mullegirri, to be erected in a most splendid manner, which is situated within the Girrewadoloosda-haspattoo; and, with the consent of the necessary villages, and many people, caused great sacrifices to be made therein, from which time also it has remained in the same state.

THE

BUDHU GUADMA'S DOCTRINE,

DRAWN UP FROM A

SINGHALESE COMPENDIUM,

BY

MODELIAR RAJAH PAXE.

THE

BUDHU GUADMA'S DOCTRINE,

ETC. ETC.

The Lord Budhu, who rules like the sun over the whole world, is a brahma of the brahmas, a god of gods, and king of kings; he subdued the five senses, and, according to the predictions of the Budhus, &c. arrived at the eminent and surpassing state of Budhu, by virtue of such beneficent acts as he performed in the unutterable number of lives through which he passed.

He became Budhu on the 15th day of the month Ursenje; and since that day he sojourned, during seven weeks, at seven different places. Among others, he remained seven days under the tree Kiripaluruke, on the south side of the tree Burweke, where he enjoyed celestial happiness. When he left this place, the god Sakdewirajun, who had become acquainted with the wish of Budhu, offered to him the medicinal gal-nut, and the nalijedawetu (a certain root), and the water of the river Anukattewille, with which he washed his face, and then took up his abode there.

On this occasion two merchants, by name Tapasjuye and Ballakeje, two brothers, who had been born and educated in the city Puskereweti Nuwara,* in the kingdom Raamanne Mandeleje, and were on their journey with a great company, and 500 loaded waggons, to trade in the country Maddemepredereje, came into the country where Budhu was. A goddess who had inhabited the earth, and who, in her former life, had been the mother of these two brothers, caused the waggons to stop. Upon this the merchants promised to make an offering. The goddess then addressed them, saying, "Hark ye, fortunate men, our Lord Budhu is under the tree Kiripaluruke, you, who go to trade, make an offering to him of fresh butter and honey,† and you

* It would be in vain to inquire where the places mentioned in these accounts are to be found. These are mysteries too great even for the priests, who generally content themselves by saying, that the places have perished in some of the destructions of the world.

† It is scarcely requisite to say, that these are and have been ever the chief offerings of the East, and are still so in Persia, to instance only the ceremonies exhibited at the entrance of

will obtain satisfaction for a great length of time."

After this, the merchants made an offering to Budhu, which he accepted, and ate out of the ruby vessel given by the god Sienwarandewirajun; he then preached his doctrine to them, by which they were converted, and became Vepasekeas.

When the merchants resumed their journey, Budhu, with his right hand, took eight blue hairs from his head, and gave them to the merchants as a pledge that they should in future promote his religion.

The merchants were exceedingly gratified at this, and conveyed the hair in a golden box to the city Puskereweti Nuwara, where they laid it at the east gate of the city, and built a tower over it, from which issues blue rays at particular seasons, and, like Budhu himself, still contribute to the delight of both gods and men. This was the first tower that was erected at Anurahde-pura.

the Shah into Teheran, &c., as detailed in Morier's "Embassy." Virgil also alludes to the sacred character of honey, when, in the Georgics, book iv. he thus sings:—

> "His quidam signis, atque hæc exempla secuti
> Esse apibus partem divinæ mentis, et haustus
> Ætherios dixere: deum namque ire per omnes
> Terrasque, tractusque maris, cœlumque profundum."

Some time after this, these merchants proceeded to their own country, and preached to the world the doctrines of Budhu. It was by them also that this persuasion was first introduced at Anurahde-pura, the country of the King Máhádharme.

Budhu arriving some time after at the temple Iswerepatnerānāyé, in the country of Benares, whither he had repaired at the request of the god Maha-Bambehee, preached a sermon to the people. He then proceeded to the temple Nisadwiam Vihari, in the country Sawetnoewere, where he preached to a merchant, by name Mahapunneje, who, being converted, became a priest that could walk on the air. He then became a member of the college of the eighty high-priests of Budhu.

After this, a merchant, by name Chulepanneje, sailing to an island to purchase sandalwood, when he had loaded his vessel, and was about to set sail, was terribly frightened by the devils who inhabited that place; but, through the power of the priest Mahapunneje, the merchant and his ship were safely conveyed to his own country; and the merchant himself was made a priest. The merchant then gave half of the sandal to the priest, with which he built a temple in the country called Sunapaṛanteratte.

He then prayed Budhu and his suite to come to the temple, intending to offer it to them.

The god Sakkraia, who knew the intention of the merchant, caused golden palanquins to come down from heaven, in which Budhu and his suite were seated. These palanquins first appeared on the rock Sachebaddepaovaba, where he converted the heathen pilgrims; and, having made them priests, he came with them to the country Sunaparante, where he accepted the offering of the temple, and made a sermon, by which a great number of souls inherited Nirwāna.

He returned afterwards to Dewram Vihari, and thence, at the request of the king of the snakes, called Narmadaanam, he proceeded to Nababhuvana, and preached there. After which, he set his feet upon a precious rock, situated on the shore of the river Narmadaanam-ganga, whence he returned to the temple Dewram Vihari.

At the request of the high priest Salchebadde Terebu, and for the welfare of many gods and men, the Lord Budhu set his feet upon the rock Sachebaddeparaweteje, and thence he proceeded to Jeeteweneraameje. After this, the principal high-priests, Punnemahaterun-wahanse and Sachebaddeterun - wahanse, promoted the persuasion of Budhu at Anurahde-pura, as well as in several other countries. This was the second propagation of the persuasion of Budhu at Anurahde-pura.

The Lord Budhu, having executed every thing for the public benefit, died in blessed state on the 15th day of the month Wesenge, at the age of eighty years.

After a lapse of 208 years, the Emperor of Jambu-dwipa, by name Dharma-Sōka Maharaja, having heard the doctrine of Budhu from the high-priest Nikgroda Terun-wahanse, was converted, and immediately set about spreading that doctrine. The high-priest Mokgeliputte-tisse Terun-wahanse, perceiving that the persuasion of Budhu was to take effect, made a sermon to 1000 rahatoons.

He afterwards sent the priests Joonekedammerakki Maharakkite Terun-wahanse, Jooneke-ratte, Sooneje Terun-wahanse, Vettereje Terun-wahanse, and Swarnebumije, in order to promote the doctrine of Budhu. This was also done at Anurahde-pura, and was the third time the persuasion of Budhu was taught at that place.

The laws and sermons of Budhu have long existed at this capital, or, as it is otherwise called, the country of the King Mahadharme, under Jambu-dwipa, and on the island of the Cingalese, according to the traditions of the priests and their posterity.

The King Walegamabaa, who descended from the first King of Ceylon, by name Vijaya-raja, had the laws and sermons called Turn-pittike written out, within the term of seven months, in the sixth year of his reign, and 450 years after the death of the Lord Budhu, by 500 rahatoons, at the temple Alu Vihari, at Maatele.

In the sixth year of the reign of the King Maha-Naaone, and in the year of Budhu 930, the high-priest Buddothegooseke Terun-wahanse, coming to the island of Ceylon, composed the books called Visuddhimarge, &c. Upon his return to Swarnabhumiye, he composed the Turnpittike also, and employed himself in teaching the doctrine of Budhu; while the King Aniniddha Maha Maja propagated the same persuasion in the country Arunardene-pureje, &c.

It might be unnecessary to add any thing more in order to shew in what manner the Budhists believe their religion to have been taught. The following is intended further to illustrate their belief as to the existence of the last Budhu.

This Guadma of such great might, who so soon attained to the state of Budhu, in mercy to mankind, having studied throughout four lacses of asankas, and done amazing works of charity in every state of his existence, departed at length from the being of Wessantera Raja, and was born again in the seventeenth heaven called Tosite Dewa-Lōka, where he enjoyed the divine bliss: and when the time to become Budhu had arrived, at the request of the deitical brahmas, and agreeably to former custom, he departed from the said heaven, and was conceived in the womb of Mahamaya Devi, the principal Queen of Suddodana, the King Nōdana Maha Raja; and having remained during a period of ten months in his mother's womb, he was born on the 15th, or full-moon day, attended by many miracles.

At length, after much reflection on the miseries and vicissitudes of human life, he was presented by God with the image of a hermit, with which he was so much pleased, that he immediately quitted his kingdom, riches, and every pleasure; and secluding himself from the laity, and assuming the habit of a hermit, he repaired to the wilderness, where, through a period of six years, he cherished the sil, or piety, and led a life of austerity and self-denial.

During this time he had many dreams and omens afforded him, which plainly foretold his promotion to the estate of Budhu, upon which he took encouragement, resolving not to forsake his station till he was initiated into that desirable state. He accordingly laid himself down, and placing his back against the bo or braman-tree, called Sri-maha-bodin-wahanse, on the 15th, or full moon, of Ursinje (May), he expired; and losing all corporeal feelings, he became endowed with the powers of omniscience, enabling him at once to view the three calpas.* After this, at the request of Brahma, he set out to Isipatanarame, where he preached from the bāna,† made by former Budhus, and thereby provided instruction for a great number of people. From this time he went preaching and working miracles, as former Budhus had done; and by continually insisting on works of charity, piety, prayer, as well as the torments of the four hells, he succeeded in affording consolation to brahmas, princes, brahminical philosophers, the sixty-two images then renowned in the world, and many others.

Budhu, by his preaching, is said to have

* Different ages or states of the world.

† The sermons extant of primitive Budhist doctrine.

saved twenty asankas of human beings; and, after the space of thirty-two years of labours, he attained to the state of Nirwāna. While attaining this state, he ordered that some relics of his body might be preserved for the adoration of mankind, which was accordingly done, and these are still kept in several temples under the name of dawtoo.

The following is an extract from a still more circumstantial account of Budhu.

The powerful gods Satagiry and Assoory, the four gods who are the supreme rulers and protectors of all the worlds, the god Sakkraia, who governs six heavens, and Maha Brahma, who illuminates all the worlds, with several other gods, went to Budhu, and bowing before him, requested the favour of a sermon from him.

Budhu, who is very experienced in such performances, and who is, moreover, lord of the three worlds Brahma-Lōka,* Dewa-Lōka,† and Manape-Lōka,‡ is also the god who guards the three worlds from all misfortune. His person is most beautiful and majestic, insomuch that, upon comparison with him, the other gods seem to

* The heaven of the brahmas.

† The next inferior heaven of gods.

‡ The residence of men.

lose all their beauty, while his alone remains resplendent.

Before he arrived at the state of Budhu, he, upon his own simple volition, abandoned all his riches, and became liberal in the extreme. After this he died; and, being born again, met the Budhu Brahma Deva, and wishing to become a Budhu, fell at his feet. After this, he met a second Budhu, named Gautama, to whom he paid divine honours, hoping some day to arrive at the same state of holiness. Continuing in this state, and fostering this desire through time immemorial, he at length found himself subject to the Budhu Diepankerenan, who, shining like the sun, was the highest ruler of the three worlds, and had his residence in the city Amarawati. He was of the brahmin class, and was called the Prince Soomedanam Budhu. Growing up under this prince, he began to have an aversion to all temporal riches, and, at the same time, conceived a desire of becoming a priest. Upon this he proceeded to the king of that country, informing him of all the wealth of his ancestors, as far as seven generations, and expressed a wish to distribute the same among the poor. The king was much rejoiced at this; and causing all the poor to be assembled by the beat of tom-

tom, caused his treasures to be distributed among them.

After this, Budhu retired to a wood, in the recesses of which he discovered a rock, upon which a building like a palace had been erected. This building was called Parne. Whatever was in this building was ordered by the god Sakkraia to be produced in the twinkling of an eye; whereupon a certain garment was brought forth and put upon Budhu, which gave him the appearance of a pilgrim, and moreover enabled him to walk in the air.

Budhu, thus elevated above other mortals, looking about him, saw the roads about the city Ramjenan adorned and decorated by the inhabitants; and asking for what purpose this had been done, he was told that the Budhu Diepankerenan was expected that way with 400,000 rahatoons. Upon this, he alighted upon the earth with a noise no less terrible than if the ring of the god Sakkraia had fallen on the ground. He then asked them to give him some employment in this way; and, in reply, he received command to fill up a valley which lay in the same road.

In this he hoped to have some assistance from heaven; but reflecting, that in order to make it a work of merit it must be his own, he took a basket, and began to carry earth to fill up the valley. In the middle of his work the Budhu Diepankerenan, with his suite, made his appearance. Budhu was rather disconcerted at this: he soon resolved upon an expedient by which the Budhu and his followers might be accommodated; he, accordingly, spread a sheet over the half-filled valley, and laying his head at the one extremity and his feet at the other, presented a bridge for the accommodation of the illustrious travellers. The Budhu arriving at his head, and inspired with delight and surprise at the sight, said: "Cast your eyes, my friends, on this happy pilgrim, who, like me, shall, after the lapse of innumerable years, arrive at the state of Budhu, and procure for many Nirwāna." He further foretold the city in which he should be born, the names of his parents, wife, and children; and also that his name should be Guadma Budhu.

After this, he walked three times round the prostrate pilgrim, made an offering of eight handsful of flowers, which was also done by the brahmins, and other people present, and then each went his way.

The pilgrim upon this got up, sat on the flowers that had thus been offered, and reflecting upon the riches which he had given to the poor, on the merit of being charitable, brave, patient, just, and industrious, and, moreover, meditating on the birth after this life, he expired, and was accordingly born again with the name of King Wessantera. In this state he gave all his riches to the poor, and died, and was again born in the fifth heaven called Tosite. Upon this occasion all the gods of the fifth heaven requested him to accept the dignity of Budhu, and to come down into the world of men. Soon after this he was conceived by the Queen Mahámáyá, and after ten months was born in the world.

The child grew and increased like the moon, and became king of the four quarters of the world. He was married to the princess Jasoda, by whom, as well as 40,000 concubines, he had children. In this state he continued till the age of thirty-one, when, seeing certain portentous signs, he retired to his country seat, and, meeting Wismekarma, who had been dispatched to him by 1000 gods in the form of a servant, he was adorned with a most magnificent dress, studded with jewels, and a crown of precious stones. At the same time, being informed of the birth of a son, he became cheerful as Sakkraia after the defeat of the Assuras.

Soon after this he met a woman called Kisa-goutame, who, in a song, represented to him all the good and evil which befal man in this life. He was so much pleased with this representation, that he took the gold chain which hung from his neck, and presented it to the woman.

He soon after arrived at his palace, which was splendid as that of the god Sakkraia; but some women being admitted in order to divert him, he took offence, insomuch that he quitted the palace without taking leave of the princess and his children, fearing they might persuade him from becoming Budhu. He accordingly ordered his servant Kantekenan to saddle his horse, which was eighteen cubits in length, and large in proportion in other respects; which being done, he mounted, and rode on till he came to a gate so large that it could not be shut by fewer than 1000 men. This gate, in consideration of his always having kept an open door to the poor, opened to him by the immediate command of God. He then rode on till he came to the banks of the river Anomanam, where he alighted, having performed a journey of 120 miles.

He then drew his golden sword, and with it cut off some of his hair, and throwing it towards heaven, it was taken up, and preserved in a golden box by the god Sakkraia.

Upon this occasion he was presented with the garment of a priest by Maha Brahma Raja, which he put on; and, from the joy he experienced on this occasion, he determined to remain where he was for the space of seven days. He then crossed the river, and arrived at the city called Rajegaha-nuwara, where he begged a handful of rice from the inhabitants, and sat near a stone till he had eaten it.

He next arrived at the city of King Bimsare, who, asking him why he begged since he was the son of a king? he answered, he did it in order to become Budhu, a state which he hoped soon to attain.

The seven succeeding years were spent in great difficulties. At length, meeting a virgin called Sujata, who made him an offering of boiled rice and cocoa-nut milk, he sat down near the river Neranjara, where he made the rice into forty-nine balls, which he ate; he then threw the golden basin which he had used into the river, laying it down as a proof, that if the basin should swim against the stream he should at length attain to the state of Budhu.

The miracle was accordingly wrought, and he then set out with fresh vigour on his journey.

After this he came to a wood of sal trees, where he rested for the day; at night, he proceeded onward to a road that had been cleared by the gods, where he found a bogas-tree. On the road thither he had been met by a brahmin, who had given him eight handsful of grain called kusatane, which he strewed on the ground near the tree; whereupon the earth clave, and a seat fourteen cubits high rose out of the ground. On this he immediately seated himself, and leaning his back against the tree, which now appeared like a column of silver, he was visited by the whole assembly of the gods, who did him homage, and bestowed large praises on his virtuous exploits.

There then appeared an elephant as large as a mountain, on which was seated a person of terrific demeanour, armed with a sword large enough to cut heaven in two; his name was Wassewarti Raja. With him was an innumerable army armed with pikes and swords, all of whom marched directly towards Budhu, in order, if possible, to dispossess him of his seat, and to put the gods to flight. But Budhu recollecting the ten virtuous deeds which he had done, they were all instantly put to flight, as though they had been attacked by ten giants. Upon this occasion it was that he received forgiveness of all his sins and became Budhu, and obtained the name of Guadma, in consideration of the good actions he had done since the time of Brahma-dewanan.

In this place he remained seven weeks; but, at the request of Maha Brahma Raja, he proceeded to Benares, where he made his introductory sermon.

On this occasion, a high-priest called Anja-kendange, with innumerable others, were converted to the faith. Many miracles were also performed, as healing the blind and lame, by which many gods and men were brought to the true religion.

Nine months afterwards, on the 17th Jan., Budhu arrived at the island of Ceylon. He first went to the devil, who resided at the spacious palace of Nangewenodennaje, which was twelve miles in length by four in breadth, where, hovering in the air for some time, he produced a thick darkness throughout the whole earth, which so much alarmed the devils, that they immediately retired. By this means he had an opportunity of alighting upon the island, and to seat himself upon a seat which again rose out of the ground for his accommodation. He next caused fire to issue from the four corners of the world, whereby the devils were more than ever alarmed; but their fear of destruction was assuaged on receiving the sentence of banishment from the island. On this occasion, the Budhu caused a wood, called Jakgierrie, to come from a distant place, and which he afterwards placed in its original situation.

After this, the Budhu preached a sermon to the gods, by which they were edified and delivered from hell. He then gave a handful of his hair to Samandewe-Raja, informing him, at the same time, that the island was now fit for the habitation of men. The Raja took the hair, and putting it into a chest with precious stones, laid it up at Mayanginne.

This is what our Budhu did when he first came to Ceylon.

Five years after this, coming from the pagoda Telewanne, he put a stop to a battle between two gods in the shape of snakes. These gods were called Chulodere and Mayodere, who had for some time kept themselves under the earth on account of the seat of precious stones. The Budhu then edified them, as well as their numerous suite, by his doctrine, and they were at length converted; when they confessed, that had either of them remained in possession of the seat, some future contest must unavoidably have arisen. They then made an offering of victuals to the Budhu, which they had the power to produce. This was accepted by Budhu, who placed himself upon the seat and ate it. He then gave a tree called Kiriepalloe, which had been used as an umbrella by the god Samane, as well as the above-mentioned seat, to the god Wismekarma, that he might obtain salvation by worshipping them. After which, he returned to the pagoda.

Some time after this he again visited the island of Ceylon, at the request of the snake-king Manaerkijeram: on this occasion, as before, he rested on his beautiful seat, where he received and ate the offerings made by the snake. During this time, also, he converted many to his religion. He then took up his residence with 500 rahatoons, upon the pagoda Balance.

The next miracle which he performed, was causing himself to appear like the moon from the top of the rock Sammantekule, which he did at the request of the god Samandewe-Raja; upon which occasion, the gods caused it to rain down flowers and precious stones.* Upon this

* This is probably the Budhist legend regarding the mark of a foot which is still said to be seen on Adam's Peak, in Ceylon. The Portuguese, it seems, upon finding such a story extant respecting Budhu, had the address to apply it to

rock the Budhu left the impression of his foot. He went, soon after, to Dieganskeje, and thence to the city Anurahde-pura, where he visited the places Srimaha Buddhistan, Ratnemalistan, Tuparamettaene, and Wonissakenaniparru Wattistan. At each of these places he remained a short time, and preached before such gods as were found there. He then returned to the pagoda, where he resided during the subsequent forty-five years, preaching and exhibiting his good works to all around him.

He next proceeded to the court of the King Mallele, and laying himself down on one of the decorated cots which stood in the hall of the palace, he began to consider in what quarter of the world his doctrine would be best received. Now, the extent of the world is 360,000,000 yoduns, each yodun being computed at four miles in length. Of this, one part, called Purewewidesije, extends 7000 yoduns; a third, called Apperego Janege, 7000 yoduns; and the fourth, called Uturukudewine, 6000 yoduns, beside 2000 small islands. After some consideration, it occurred to his omniscience, that his doctrine would flourish most in the island of Ceylon, and

Adam, hoping by this means to soften the prejudices of the people against Christianity.

it would continue there for the space of 5000 years. This he declared to the god Sakkraia, and moreover appointed him the tutelary deity of the island. The care of the island was afterwards intrusted to the god Vishnu.

Soon after this, and on the 15th day of May, the Budhu died in happy state, having edified the gods of the highest heaven with his sermons. His body was deposited in a golden coffin, and burned by the Chakkeneassen brahmins, and others, who had come from 10,000 worlds. The funeral pile was of sandal-wood, and was in height 120 cubits. The three weeks following were occupied in offering sacrifices to the departed Budhu.

The following is a short enumeration of his good works: to enumerate the whole would be impossible, being more in number than the sum of the solid contents of the earth, the depths of the sea, the height of heaven, or the abundance of the atmosphere. He was guiltless of slaying any thing that enjoyed life, of the commission of theft, fornication, lying, slandering, obscenity, of eating at night,* of dancing, singing, playing, smelling flowers and other odoriferous sub-

* This is thought so great a sin among the Cingalese, that a fine is said to be imposed on any one who should be guilty of it.

stances; of sitting on any place higher than a cubit,* of being covetous of gold and silver, of desiring all sorts of paddy, slaves, goats, lambs, fowls, hogs, elephants, horses, cows, buffaloes, gardens, and fields; of delivering away writings or presents, of taking or giving any treasures, of keeping false weights and measures, of disinheriting any heir, of deceit in falsifying gold and precious stones, of taking villages, and other possessions; besides all this, he persevered in every good and laudable action, as the priests of Budhu, who still keep his laws, continue to do.

Here follows a summary of the high doctrine of Budhu, which is but as a drop of the ocean.

1st. Whoever kills any living thing, or causes the same to be done, shall undergo much oppression in this world, and at length shall be born again in hell. After atoning there for his sins, he may again be born in the world; and although this might happen in a good family, still he shall experience nothing but wretchedness.

* We must, of course, except the seat of precious stones, said to have been fourteen cubits in height, which is the same throne or mystic couch on which all the statues of the Budhu are placed.

2dly. Whoever steals shall be punished in this life by the amputation of his hands and feet, and other castigations; after this, he shall be born in hell; then, after much suffering, he may be born again in the world, where his portion will be to beg, but shall receive nothing either to satisfy his hunger or cover his nakedness.

3dly. Whoever is a slave to lusts shall suffer many oppressions in this life. After this, he may be born 100 times into this world in the shape of a young woman, yet shall he be unnoticed and undergo many vexations.

4thly. Whosoever speaks lies shall die in his sins, and be born again in hell. Having made atonement there for his sins, he may again be born in the world, but shall possess neither a fine figure nor fine voice, his tongue shall be forked like that of a snake, his breath shall be offensive, and he shall not be believed although he speak the truth.

5thly. Whosoever gets drunk loses his understanding and is detested by all; such a one, also, treats both his parents and master unjustly. After his death, and in his journey to heaven, he shall meet with impediments on his way as jungles.

The wicked thoughts of the drunkards shall

become worse and worse: besides this, the killing of cattle, committing robbery, adultery, speaking lies, slandering, speaking unnecessary and idle words, coveting the wealth of his neighbour, envying the good works of his neighbour, as well as imagining himself without sin, and in the way of salvation, is all prohibited by the law of Budhu; so that whoever dies in any of these sins shall be born again in hell: after atonement there, he may again appear in the world only to undergo new scenes of suffering.

All, therefore, who seek wealth by selling liquor, beef, living cattle, arrows and bows, firelocks, or such arms wherewith birds may be shot, should leave it off, and turn their attention to the following:—To seek to acquire good riches by the labour of their own hands; such as sowing, reaping, and carrying on honest trades, to give cheerfully to the poor, to think of Budhu, to maintain his doctrine, assist his adherents, keep his laws, and be equally charitable to all men; to honour parents, masters, Budhu, and his followers, and to do them good to the best of their ability; to teach his doctrine to others; to listen attentively to the instructions of his priests; and constantly to place faith in their doctrine. He who thus lives, shall, after this life, go to heaven, where he shall enjoy every good thing for ever and ever.

A further account of the doctrines of the Budhists, originally written in the Dutch language in questions and answers, as proposed to the Candians, and answered by them.

Do the learned acknowledge a most high and sole supreme being? and how do they describe him?

No; at least no such conclusion is to be drawn from their writings. They acknowledge one Sagampati Maha Brahma, as the first and chief of all the gods; and they say, that both he and his servants have neither flesh nor bone, that they have a shining skin, teeth in their mouth, and hair on the head and body, which are not to be felt, but are mere appearances; hence it should seem they consider them as spirits, though this is not positively asserted in their writings. Budhu, who is described as having been human, is, nevertheless, superior to Maha Brahma in knowledge, as well as in other respects. He has, moreover, the power of omniscience, so that he is able to be present in the ninth heaven, where Brahma keeps his court, and, at the same time, to surpass him both in splendour and dimensions.

It is further said, that Budhu (we speak of the last Guadma Budhu) after attaining Nirwāna in the glory-hall Moksé, a place higher and more excellent than the twenty-sixth heaven, was born again, and is still living there in joy, magnificence, and immortality; and that his doctrine, which is still maintained in full lustre, should, according to his prophecy, last 5000 years after he attained Nirwāna; so that it shall still continue 2,623 years, as, according to the chronology of the Cingalese, 2,377 years have already elapsed since the decease of Guadma Budhu. A long time after these years shall have expired, another Budhu is to be born, who shall be called Maitréya. After an unutterable number of ages the superintendence of Maha Brahma shall cease, when the world shall perish, and another shall arise in its place. After this, Maha Brahma shall, by degrees, ascend through the seventeen superior heavens, till he shall at last arrive at the state of Budhu. The names of these heavens, beginning with the lowest, and ascending to the highest, are the following:—

1. Chatturmaharajekije.
2. Tawetiengseje.
3. Iameje.
4. Tusitteje.

5. Nirmaneratije.
6. Parrenirmitre Wassewartie.

These are called Kama-Lōkas, and are the residences of inferior gods: women are said to be found in these places.

7. Brahmeparisatjeje.
8. Brahme Puruhiteje.
9. Brahme Kajekanam.
10. Paritrabheje.
11. Appemanibheje.
12. Abhassereje.
13. Parrite Subheje.
14. Appemane Subheje.
15. Subhekiemeje.
16. Whabheliege.
17. Assanjasattheje.

These are called Brahma-Lōkas, also Roopa-Lōkas, that is, heavens of superior gods.

18. Arriheje.
19. Attapheje.
20. Suddasseje.
21. Suddasseje.
22. Akkenieshkeje.*

* The doctrine of Budhism, although it inculcates practically the tenet of materialism, yet contains a germ of ancient doctrine in these triumphing heavens —mansions for the souls

The numbers 18, 19, 20, 21, and 22, designate the triumphing heavens.

23. Akasanancha Jattenieje.
24. Winjannancha Jatteneje.
25. Bkinchanija Jatteneje.
26. Newesanjan Samijajatteneje.

Aroopa-Lōkas—these are heavens above all heavens, or worlds above all worlds. There are in some, souls without bodies; and in others, bodies without souls, which live notwithstanding. The Cingalese believe that the world has been destroyed and restored several times under the direction of one or more, if not fewer than five, Budhus; and although no Budhu has now the care of it, yet a Maha Brama is always to be found who has.

Have the Cingalese any notion of a ghost or immaterial being?

No: it does not appear from any of their writings that they have; yet, from their description of the gods, they seem to consider them as immaterial beings.

Did the Supreme Being create the inferior gods?

No: in the first place, a supreme being is

who shall survive the great catastrophe of the destruction of the universe.—Vide "Doctrine of Budhism," p. 74.

denied; and, in the second, no god has the power of creating any inferior being. On the contrary, all proceed from nature. When men die, such, for instance, as are of the lower heavens, they are first judged according to their works; and, in proportion as these are found good or evil, they are again born into the world, either as rational or irrational creatures. This death and regeneration takes place several times, till the objects of such probation gradually ascend through all the Brahma-Lōkas, and at length arrive at the highest heaven; so that the regeneration only takes place in such as are inhabitants of the Dewa-Lōkas, and in no other. The Budhists, moreover, believe in no such thing as the creation of souls. The breath of life, say they, by which they mean the soul, loses not its hold on this life, till it has a prospect of enjoying some other, just as a leech loses not his hold at the head till he has fastened on some part with the tail. Hence they conclude, that the soul, before it leaves this mortal body, has either a prospect of getting to heaven, or is conscious of its liability to the torments of hell.

Is the Supreme Being also creator of heaven and earth, and does that Supreme Being still interfere in the direction thereof?

A supreme being is denied, and, as aforesaid, all proceeds from nature, for these reasons: if there were a creator, the world could not perish, but would by him be kept permanent and entire; but the direction of heaven and earth is in the first case subject to the Budhu; after him, Sagampati Maha Brahma has the rule; and after him, the gods in their several order.

The Candians speak of four gods as chiefs and directors of the world; who are they?

The names of these gods are Dertheraachtirre, Viruddhi, Vesoepaeskani, and Waysrewenne.

Are these gods equal to each other in power? and what are their chief transactions?

They are independent of their chief god Sakkraia, who is director of the world, and of the lowest heaven called Chatturmaharayéā, where he resides with the four gods just mentioned. These four gods, who are equal in power, employ themselves constantly in guarding their superior god; and, as he presides over the four quarters of the world, each of them has one quarter assigned to him.

The first of these gods, who is called Dirtheraachtirre, has his residence in the east; himself, his clothing, servants, horses, carriages, &c., are all white; his weapons are of white crystal; while his office is that of presiding over all music, both vocal and instrumental.

The second, who is called Viruddhi, hast he superintendence of the south; his colour, as well as that of his servants, is sky-blue; he is also head of a great number of angels called Kumbandijo.

The third, called Vesoepaeskani, directs the western part: his distinguishing colour is that of red coral; he, moreover, presides over the Nagebattejo, a sort of snakes said to be in the heavens: the upper portion of their body resembles that of a man; the lower, that of a snake. The servants of this deity are said to have the power of transforming themselves into men, birds, quadrupeds, reptiles, &c., and even to become wood or stone.

The fourth and last of these gods is called Waysrewenne: his province is the north; he has the superintendence of the devils; and his distinguishing colour is that of gold.

The office of these four gods is to guard their chief god Sakkraia against the attacks of his enemy, the god Wessetjiette Assurendria, who is equal in power to Sakkraia himself, and whose residence is lower than the world called Assura-Lōka, and deeper than the bottom of the sea. The four gods above mentioned send out their emissaries on or near the day of the new moon, in order to take an account of the actions of men: on the first eight days they investigate and record the sins committed by them; on the eight following they go about in order to confirm or correct their account. After this, the statement is presented to the god Sakkraia in council, who is attended with thirty-two gods, superior in rank to the above-mentioned four. On this occasion, should the virtuous men be found more in number than the vicious, there is great joy in heaven; if the contrary, there is much sorrow.

Is any book extant said to be written by Sakkraia? and if so, in what language?

There are many such books in the possession of the priests of Budhu. They are in the Pali language, and are to be had in Ceylon, of which the book Deewadutesustere is one.

How many inferior gods are there besides the four above mentioned?

The number, with that of their attendants, is unutterable. Those whose names are known amount to 120,535.

Of these, 35 reside in the Dewa-Lōkas, or inferior heavens........................	35
120,500 reside on the earth, viz., in the kingdom of Kimbulwatnuwere*	7,000
The gods that reside in the unknown southern countries amount to.....................	113,500
	120,535

Viz., in a rock called Himaleparkwete	10,000
In a rock called Satagirenampartwete.....	3,000
In a rock called Wissameteparkwete......	500
In the rock called Wepuleparkwete	10,000
Total........	120,535

The gods that reside on the earth may, if they choose, ascend to the Dewa-Lōkas, or six inferior heavens.

Do these inferior gods, like our angels, execute the will of the Supreme Being?

Neither the superior nor inferior gods are angels; their servants are the angels, and are therefore called Kumbandijo. These angels, as well as the inferior gods, obey the commands of their superiors; and they succeed each other in rank, in the following order:

1st, Budhu; 2d, Mahabrahma; 3d, The gods of Dewa-Lōka; 4th, thirty-two counsellors,

* This kingdom is said to be situated on the south of Hindoostan; but, from the change of names which those places have undergone, is not now to be found.

or Chaen; 5th, the before-mentioned four gods; 6th, the other inferior gods; 7th, the Kumbandijo; 8th, the gods on earth, with their servants.

Is there any book extant giving an account of these gods? and in what language is it written?

In Candia, and in the district of Matura, such books are to be found, written both in the Pali and High Cingalese languages, particularly the books Diksangieje and the History of Maha Sameje Sastra.

Does it appear in the Cingalese books that there were more Budhus than those that were in Ceylon?

This question will be more fully answered in the sequel, and is merely touched upon here to shew that the word Budhu signifies omniscient, a saint superior to all saints, and even superior to the chief god Mahabrahma. Still the Budhu, properly speaking, is no god, but is considered as having been born human, and in process of time attained to the state of Budhu. This power, however, was not given him by any superior being, but he took it of his own sovereign will.

Is Budhu descended from gods or men?

He was god before his birth as man, and had the superintendence over the gods in the heaven Tusitieje. Afterwards, at the request of all the gods, he was born of the Princess Mahamáyá, and as son of the King Suddodana Rajah. The manner of his birth differed not from that of other men; so that the opinion of some, that he was born from the left side of the princess, is false.

Is he not to be considered as one sent from heaven to publish to men the way of salvation?

No: in the fulness of time, and according to the predictions of numberless ages, at the request of the said gods, and by his own sovereign will, he became man, for the salvation of all who should embrace his doctrine.

How many such Budhus have there been?

According to the Cingalese writings, there were twenty-two Budhus before the creation of the present world. These Budhus lived during the ten creations and destructions which preceded the present creation. It is also believed that many creations and destructions have preceded the ten above referred to; but there is no account of the Budhus who existed during this time. For the direction of this world, however, five Budhus have been appointed, of which four have already appeared, whose names are these—Kakusande, Konagamme, Diepankerenan, and

Guadma. The fifth, called Maitri, is still expected; he is said to be now in heaven, and is to be born of a brahmin woman.

Who was the Budhu Diepankerenan?

He was the principal of the above-mentioned twenty-two Budhus, which he became on account of his great personal beauty, and because the number of people in his time is said to have been greater than in the time of any other Budhu. His doctrine, however, differed not from that of other Budhus; nor did he possess any peculiar privilege relative to the point of salvation.

Was he on Ceylon?

Yes: as were Guadma and the other Budhus, where they proceeded whithersoever they pleased, for the purpose of promulgating their doctrines.

What has he done upon earth?

He published his doctrine and saved men.

Are there any books at hand treating of him and his doctrine?

Yes, there are many, particularly those entitled Satyadharma, Ratnavali, Thuparvanyse, and Buddhavansá, which are all written in the Pali language.

Is it not Guadma Budhu who, in the Siamese language, is called Sammona Kodom and Pootisat?

It is; yet it is not in the Siamese, but the Pali language, that he is so called. Sammona signifies a principal saint known by his dress; Kodom (*i. e.* Gautame) is a proper name; Pootisat is a title given to all Buddhisatwe before they arrive at that state in heaven.

What is that god which is worshipped at Katteregam?

He is one of the gods of the earth. His place of residence is near a rock called Maha Mirreparkesette, situated between the bottom of the sea and the lower world, called Assura-Lōka.

What is his name?

Kande Kumara. He has six heads and twelve hands. In his hands he has ten weapons, namely, 1, a trisuli, or harpoon; 2, a pallas; 3, a large ring, or spring, called parawallalle, which is sharp on the outsides, and which, by turning it round on the finger, is thrown at the enemy; 4, a javelin; 5, a line; 6, a leg-breaker; 7, a standard, with a cock painted on it; 8, a throwing chain; 9, a bow; 10, an arrow. He is further delineated as standing, or riding, on a flying peacock, with such other insignia as his good works in this world merited. These insignia are generally some of the following: a god of great courage has on his shield a lion; a believer has an eagle; one who has performed laborious exploits, an ox; and so on.

What good works is this god said to have done?

It is said, that when Guadma Budhu was in his pagoda at Kattegeram, Kande Kumara was on guard, on the tree called bogaha,* sometimes called devil's tree; and that, upon making his obeisance to Budhu, he obtained the power of healing the sick, particularly such as are of royal blood; of performing miracles; of doing good to irrational beings, and to men in distress: with this caution, that he should never aspire to the honour of being worshipped as a god; but might claim such respect from the followers of Budhu as is generally given to other inferior gods. Hence it was that the offering-house at Katteregam was consecrated to him, and which is held in greater esteem than the temple at Candy, insomuch that the king himself not only sends presents to it, but permits his subjects to visit it in great numbers.

Does his power still extend to the world, and is it exerted for the good of the creatures?

* Every Budhu is said to have a tree sacred to himself, which, when it has been consecrated, never perishes. The tree to be chosen by the last Budhu, Maitri, is the ironwood tree, called nagaha.

Yes: he heals the sick, and performs miracles.

How is he worshipped in his temple?

The first day after the new moon in July is that on which the ceremonies begin. Should the astrologers, however, determine that day to be unlucky, the ceremonies are deferred to the day of the new moon in the following month, when people, in great numbers, assemble from all parts. Budhists, brahmins, Gentoos, pattanies, and Moors,* are found among the concourse, as well as many who come out of curiosity from the coasts of Madura and Coromandel. On the day appointed for the ceremonies, the following order is observed: The three principal officers of the place, called the Maha Bitmeralehaine, the Kuda Bitmeralepami, and the Basnaykeralehami, meet the three inferior officers, called the Maha Kappuraales, and Kuda Kappuraales,† as well as the other inferior servants, and sixteen married women chosen to prepare the procession. Three elephants, with tusks, one larger in size, the other two smaller, are also

* The Moors (*i. e.* Mahometans) are said to affirm that the temple at Katteregam formerly belonged to a nabi, or prophet of theirs.

† These temple-servants will be described in a subsequent tract.

provided. The large elephant is adorned with seven valuable pieces of cloth, with golden flowers, and other valuable ornaments, consisting of pearls, precious stones, gold chains, and jewels. On the elephant's back is placed a bench, wrought with gold, silver, and precious stones. Upon the extremities of the bench are placed six supporters, and over these is laid an arched roof, the covering and curtains of which are of very costly silk. On the bench is laid a golden sword.

On each side of the large elephant the smaller ones are placed, in their usual accoutrements. Upon each of these sits a Kappuraale, having in his hand a tail of the chamara,* with which they fan the sword. On this occasion, many open umbrellas are held near the great elephant, in order to protect the sword.†

The sixteen women then divide themselves

* This animal is said to be found only in Hindoostan, and that its hair is of such an extraordinary length as frequently to entangle the animal in the jungles; and that, rather than disturb the hair, it submits to be taken, which is, therefore, frequently done. It is the same as the yak, which is described in the "Asiatic Researches."

† Herodotus affirms that the Scythians worshipped their war-god under the symbol of a sword.

into two companies, placing themselves on the right and left of the elephants, and carrying in their hands brazen bowls filled with saffron-water. As the procession moves on, it is the business of the women to pronounce short benedictions on the people, such as, May those who are assembled here prosper! In this manner, and attended by drums, trumpets, and other musical instruments, as well as colours flying, the procession proceeds through the four principal streets, and as the sun has by this time set, the houses are brilliantly illuminated, and many of the attendants are provided with torches for the occasion. This procession is repeated through the following fifteen days successively, or till the next day of full moon. On the last day of the procession, the ceremonies continue till the morning of the following day, when the gold sword, &c. is taken from the back of the elephant, and is put into a magnificent palanquin provided for the purpose.

The palanquin is then carried in procession by two kapuwas to a shallow river, which is about a mile from the temple, and is thrown into the water; upon which one of the kapuwas, called Diejekappenerale, or wood-cutter, steps into the stream, and taking the golden sword from the scabbard, strikes the water, which immediately stands still. This miracle is generally believed; and those who doubt, account for the phenomenon by saying, that as the people all rush into the stream on this occasion, a temporary stagnation is produced, which does not amount to a miracle.

This ceremony generally ends about seven in the morning, when the palanquin and sword are carried back in great pomp to the temple. The people now assemble for the purpose of making the usual offerings, which consist of gold coin, gold and silver in bars, slaves, &c.: fields and gardens are also given for the use of the temple. Those who are sick either come in person or send images of gold and silver, with their names, to be offered in the temple, in order to obtain a recovery, or to avert death. For the purpose of getting relief for animals, images of them are sent with their names and presented to the priests.

Three bowls are provided, in which the offerings are collected; the first is of gold, and in it are collected the offerings of the nobles and wellales; the second is of silver, and is used to collect the offerings of the fishermen, chandos, and superior castes; the third is of inferior metal, and receives the offerings of the berrewais and low castes. When these bowls are filled, they are emptied by the servants in attendance, and are again placed on the offering-bench.

These presents serve to defray the expenses of the temple, as well as to maintain the superior and inferior officers, who act as judges to the people. There is, moreover, a vessel filled with a part of these offerings, and sent to Candia for the use of the temple there.

After the ceremonies are ended, it is expected that the people depart for their respective homes on the day following, which is the ancient custom. Such as are sick are permitted to suit their convenience in this particular.

There is, beside the above-mentioned ceremonies, a general illumination, in the month of November, at Katteregam, as well as at the three other principal temples of Ceylon.

What do the Candians believe of devils?

They believe that there are devils in the world, but, according to the doctrines of Budhu, they are not permitted to honour them.

What is the origin of devils? did the Supreme Being create them, or are they from eternity, or are they fallen gods or angels?

They say, that when nature produced the sun, moon, and stars, the devils were human beings, and, on account of their horrible sins, did fall from their state of happiness. But their having been gods, or fallen angels, or having been created, or existing from eternity, is denied. They also say, that devils who commit greater sins than those already committed by them, are condemned to greater suffering. Men who have been condemned for their sins are also said to be placed among the infernal devils. On the other hand, such devils as have died and been born again as men, and have not committed sin, are finally restored to their former happy state. Indeed, angels, as well as devils, rank in exact proportion to the good or evil done by them, and not according to imputation of either the one or the other.

What is the employment of the devils?

They obey their chief, the god Waysrewenne; they make war against the enemy of the god Sakkraia, namely, the god Wessetjiette Assurendria; they eat the flesh of the dead, and although the doctrines of Budhu forbid divine honours being paid to them, the Cingalese do, notwithstanding, shew them some honours, because, as they have the power of inflicting sickness, &c. on human beings, they think it best to conjure them, and then to make to them offerings of money, of boiled and unboiled meat, and to pay them some other honours. They also cause the throat, arms, legs, and other parts of the sick man's body, to be tied about by the conjurors with necklaces or threads dyed with saffron-water.

What do the Candians further believe of devils?

According to the doctrine of Budhu, they believe nothing but that they are enemies to the human race.

How is the most sacred law-book or Scripture of the Cingalese called?

Abidarmepeteke Sattaperkarreneje.

In what language is it written?

In the renowned Pali or Mágadi language, in which Budhu first preached his doctrine.

Is the book to be had here?

In Candia it is to be had complete: at Mulgirigalle, or Adam's Hill, it is not complete.

Is it not the same that the brahmins have, and which they call the Vedam?

No; the book of the brahmins called Vedam is a collection of secular learning:* there are many such books.

May any one read this law-book or bible?

None but the learned, who can understand it, are permitted to do so.

* It was doubtless the exalting of the Bānas of the Budhu above the Vedam of braminism, which drew on the Budhists their relentless persecutions.

When was the world or universe created, or, according to the Cingalese system, produced by nature?

In order to state this correctly, it would be necessary to know how long the world was without a ruler after the above-mentioned four Budhus; but this is not possible for want of a complete copy of the Cingalese Scripture.

In what manner did nature produce the world?

The worlds which preceded the present (for besides this there were, and there are, many others, as the sun, moon, and stars, &c.), all perished by wind, fire, and water, excepting hell only, which is said to have lain concealed beneath the abyss of the earth. The gods whose time had arrived for their removal to the triumphing heavens, were removed thither; the others were sent to the unknown worlds. Whereupon a violent motion took place by means of the wind. Seven suns, or pillars of fire, upon this descended on the earth, which burnt every thing to ashes, and, at the same time, destroyed the fourteen lower heavens. After this, a general deluge took place, or, to express it in the words of the Cingalese, the whole was filled up with the general rain of the world called Sampattiekere Mahamege.

Some time after this, hitherto undetermined, the gods who were in the heaven Subhekierneje, to which the waters had nearly risen, seeing the lotos floating on its surface, supposed, for the first time, that a new earth existed beneath. Such, therefore, whose time had expired for quitting this heaven, seated themselves upon the flowers, and, as the waters descended, arrived at length at the surface of the earth.* The gods, who were then without bodily parts or passions, and reflecting from themselves light sufficient without the aid of the sun or moon, were much delighted with their new situation. After a while these gods became so much inflated with pride, and debased by lust, that they were changed into human beings of both sexes. Their resplendent properties being now gone, they

* The Cingalese suppose that the whole surface of the earth is flat, and that it is terminated by the circle which the horizon seems to present. All beyond this circle, though it might be inhabited, is in another world, and so separated from this, that none but the gods can pass from the one to the other. They also believe, that though a great part of the sea lies without this circle, it is still attached to the earth. The four parts of the world, they say, are enlightened by the reflection of four precious stones. Asia, Africa, Europe, and America, are indebted for their light to the blue sapphire: white sapphire, ruby, and topaz, enlighten the rest, which, according to them, is unknown.

lived a great length of time in entire darkness, until the sun, moon, and stars, were produced by nature. Their god was the clay of the earth, which was at this time sweet; but, on account of the avarice of these gods in accumulating great quantities for their pleasure, it was rendered tasteless for their punishment. After this, they subsisted on a kind of shrub, which, for similar reasons, also became tasteless. A sort of kampernulje, commonly called devil's bread, or paddestulen, was their next food; but, conceiving an aversion to this, they were supported on a sort of seed, in the use of which they grew more wicked than formerly, and were accordingly condemned to till the ground for their future maintenance.

As the supreme god is perfectly good and holy, and consequently has a great aversion to sin, from whence then came sin?

The origin of sin is to be attributed to the mischievous and corrupted temper of man.

Is the devil, or any other powerful spirit, the cause of sin?

By no means.

What are the principal precepts of Budhu, and where were they given?

They are the following, which are ten in number, and considered threefold: 1st, extending to the thoughts; 2d, to the words; 3d, to the works.

1st. Call not truth by the name of falsehood, and be not suspicious.

2d. Desire not the wealth of others.

3d. Never wish for the death of your enemies.

4th. Avoid lying.

5th. Betray not the secrets of others.

6th. Avoid all injurious and foul words.

7th. Abhor all idle conversation which may tend to the ruin of yourself and others.

8th. Commit no murder.

9th. Do not steal.

10th. Commit neither fornication nor adultery.

This is the moral law of the Budhists, which was given from time to time by the several Budhus, and last of all by Guadma Budhu, in the kingdom of Rájaguham.

Is there any life to be expected after this? If so, are rewards and punishments to be expected for the good or evil done in this, and what are those rewards and punishments?

There is, undoubtedly, a life after this, in which the virtuous may expect the reward of their good deeds; but that reward is not to be enjoyed till they have died many times, and been born again in the six Dewa-Lōkas, and again born into the world. After they have thus enjoyed the eleven Brahma-Lōkas, and a foretaste of felicity, they arrive at the five upper Brahma-Lōkas, or triumphing heavens, where the transmigration ceases, and they remain for ever in felicity. Wicked men, on the contrary, are, after their death, born in hell, as irrational animals. If they have done any good thing during their lifetime, they are, after a long time, released from this hellish banishment, and are born again into the world as men. If, in this state, they abstain from evil and do good, it is possible for them to arrive at the state of felicity.

What and where is paradise? what and where is hell? and what is believed concerning them?

The Cingalese know neither the name nor the situation of paradise. They suppose it to be a place full of joy and delight. Nirwāna, or Moksé, is the place of departed Budhus; and, according to the doctrine of the last, is situated above the twenty-sixth heaven, and is magnificently adorned with gold, silver, and precious stones.

With regard to hell, it is, as aforesaid, situated beneath the abyss of the earth, and is continually agitated by winds, more violent than the strongest hurricane.

According to the doctrine of Budhu, there are eight large hells, in each of which there are sixteen smaller ones. Part of these hells is square, and is walled round with walls of iron, thirty-six miles thick. The floor and roof are of the same materials and thickness. In each of the walls there is a gateway. The punishments inflicted in each of these places are such as are proportionate to the crimes of the damned. In the hell called Awitgege, the greatest punishments are inflicted with bills, sledges, bone-breakers, hammers, pincers, spits, &c. The skin is also taken off occasionally from head to foot, and melted lead poured down the throat.

Is a last judgment and resurrection of the body to be expected?

No; that judgment immediately follows death; and this is pronounced by the inferior god Wassewartija on such as may have done some good in their lifetime, and may have hopes of arriving at last at the Brahma-Lōkas; but the flagrantly wicked shall go to hell unheard.

Have the Cingalese any peculiar form of prayer?

No: they have, however, many prayers for both public and private use, which were given by Guadma Budhu, as occasion required.

These prayers were published 433 years after his death by the King Wattegemmoense Abejereje,* who is said to have been the inventor of writing.

Are there stated times of prayer? and if so, what are they?

The stated times of prayer are three daily, namely, in the morning at half-past four or five o'clock, at noon, and in the evening at half-past six. Some, however, who wish more particularly to obtain the favour of Budhu, pray much more frequently.

To whom do the Cingalese pray?

To Budhu; to his arhatas, or saints; to his doctrine, law-book, and other relics: these latter are addressed without attributing any miraculous power to such relics, &c.

Are any days set apart for public prayer?

Four days in every month are thus set apart, namely, the new and full moons, and the others in the first and last quarters, when the people assemble in the temples for religious service. Such as are unable to go

* The accuracy of this date is confirmed by the Mahavansi.

to the temples, perform their services at home.

Are there any appointed festivals?

Besides such as have been above noticed, any one may, by meditation and abstinence from sin, set apart any day for prayer and fasting in honour of Budhu.

In what manner do they perform their religious services in the temples?

It has been said that the Cingalese pray three times a-day. In the morning, from eight to eleven o'clock, dressed victuals are offered for the priests, whose duty it is to keep the temples clean, and to perfume the altar and images with incense.

In the afternoon, offerings of flowers are made. When the priests worship, all others are excluded; but when the people worship, one priest remains, who instructs the ignorant what to say in their prayers, which is to this effect: "The health and salvation of Budhu befal me; and for this end, may his doctrine and rahatoons assist me."

When this has been said, vows are sometimes made not to sin in thought, word, or deed, and to keep the five following commandments:

1st. Kill neither man nor beast.

2d. Do not steal.
3d. Do not commit adultery.
4th. Tell no lies.
5th. Drink no intoxicating liquors.

Others undertake to observe eight commandments, adding three more to the above-mentioned.

Those who are still more rigid, add the two following commandments, making in the whole ten:

1st. Smell no odoriferous flowers, &c.
2d. Wear no sumptuous apparel, gold, silver, or precious stones.

To these they add some other austerities, such as to eat no dressed victuals after noon, but to subsist upon the juice of fruits, excepting the milk of the young cocoa-nut, the juice of cucumbers, and some others.

To attend no pleasure parties of dancing, singing, &c., and to sleep upon no bed more than a cubit in height.

In what way do they perform their religious services in the dewales and kowiles?

In the dewales, drums and tom-toms are beaten in honour of the god to whom the place is dedicated. In the morning and evening, trumpets and horns are sounded. In the month of July, as before-stated, the great offering takes place; and in November there is a general illumination. But as the dewales are held by inferior servants only, the priest's service is not performed there.

The kowiles are mere chapels, situated in hamlets and villages, where no other religious service is observed except that of a few offerings of boiled food, for the maintenance of the officers who reside there.

Do the Budhists do penance for sin, use holy water, or any other preservatives against wicked spirits, &c., as the brahmins do, who rub their forehead with ashes for this purpose?

No: these outward ceremonies are, by the Budhists, considered as superstitious, and therefore rejected.

Why have the Budhists such respect for cattle?

Not because they suppose any peculiar virtue inherent in them, but from gratitude. The great services which these animals render, in ploughing the ground, &c., as well as the milk they afford for sustenance, is with them reason sufficient for such a conclusion.

It is also said by the learned, that there is a prohibition regarding the slaughter of cattle, made formerly by a king, whose name is unknown. This king gave order for a general illumination in honour of Budhu, for which the lamps were to be supplied with butter. He was told by his ministry that it was impossible this order could be executed, unless he issued another prohibiting the slaughter of cattle. With this the king complied; and, since that time, none but the lowest castes, such as tom-tom beaters, have taken the liberty to eat beef.

Is suicide considered as a crime amongst the Budhists?

It is considered a greater sin than even murder.

Have the Candians any knowledge of Adam and Eve? Was Paradise on Ceylon, and did Adam leave the imprint of his foot on the hill called Adam's Peak? Is the lake found there said to have originated from the tears shed by Eve, on account of her sins? Are Adam and Eve represented by the images in the temple of Mulgiri-galle? What idols are those which have the shape of women?

The Candians have no knowledge of Adam or Eve, &c. The footstep visible on the hill called Adam's Peak is that of Guadma Budhu. The large images in the temple of Mulgiri-galle are images of Budhu alone; the smaller ones are those of the inferior gods. Wherever pictures of women are found painted on walls, they represent former queens and princesses, of whom accounts are to be found in Cingalese books.

PALI AND CINGALESE BOOKS

CONTAINED IN

THE VIHARIS

OF

1. *Mulgirri Galle Vihari.*
2. *The Chief Vihari in the District of Matura.*
3. *The Galapata Vihari in the District of Bentotte.*

As the only information respecting the contents of these Pali and Cingalese works is contained in the scanty notices comprised in the Series of Tracts No. II., which follow the List of the Collections in possession of the Viharis of Mulgirri Galle, of Matura, and of Bentotte, the numbers added are intended to facilitate a reference to these notices, as their information becomes valuable by supplying a key to their contents which we cannot otherwise possess: in this view the reference-figures on the left margin of the text shew the number of the Tract in the Second Series which contains any matter referring to the work that it precedes. It also has been considered a matter of utility to ascertain the books composing the collection of the three Viharis named in the Title, which being the chief Temples of Ceylon, and superintended by the most learned of the Budhist priesthood, it is fair to conclude, that the works which are found in the whole three Viharis are books particularly in estimation. No. 1, therefore, shews that the book is in the collection of the Vihari of Mulgirri Galle; No. 2, of the Vihari of Matura; No. 3, in that of Bentotte; and consequently indicates that such work is in all three of these religious establishments whenever the three figures follow a title.

A LIST

OF

RELIGIOUS BOOKS, &c.

IN

The Temple of Mulgirri Galle, No. 1.
The Temple of Matura, No. 2.
The Temple of Bentotte, No. 3.

---

6. Digsangiya. 1 2 3.
6. Maidum-sangiya. 1 2 3.
6. Sanyut-sangiya. 1 2 3.
6. Angottra-sangiya. 1 2 3.
Samanda-pasadicanan-atuwa. 1 2 3.
1. 6. Sumangala-wilaseninan-atuwa. 1 2 3.
Prapama-sudatiṅan-atuwa.
Manorata-puraninan-atuwa. 1 2 3.
Mangaladipaninan-atuwa. 3.
Wimatiwinodaninan-atuwa. 3.
Pansiya-panas Jataka-atuwa. 1 2 3.
6. Sarartadipaninan-atuwa. 1 2 3.
2. 6. Dampiya-atuwa. 1 2 3.
6. Terigata-atuwa. 1 2 3.

6. Teregata-atuwa. 1 2 3.
Tikamaha-wanse. 1 3.
6. Jataka-tika.
Piriwana. 1 2 3.
Abidarma-pitaki. 1 2 3.

The above-mentioned books are in Pali language, and contain each from 4 to 800 leaves of one cubit's length.

Wisuddi-magge-pela. 1 2 3.
6. Aratasalininan-artawarnana. 1 3.
6. Parayika. 1 2 3.
Pawiti. 1 3.
6. Maha-waga. 1 2 3.
6. Suluwaga. 1 3.
6. Pariwara-pate. 1 2 3.
Palimuttaka-wine. 1 3.
Canka-witarane. 1 2 3.
6. Winaya-winitche. 1 3.
2. Maha-wanse. 1 2 3.
6. Suttra-nipate. 1 2 3.
6. Upasaka-Janalankare. 1 2 3.
6. Wisuddimarga-tika. 1 2 3.
Milindapprasne. 1 2 3.
6. Wimana-wastu. 1 2 3.
6. Preta-wastu. 1 2 3.
1. 6. Sarasan-grahe. 1 2 3.
Maha-bodiwanse. 1 2 3.

6. Rasa-wahini. 1 2 3.
6. Bodiwanse-tika. 1 2 3.
6. Abidarma-arta-sangrahi. 1 2 3.
Jina-lankare. 1 2 3.

The above books are likewise in Pali language, and contain each about 250 or 300 leaves of a cubit and a half in length.

6. Parajika. 1 2 3.
Mangala-dipaninan-atuwa. 1 2 3.

These two books, which were brought from Camboya country, are in Camboya language, and contain each about 200 or 300 leaves.

Sataramaha - sangiyehi - linarta - warnana. 1 3.

This book is written in Pali language, and contains 200 leaves of two cubits long.

1. Pansiya-panas Jateke. 1 2 3.

This book is written in Cingalese, and contains 1500 leaves, each a cubit and a half long.

3. Puja-waliya. 1 2 3.
Ratana-waliya. 1 2 3.
Saddarma-ratanakare. 1 2 3.
Sararta-sangrahe. 1 2 3.
Wisuddimarga-sanne. 1 2 3.

Wimana-wastu-prakarane. 1 2 3.

These books are written in Cingalese, and contain each about 500 or 600 leaves of one and a half cubits long.

Teleatara-gata-sanne, or explanation. 1 3.
Dampiya-sanne, or ditto. 1 2 3.
Amawatura. 1 2 3.
Paritcheda. 1 2 3.
Tupa-wanse. 1 2 3.
Carma-wibage. 1 2 3.
6. Anagata-wanse. 1 2 3.
Saddarma-dipica. 1 2 3.
2. 7. Brahma-jalasustra-sanne, or explanation. 1 2 3.
Raja-ratna-kara. 1 2 3.
Sanga-sarane. 1 2 3.
Gehiwini. 1 2 3.
Attanagalu-wanse. 1 2 3.

These books are written in Cingalese, and contain each about 100 or 150 leaves of one cubit long.

Gatipattana-suttra-sanne, or explanation. 1.
Salaya-suttra-sanne. 1 2 3.
Chulakamma-wibanga-suttra-sanne. 1 2 3.
Singa-lowada-suttra-sanne. 1 2 3.

Cala-carama-suttra-sanne. 1.
Chula-hattipadoma-suttra-sanne. 1.
Mangala-suttra-sanne. 1.
Aloka-suttra-sanne. 1.
Daksina-wibanga-suttra-sanne. 1.
Damsakpawatun-suttra-sanne. 1 2 3.
Uposata-suttra-sanne. 1 2 3.
Balapandita-suttra-sanne. 1 2 3.
6. Kudusika-sanne. 1 3.
Angúlimala-suttra-sanne. 1 3.
6. Mulusika-sanne. 1 2 3.
Prati-moksa-sanne. 1 2 3.

These books are written in Cingalese, and contain each about sixty or seventy leaves of one cubit long.

Sadu-charitode. 1 2 3.
Cudu-sika. 1 3.
Mulusika. 1 2 3.
6. Prati-mokse. 1 2 3.
Dampiyawa. 1 2 3.
Sikkapada-walawjani. 1 2 3.

The above books are written in Pali language, and contain about fifty or sixty leaves of one cubit long.

Abidane. 1 2 3.
Amara-sinhe. 1 3.

Pada-sadane. 1 2 3.
Saibda-lakkate. 1 2 3.
Sandicappe. 1 2 3.
Prayoga-siddiya. 1 2 3.
Balawa-tare. 1 2 3.
Nigandu-sanne, or explanation. 1 3.
Saibda-lankata-sanne. 1 2 3.
Balawatara-sanne. 1 2 3.
Wratto-de. 1 2 3.
Wratta-ratnakari. 1 2 3.

These books are written in Pali-waikarna, and contain about 100 or 200 leaves of one cubit long.

A List of the Religious Books which are in the Temples in the District of Matura.

6. Damnia-sangani. 2 3.
6. Arta-salini. 2 3.
   The explanation of the same. 2.
6. Wibaneja-prakaranaya. 2 3.
6. Sammoha-winodani. 2 3.
6. Catawastu-prakaranaya. 2 3.
   The original of the same in Pali. 2.
6. Datuprakara-naya. 2.
   The original of the same in Pali. 2.

6. Pattana-prakaranaya. 2.
The original of the same in Pali.
6. Abidarmawa-taraya. 1 2 3.
The original of the same in Pali. 2.
The explanation of the same in Cingalese. 1 2.
6. Abidarmarta-sangrahaya. 1 2 3.
The explanation of the same in Pali. 2.
The explanation of the same in Cingalese. 3.
6. Abidarma-pitapota. 1 2 3.
6. Maha-waga. 1 2 3.
6. Sulu-waga. 1 2 3.
6. Parajika. 1 2 3.
Paçhiti. 1 2 3.
Samanta-pasadika-atuwa. 1 2 3.
6. Sararta-dipanitika. 1 2 3.
6. Wajira-bodi-tika. 2 3.
Wimati-winodani-tika. 2 3.
Canka-witarani. 1 2 3.
Pali-muttaka-winaya. 1 2 3.
The explanation of the same in Pali. 3.
Budda-sikka. 2 3.
The explanation of the same in Pali. 2.
The explanation of the same in Cingalese. 2.
Sikkapada-walanjiniya. 1 2 3.

The explanation of the same in Cingalese. 2.

6. Mulusika. 1 2 3.
The explanation of the same in Cingalese. 2.

6. Prati-moksaya. 1 2 3.
The explanation of the same. 2.

6. Diksangiya. 1 2 3.
Sumangala-wilasini. 1 2 3.
The explanation of the same in Pali. 2.

6. Maidum-sangiya. 1 2 3.

6. Prapancha-sùdani. 1 2 3.

6. Saruju-sangiya. 1 2 3.

6. Sararta-prakasani. 2.

6. Angottara-sangiya. 1 2 3.

6. Manorata-purani. 1 2 3.

6. Dampiya-pela. 1 2 3.
The original of the same. 2.
The explanation of the same. 2.
The explanation of the same in Cingalese. 2.

6. Maha-nerdesaya. 2 3.

6. Chula-nerdesaya. 2 3.
Pansiya-panas-jataka-atuwa. 1 2 3.
The explanation of the same. 2.
The explanation of the same in Cingalese. 2.

6. Teregata-atuwa. 1 2 3.
6. Terigata-atuwa. 1 2 3.
6. Wimana-wastu-atuwa. 1 2 3.
The explanation of the same in Cingalese. 2.
Patisampida-pela. 2 3.
The original of the same in Pali. 2 3.
Nettipprakaranaya. 2 3.
6. Udana-atuwa. 2 3.
6. Etiwuttaka. 2 3.
6. Pretawastu-atuwa. 1 2 3.
6. Suttra-nipata-atuwa. 1 2 3.
The explanation of the same in Cingalese. 2.
6. Budda-wansa-atuwa. 1 2 3.
6. Chariya-pitaka-atuwa. 2 3.
6. Wisuddi-margaya. 1 2 3.
Paramarta-manjusa. 2 3.
The explanation of the same. 2.
Piriwana. 1 2 3.
Melindapprasnaya. 1 2 3.
The explanation of the same. 2.
1. 6. Sara-sangrahaya. 1 2 3.
Saddarma-sangrahaya. 2 3.
Jina-lankaraya. 1 2 3.
Maha-bodi-wansaya. 1 2 3.
The explanation of the same in Pali. 2.

The explanation of the same in Cingalese. 2.

6. Rasa-wahini. 1 2 3.

6. Upasaka-janalankaraya. 1 2 3.

2. Maha-wansaya. 1 2 3.

Data-wanseya. 2 3.

The explanation of the same in Cingalese. 2.

Padda-maduwaya. 2 3.

The explanation of the same. 2.

Jina-charitaya. 2 3.

The explanation of the same. 2.

Sadu-charitodaya. 1 2 3.

Saddammo-payanaya. 2.

The explanation of the same. 2.

Saddarma-ratana-waliya. 1 2 3.

Butsaranaya. 2 3.

2. Saddarma-lankaraya. 2 3.

Daham-saranaya. 2 3.

3. Puja-waliya. 1 2 3.

Paritchedaya. 1 2 3.

Sanga-saranaya. 1 2 3.

Ama-watura. 1 2 3.

Tupa-wanse. 1 2 3.

Carma-wihagaya. 1 2 3.

Anagata-wanseya. 1 2 3.

Saddarma-pradipikawa. 2 3.

3. Raja-ratna-karaya. 1 2 3.

Gehi-winaya. 1 2 3.

Attanagalu-wanseya. 1 2 3.

The explanation of the same. 2.

Sarata-sangrahaya. 1 2 3.

Abidana-pradipikana. 1 2 3.

The explanation of the same. 2.

Sandikappaya. 1 2 3.

The explanation of the same. 2.

Muka-matta-dipaniya. 2 3.

Maha-rupa-siddiya. 2.

The explanation of the same. 2.

The better explanation of the same. 2.

Balawa-taraya. 1 2 3.

The explanation of the same. 2.

Another explanation of the same. 2.

Maha-sannaya. 2 3.

Datu-manjusuya. 2 3.

Datu-pataya. 2 3.

Sabda-laksanaya. 1 2 3.

The explanation of the same. 2.

Pada-sadanaya. 1 2 3.

The explanation of the same. 2.

Prayoga-siddiya. 2 3.

Panebi-cawa. 2 3.

The explanation of the same. 2.

Wrattodaya. 1 2 3.

The explanation of the same. 2.

2\. Brahma-jala-suttraya. 1 2 3.

Singalowada-sannaya. 1 2 3.
Salaiyaka-suttraya-sannaya, or explanation. 1 2 3.
Werawjaka-suttra-sannaya, or ditto. 2 3.
Uposata-suttra-sannaya, or ditto. 1 2 3.
Chula-camma-wibanga-suttraya. 1 2 3.

List of the Cingalese Books belonging to the Temple Galapata Vihari, in the District of Bentotte.

Pansiya-panasjataka. 1 2 3.
Ratnahwahlija. 1 2 3.
3. Poojahwahlija. 1 2 3.
Angottra-sangiya. 1 2 3.
6. Madoon-sangiya. 1 2 3.
6. Sanyot-sangiya. 1 2 3.
6. Dicksangiya. 1 2 3.
6. Parpancha - soodaneenam - attoowahwa. 2 3.
Sawmantepawdee - kawnam - attoowahwa. 1 2 3.
6. Dampeeyaw-attoowahwa. 1 2 3.
Saddarma-rattanakary. 1 2 3.
Madoorawrta-deepaneeya. 3.
Soettraneepawta. 1 2 3.

Meeleendapprasna. 1 2 3.
Aloopotwahansa. 3.
Peeroewana-potwawhansa. 1 2 3.
Pawleewimawna-wastoowa. 3.
Aloowimawna-wastoowa. 3.
1. Predeepikawwa. 3.
Jeena-awlankawra. 1 2 3.
Maha-awnawgata-wansa. 1 2 3.
Saddarma-awlankawra. 2 3.
Satty-pattana-soostra-sanna. 3.
Unmagga-jawtaka. 3.
Brachma-jawla-soostra-sanna. 1 2 3.
Rattapawla-soostra. 3.
Bawlapanditta-soostra-sanna. 1 2 3.
Soostra-sanna. 3.
Anawgata-wansa. 1 2 3.
Satty-pattawna-soostra-sanna. 3.
Toopaw-wansa. 1 2 3.
Boodsawrana. 1 2 3.
Pawreechada-potwawhansa. 1 2 3.
Coosala-soostra. 3.
2. Brachmajawla - soostra - pawda - anoema. 1 2 3.
Rawna-dawham-potwawhansa. 3.
Attanagalloe-wansa. 1 2 3.
6. Cawtaw-wastoo-potwahansa. 2 3.
Sangrahaw-potwawhansa. 3.
Mangala-soostra. 1 2 3.

6. Rawsa-wawhena-potwawhansa. 1 2 3.
Waranjaka-soostra. 2 3.
Damsakpawatoon-soostra. 1 2 3.
Sooba-soostra. 3.
Dampejaw-pawle-potwawhansa. 1 2 3.
Sanna-potwawhansa. 3.
Sooroochy-rawtaw-potwawhansa. 3.
Pawleeneegandoewa. 3.
Bawlawatawra-pawle-potwawhansa. 3.
Sanna-potwawhansa. 3.
Maittrewarnaw-potwawhansa. 3.
Sangee-sawkrata-aksarawdeya. 3.
Brachmawyoe-soostra. 3.
Singawla-wawda-soostra. 1 2 3.
Awlawaka-soostra. 3.
Maha-damma-sawmawdawna-soostra. 3.
Angoely-mawla-soostra. 2 3.
Sawrawrta-sangraba. 1 2 3.
Amaw-wawtoora-potwawhansa. 1 2 3.
1. 6. Sawra-sangraba. 1 2 3.
Negandoe-sanna. 1 2 3.
Ratty-kawneesansaw-potwawhansa. 3.
Wena-potwawhansa. 3.
Bawwoodda-sawtaka. 3.
Annorda-sawtaka. 3.
Sooreeya-sataka. 3.
Nawmasta-sawtaka. 3.
Wasana-sataka. 3.

Caumene-kondala. 3.
Cawuya-maneemawlawa-sanna. 3.
Wawrayogawsawra. 3.
Yogasawtaka. 3.
Yogaratnawkawra. 3.
Goenados-sangraha. 3.
. Digsangiya. 1 2 3.
. Maidun-sangiya. 1 2 3.
. Sanyut-sangiya. 1 2 3.
6. Angottra-sangiya. 1 2 3.
Samantapasadikanan-atuwawa. 1 2 3.
6. Sumangala-wilasininan-atuwa. 1 2 3.
6. Prapancha-sudaninan-atuwa. 2 3.
6. Manorata-puraninan-atuwa. 1 2 3.
Mangala-dipaninan-atuwa. 1 3.
Wimati-winodaninan-atuwa. 2 3.
Pansiyapanas-jataka-atuwa. 1 2 3.
6. Sararta-dipaninan-atuwa. 1 2 3.
6. Dampiya-atuwa. 1 2 3.
6. Terigata-atuwa. 1 2 3.
6. Teragata-atuwa. 1 2 3.
Tika-wahanse. 1 2 3.
6. Jataka-tika. 1 3.
Piriwana. 1 2 3.
Abidarma-pitake. 1 2 3.

The above-mentioned books are written in the Pali language; some of them contain about 400 or 500 olas each, others about 700 or 800; and they are about a cubit and a half in length.

6. Wisuddi-mangepela. 1 2 3.
6. Artasalininan-artawarnana. 3.
6. Parajikanan. 1 2 3.
Pachiti. 1 2 3.
Mahawaga. 1 2 3.
6. Suluwaga. 1 3.
Pariwara-pate. 1 2 3.
Palimuttaka-wine. 1 2 3.
Kanka-witarane. 1 2 3.
6. Winaya-winiche. 1 2 3.
2. Maha-wanse. 1 2 3.
6. Suttra-nipate. 1 2 3.
6. Upasaka Janalankare. 1 2 3.
6. Wisuddi-marga-tika. 1 2 3.
Milindapprasne. 1 2 3.
Wimana-wastu. 1 2 3.
6. Preta-wastu. 1 2 3.
Sarasangrahe. 1 2 3.
6. Mahabodi-wanse. 1 2 3.
Rasa-wahini. 1 2 3.
6. Bodiwanse-tika. 1 2 3.
6. Abidarma-sangraba. 1 2 3.
Jinalankare. 1 2 3.

The above-mentioned books are also written in the Pali language; they contain about 250 or

300 olas each, about a cubit or a cubit and a half in length.

6. Parajika, which had been brought from the Camboya country, after having been written in the same characters. 1 3.

Mangaladipaninan-atuwa, which had also been brought from the above country, after having been written in the same characters. 1 2 3.

These books are written in the same language, and contain each about 200 or 300 olas, about a cubit and a half in length.

Sataramaha-sangiyehi-linarta-warnana; this book is written in the Pali language, and contains 200 olas, and are in length two cubits. 1 3.

Ratana-waliya. 1 2 3.

Saddarma-ratnakara. 1 3.

Sarartasangraha. 1 2 3.

6. Wisuddimarga-sanne. 1 2 3.

6. Wimana-wastuprakarane. 1 2 3.

These books are written in Cingalese, and contain about 500 or 600 olas each, about one or two cubits in length.

Telcatara-yatasanne. 1 3.
Dampiya-sanne. 1 2 3.
Amawatura. 1 2 3.
Paratchida. 1 2 3.
Tupawanse. 1 2 3.
Carma-wibage. 1 2 3.
6. Anagata-wanse. 1 2 3.
Saddarmapradipika. 1 2 3.
Brahmajala-sustrasanne. 1 2 3.
3. Raja-ratnakare. 1 2 3.
Sangasarane. 1 2 3.
Gehiwine. 1 2 3.
Attanagala-wanse. 1 2 3.

The above-mentioned books are written in the Cingalese language, and contain each about 100 or 150 olas, about one cubit in length.

Satipattana-suttra-sanne.
Saleya-suttra-sanne. 1 2 3.
Chulakamma-wibanga. 1 2 3.
Suttra-sanne. 1 2 3.
Singalowada-suttra-sanne. 1 2 3.
Calakaracha-suttra-sanne. 1 3.
Chulahattipadoma-suttra-sanne. 1 3.
Mangala-suttra-sanne. 1 2 3.
Aloka-suttra-sanne. 1 3.
Daksinawibanga-suttra-sanne. 1 3.

Damsak-paiwatun-suttra-sanne. 1 3.
Uposata-suttra-sanne. 1 2 3.
Balapandita-suttra-sanne. 1 3.
6. Cudusika-sanne. 1 3.
Angulimala-suttra-sanne. 1 3.
6. Mulusika-sanne. 1 2 3.
Pratimoksa-sanne. 1 2 3.

These books are written in Cingalese, and contain each about sixty or seventy olas, about one cubit in length.

Sadu-charitode. 1 2 3.
Kudusika. 1 3.
6. Pratimokse. 1 2 3.
9. Dampiyawa. 1 2 3.
Sikkapada-walanjene. 1 2 3.

These books are written in Pali, and contain each about fifty or sixty olas, about one cubit in length.

Abidane. 1 2 3.
2. Amarasinhe. 1 3.
Padasadane. 1 2 3.
Saibdalakkate. 1 2 3.
Sandikappe. 1 2 3.
Prayoga-siddiya. 1 2 3.
Balawatare. 1 2 3.
Nigandu-sanne. 1 2 3.

Padasadane-sanne. 1 2 3.
Saibdalakkane-sanne. 1 2 3.
Balawatare-sanne. 1 2 3.
Wrattode. 1 2 3.
Wratta-ratnakare. 1 3.

These Pali-waikarne books contain each about 100 or 200 olas, about one cubit in length.

6. Damma-sangane. 2 3.
Arta-salini. 2 3.
The explanation of the same. 3.
6. Wibangaprakaranaya. 2 3.
6. Sammoha-winodani. 2 3.
Catawastu-prakaranaya. 2 3.
The explanation of the same in Pali. 3.
6. Datu-prakaranaya. 2 3.
The explanation of the same in Pali. 3.
6. Yamaka-prakaranaya. 3.
The explanation of the same in Pali. 3.
6. Pattana-prakaranaya.
The explanation of the same in Pali. 2 3.
6. Abidarmawa-taraya. 1 2 3.
6. The explanation of the same in Pali. 1 2 3.
The explanation of the same in Cingalese. 3.
Abidarmarsta-sangrahaya. 3.

The explanation of the same in Pali. 1 2 3.

The explanation of the same in Cingalese. 3.

Abidarmapita. 3.

Mahawaga. 1 2 3.

6. Sulumaga. 1 2 3.

6. Parajika. 1 2 3.

Pachiti. 1 2 3.

6. Pariwara. 1 2 3.

Samantapasadika-attuwa. 1 2 3.

Sarartadipini-tika. 1 2 3.

6. Wajirabode-tika. 2 3.

Wimatiwinodani-tika. 2 3.

Kanka-witarani. 1 2 3.

Palimuttaka-winaya. 2 3.

The explanation of the same in Pali. 3.

Budda-sinka. 2 3.

The explanation of the same in Pali. 3.

Sikkapada-walanjanaya. 3.

The explanation of the same in Cingalese. 1 2 3.

Prati-moksaya. 1 2 3.

The explanation of the same in Cingalese. 3.

Mulusika. 1 2 3.

The explanation of the same in Cingalese. 3.

Sumangala-wilasini.
The explanation of the same in Pali. 1 2 3.
Maidum-sangiya. 1 2 3.
Prapancha-sudani. 1 2 3.
Sanyut-sangiya. 1 2 3.
Sararta-prakasani. 1 3.
Sangottara-sangiya. 3.
6. Manorata-purani. 1 2 3.
Dampiya-pela. 1 2 3.
Attuwawa. 3.
The explanation of the same in Cingalese. 3.
Mahanirddesaya. 2 3.
6. Chulanirddesaya. 2 3.
6. Teragata-atuwa. 1 2 3.
6. Terigata-atuwa. 1 2 3.
6. Wimana-wastu-attuwa. 1 2 3.
The explanation of the same in Cingalese. 3.
6. Patisampida-pela. 2 3.
The explanation of the same in Pali. 3.
Netti-prakaranaya. 2 3.
6. Udana-atuwa. 2 3.
6. Eti-wuttaka. 3.
Preta-wastu-atuwa. 1 2 3.
Suttra-nipata-atuwa. 1 2 3.

The explanation of the same in Cingalese. 3.

6. Buddawansa-atuwa. 1 2 3.

6. Chariapitaka-atuwa. 1 2 3.

Wisuddi-margaya. 1 2 3.

Paramarta-manjussa. 3.

The explanation of the same in Cingalese. 2 3.

Piriwana. 1 2 3.

Milindapprasnaya. 1 2 3.

Explanation of the same. 3.

Sarasangrahaya. 2 3.

Saddarma-sangrahaya. 1 2 3.

Jinalankaraya. 1 2 3.

Mahabodi-wanseya. 1 2 3.

The explanation of the same in Pali. 3.

The explanation of the same in Cingalese. 3.

6. Rasa-mahini. 2 3.

Upasaka-janalankare. 1 2 3.

Maha-wanseya. 1 2 3

Data-wanseya. 1 3.

The explanation of the same in Cingalese. 3.

Paddai-maduwaya. 1 2 3.

The explanation of the same. 3.

Jina-charitaya. 1 2 3.

The explanation of the same. 3.

Saducharitodaya. 1 2 3.
Saddammopayanaya. 2 3.
The explanation of the same. 3.
Saddarma-ratanawaliya. 1 2 3.
Butsaranaya. 1. 2 3.
2. Saddarmalankaraya. 2 3.
Saddarma-ratnakaraya. 1 2 3.
Daham-saranaya. 2 3.
3. Pujawaliya. 1 2 3.
Paritchedaya. 1 2 3.
Sanga-saranaya. 1 2 3.
Ama-watura. 1 2 3.
Tupa-wanseya. 1 2 3.
Karma-wibagaya. 3.
Anagata-wanseya. 1 2 3.
Saddarma-pradipikawa. 2 3.
Raja-ratnakaraya. 1 2 3.
Gihi-wineya. 1 2 3.
Atwanagalu-wanseya. 1 2 3.
The explanation of the same in Cingalese. 3.
Sararta-sangrahaya. 1 2 3.
Abidana-pradipikawa. 1 2 3.
The explanation of the same. 3.
Sandi-kappaya. 1 2 3.
The explanation of the same. 3.
Mukamatta-dipaniya. 2 3.
Maharu-pasiddiya. 2 3.

The explanation of the same. 3.
The better explanation of the same. 3.
Balawataraya. 1 2 3.
The explanation of the same. 3.
Another explanation of the same. 3.
Maha-sannaya. 2 3.
Datu-manjusaya. 2 3.
Datu-pataya. 2 3.
Sabdu-laksanaya. 1 2 3.
The explanation of the same. 3.
Padasadanaya. 1 2 3.
The explanation of the same. 3.
Prayoga-siddiya. 1 2 3.
Panchikawa. 2 3.
The explanation of the same. 3.
Wartodaya. 1 2 3.
The explanation of the same. 3.
Brahmajala-suttra-sannaya. 1 2 3.
Singa-lowada-sannaya. 1 2 3.
Saleyyana-suttra-sannaya. 1 2 3.
Werajaka-suttra-sannaya. 2 3.
Uposata-suttra-sannaya. 1 2 3.

NOTICES OF SEVERAL

OF THE PRECEDING

PALI AND CINGALESE WORKS

ON

DOCTRINE AND GENERAL LITERATURE.

I.

The brief account of the religion of Budhu agrees with and may be seen at large in the following books:—

Pradiepika,
Saurasangraha,
Sumangala-wilasinie,
The Commentary of the book Pansiya-pana-jutakas.

Saddharma-alancaraya, signifying an illustration of the genuine writings which relate the thirty-two majestic bodily perfections in Budhu, eighty simple perfections, and 216 other simple natural signs in Budhu; the merits due in the next world for the honour, respect, homage, &c., paid to Budhu and other sacerdotal characters; the blessing already obtained in the preceding state of life, by those who had done in the like manner; also the good resulting to those who followed the doctrine of the religion, and the evil resulting to those who sinned against the same; the reward or punishment that is expected by those who do good or commit sin here, in the future state of being.

II.

1. Dampiyawa.—This book contains sermons of Budhu to his priests, and other people, with rules of life.

2. Brahmajala-sustraya.—This book shews how the priests are to preserve the commandments of Budhu, and how to abstain from sins; and also the fraud of the sixty-two other religions.

3. Mahawanse.—This book contains the histories of the kings; and it also appears there, how those kings believed in Budhu's religion, and continued to preserve it.

4. Saddarma-lankare.—This book contains histories about Ceylon, and some about Jambudwipa.

5. Wakkai-potta.—This book teaches how to calculate the years, months, and days.

6. Guna-pata.—This book gives a description of the effects of different sorts of medicine.

7. Wattoru-weda-pota.—This book contains accounts of different sorts of the choicest medicines.

8. Nidana-pata.—This book contains an assertion of the truth of Budhu's religion.

9. Yantra-pota.—This book contains a collection of figures, one of which is to be copied out, and tied on the body of the sick person, when the cause of his disorder is supposed to have arisen from any evil spirit.

10. Amara-pura-warna-nawa.—This book shews how the inhabitants of Amara-pura began first to embrace the Budhu's religion.

11. A List of Lands.—A list of all the lands that belong to the Budhu temples in the district of Matura.

12. Graha-chare, or Almanac.—The Cingalese Almanac.

13. Anne-pana-tikitsawa.—This book contains an account of the effects of different sorts of food.

III.

A Sketch of the contents of the Cingalese Book called Rajaratnakare, according to the statement of the chief priest of Galle.

Paryepty, Pretypanty, and Pretiwaide.

Paryepty signifies the scripture of the Budhist religion.

Pretypanty signifies the mode of exercising the same.

Pretiwaide signifies the good fortune that awaits good deeds.

It appears, says the priest, that when the wicked, that cared not themselves, and deviated from these three principles, were multiplied to a considerable number, this book was written by one Abeyeraje Pariwainaste (a high priest) in the reign of one of the kings of the royal family of Sriesangebo, for the purpose of reforming them, and re-establishing the law.

The chief priest of Galle, and every other of his profession, regard the contents of this book as a true and holy Scripture.

IV.

Manjoosey.—First book of the doctors, by which every thing about physic may be known.

Weeraha-meerey.—By which astronomical matters may be known.

Abidarmepitteka.—Praise to the idols.

Wineepitteka.—Praise to the priests.

Soottrepitteka.—Praise to the men.

V.

Sudderme-alancalny.—Sermons, or Bana of Budhu.

Brachmagahle Locha.—A dialogue between a Budhu priest and a bramin, in which the brahmin is at last converted.

VI.

A List of the different sorts of Books amongst the Cingalese.

Bannepot, or religious books, are of three different sorts, namely, Wineepitteka, Soottrepitteka, and Abidarmapitteka.

Wineepitteka consists of the following books :—

Pawrajikaya, Pachittia, Suluwarge, Mahawarge, Pariwarepawtte, Samantasawjikawe, Wajirabuddhia, Sawrartediepania, Wineawinisiea, Wineasangrahaya, Pawti-moksea, Wankawtinaranea, Wineyalankaria, Kudusikaya, Mulusikaya, Wineyartechaksusawe.

Soottrepitteka consists of—

Dicksangia, Medunsangia, Angottrasangia, Sanyutsangia, Buddahpawte, Dampiyawe, Oedawney, Ittiœtteke, Suttra-nipawne, Wimawnewastua, Praytewastua, Theregata, Theerigata, Jawtekka, Chulanerdeve, Mahanerdese, Pattisambidawmarge, Apadawne, Buddahwanse, Anagatawanse, Bodiwanse, Diepawanse, Kaisa-dawtoo-wanse, Lallatte-dahtoo-wanse, Charria-pitteka, Sumangala-lasania, Prapancha-soodana,

Manoratta-poorania, Sawrawrta-prakawsania, Rassawahinee, Buddeke-pawteya, Oepawseke-janawlankawre, Sawra-sangrahe, Wissuddhi-marga.

Abidarmapittekka consists of—

Paramawrtajotikawe, Dahrmasangranippre-karane, Wibahnga-prekarane, Kattawwastuppra-karane, Puggalla-prag-gnaptia, Dawtoo-preka-rane, Yamakapprakarane, Pantawnapprakarane, Artasalia, Sammoha-winodania, Abhidahrma-wetawre, Abhidarma-sangrahaye, Mạni-diepe, Manimanjuse, Abhidahrma-wikawsania, Gœla-hattawdiepennia, Satcha-sanke, Sankawpewarne-nawe, Paramawrta-winischea, Suchittaw-lan-kawre, Dhawtoo-kattaw-warnenawe, Madoosaw-ratta-diepania, Apeggoe-sawre, Pantawnasawra-dienia, Mahanayasawra-gooua, Cheeda-wiha-sania, Abhidarma-prakawsenia.

Weddepot, or medical books.

Charawke, Mœla-game, Helay, Buddah-gaggia, Buddah-wedeke, Halœke, Assina-saw-hitawe, Kahra-nawde, Catchayaniea, Waidawp-pieya, Mahakassapia-kahra-pawne, Preyoga-kose, Bissak-muttia, Chickit-cha-kalli-kawe, Wara-rooche, Watcha-kassapia, Preyoga-ratna-wallia, Ammette-mawlawe, Can-cawnia, Harriettee,

Chandettee, Sussutte, Yogakose, Maha-yawne, Boja-rajia, Jawtoo-kannia, Bindhu-sawre, Waray-awne, Sussutta-bahatte, Pawta-suddia.

Nacksastrapot, or astrological books.

Dhywag-gne-kawme-deenua, Waraba-meree, Dosesan-grahe, Hora-bharene, Dose-winischea, Nacksastra-diepa-mawlawe, Santawne-diepikawe, Soorye-siddahnte, Chandra-siddahnte, Nawe-pat-tawle, Chandra-charne, Soorye-charne, Prasna-sawre, Bahg-gyesanhitawe, Siridhare, Why-kon-tye-alankawre, Sawhit-thyea-chooda-mania, Jo-teaw-lankawre, Saw-raw-wallia.

Cahwye-sastra-pot, or poetical books.

Caw-silu-mina, Moowe-dew-daw-watte, Sa-sanda-watta, Yamakap-prati-hawrye-satteke, Cawye-sekkere, Girra-sandese, Selle-lihini-san-dese, Parrewi-sandese, Tisserre-sandese, Cowul-sandese, Lowe-wedde-sangrahe, Himawle-wis-terre, Cauminny-condelle, Cau-minny-mal-dam-me, Caumoot-harre, Lanka-wisterre, Gannedewi-helle, Wadan-kawi-potte.

Halipot.

There are several historical books amongst the Cingalese (wherein the histories of Ceylon are recorded), namely:—

Maha-wanse, Mahawanse-tiekawe, Rajaratnakare, Raja-wallia, Siehelle-wastua.

Wye-carne, or grammatical books, are of three different kinds, namely, Pali, Sangiskritta, and Elua.

Pali Wye-carne consists of—

Sandy-cahg-ghe, Maha-roopa-siddia, Choola-rupa-siddia, Balawe-tawre, Mooka-matta-die-pania, Sebdhe-niddhese, Casawne-chede, Gandha-charne, Abhidahane-warne-nawe, Sebde-nietiya, Sambandha-chintawe, Sadda-sawratwa-jalinseya, Sad-dwanta-cheede-chintawe, Wache-natwe-jotikawe, Wachekopedese, Abhi-dhne-pra-diepi-kawe, Waran-negilla, Dahtoo-pawya, Dah-too-manjoose, Samaya-chakkre.

Sangiskritta consists of—

Ammara-sinhe, Dor-ge-sinhe, E-kawksera-kose, Kriya-mawlawe, Roopa-mawlawe, Chandra-cau-mudia, Saras-wettiya, Maha-siddahnte-cau-mudia, Chula-siddahnte-kau-mudia, Moogdha-chode, Buddha-garge, Sakkas-kadda, Nawe-ratne, Wye-sene-sattekke, Naw-maws-ta-sat-tekke, Anoo-rud-dha-sattekke, Baud-dye-sat-tekke, Soor-ye-sattekke, Wartha-maw-lawk-kye-we, Wartha-ratna-kerre.

Elua consists of—

Sidat-sange-rawe, Lack-senne-sawre, Cauye-ratnemaw-lawe, &c. &c. &c.

Soostrakienne-pot, or astrological books.

Garbad-dware, Panche-pakse, Dandoo-marenne, Indra-gurullua, Sareve-to-chaddre, Niwitty-potte, Baw-daw-wallia.

VII.

Brachmah Jawle Sootra consists of a dialogue between two bramins respecting the principles of the Budhu religion, originally written in Pali: it is written in this book both in Pali and Cingalese; the Pali and Cingalese words being placed alternately. The disciples of Budhu are supposed to have heard all that was urged against their religion, which they then related to the Budhu, who controverts the objections.

Kaala Karame Sooha contains sermons, almost all of which are written in Cingalese, only a small portion being in Pali.

VIII.

The Books belonging to the Temple of Calany.

Rattana-walliya.
Saddarma-lankawra.
Pujawalliya.
Pradipikahwa.
Rasa-wawhina.
Amaw-watoora.
Brammajawla-soostra.
Sawtipattana-soostra.
Sawleiya-soottra.
Singawla-wawla-soottra.
Angoly-mawla-soottra.
Dahansappawatun-soottra.
Soeba-soottra.
Piroewawhanaw-potwawhansa.
Kadusika.
Mulusika.
Jawtaka-potwawhansa.

In this temple were several other books, which were lost when the priests were imprisoned.

IX.

An explanation of the contents of the book called Dampiyawa, which had been preached by Budhu, who was the chief of all the worlds, and displaying the doctrine in the said book.

Thought is the root and the principal thing which marks every intention.

A person commits the four following sins by words, viz. speaking falsehood by hiding the truth; speaking falsehood with an intention to deprive friends of their friendships; abusing a person as if he had pierced into his heart by a weapon; and by vain talking in such a manner as is of no use to himself nor to any one else.

A person commits the three following sins by his body, viz. either by punishing another severely; by teasing or killing any living thing; taking away the property of other people either by theft or force; and by enjoying carnal pleasure with women belonging to others.

A person commits the three following sins by his thoughts, viz. by covetousness to get the wealth of other people; by wishing for another's death; and thinking to one's-self that there is no sin, there is not a good act, there is nothing in this world, there is nothing in the other world, there are no good priests nor brahmins, and there is nothing to expect in return from charity that is given to the poor; and also by persuading a person to believe another religion.

Thus the people commit the said ten different sins by their bodies, words, and thoughts, on account of their ignorance, and by which means they descend themselves into the four following hells, viz. Narakaya (or bad), Tirisanyoniya (or that of becoming beasts), Pretalokeya (or the place of inferior devils), and Asurakaya (or the place of another sort of devils called Asurayas); and though they be born in a world where men are, yet they are exposed to many vices, griefs, troubles, pains, and diseases. Moreover, when such a sinner is born at any time in the habit of a man, there he again follows his old custom of committing sins, which are greater than what he had committed in the other world. For an example; as the wheels of a cart follow always the bullocks wherever they draw it, a person who has once committed such sin, follows his custom of committing sins wherever he is born again.

A person performs the following four good acts by his words, viz. speaking always what is true without any falsehood; persuading those that are on bad terms to live amicably; speaking in such a manner as always to please the hearer; and by conversing about matters which are either useful to himself or to others.

People who observe these will enter into Nirwāna (or the place of everlasting happiness), after having enjoyed much happiness and pleasure as gods and men. For an example; as the shadow of a man will not leave him at any time, a person who has once done a good act, as above-mentioned, will not forget to do good acts always wherever he is born.

A person, either a priest or a common man, gets himself into a passion by the following means, viz. either when he is affronted or abused; when he is beat, kicked, or flogged; when he is stabbed or wounded; when he has lost his case on account of the false evidence of another; or when he is robbed either of his movable or immovable property; which passion often turns into hatred, and which hate he hides in the bottom of his heart, as a lump of spoiled flesh hidden under some straw, and this bad passion increases day by day, as the scent of the flesh so hidden increases.

When a person, either a priest or a common man, is so treated, in either of the modes named, if he thinks to himself, This is nothing, the life of this world is nothing, and I am so treated now by them as they were treated by me in the other world, so I deserve thus to be treated, and then drop off the hatred from his heart, the passion will also decrease, and will not increase, as the fire cannot be much where there is no firewood.

Hatred which the people of this world bear in their hearts, can never be turned into goodwill through the hatred itself, but by good acts, patience, compassion, and wisdom,—as a place filled with filth can never be cleaned by filth itself, but by clean water.

The ignorant people of this world often make quarrels without ever considering that they are mortal; but those that are wise will always endeavour to avoid quarrels, considering to themselves, "What is the use of making quarrels when we are all mortal?" and by which means a person who bears an ill-will towards a wise man will, in a short time, be his good friend.

The great Budhu often preached thus, "Ye priests, live together amicably without quarrelling or bearing in your heart any hatred;" but if a priest should happen to make a quarrel by accident or impatience, he will soon appease it by his wisdom.

X.

The book called Dampiyawa contains twenty-six sorts of Budhu's exhortations.

1. Is called Yamakka; of this sort there are twenty exhortations having double meanings in each.

2. Appamada; of this sort there are twelve exhortations concerning things which ought not to be delayed.

3. Chitta; of this sort there are eleven exhortations concerning the different thoughts of a person.

4. Puppa; of this sort there are sixteen exhortations in comparison to flowers.

5. Bala; of this sort there are seventeen exhortations in comparison to fools.

6. Panditta; of this sort there are fourteen exhortations in comparison to wise men.

7. Arrehantakka; of this sort there are ten exhortations in comparison to Budhu priests, who can walk on the sky.

8. Sahassa; of this sort there are sixteen exhortations in comparison to number.

9. Papa; of this sort there are thirteen exhortations concerning sins.

10. Danda; of this sort there are seventeen exhortations concerning punishments.

11. Jarrah; of this sort there are eleven exhortations concerning infirmities.

12. Atta; of this sort there are twelve exhortations concerning the soul.

13. Loka; of this sort there are twelve exhortations concerning the world.

14. Budhu; of this sort there are sixteen exhortations concerning Budhu.

15. Sooka; of this sort there are twelve exhortations concerning health.

16. Piya; of this sort there are twelve exhortations concerning love.

17. Kroda; of this sort there are fourteen exhortations concerning anger.

18. Mala; of this sort there are twenty exhortations concerning blemish.

19. Dammatta; of this sort there are seventeen exhortations concerning justice.

20. Magga; of this sort there are sixteen exhortations on good behaviour.

21. Pakinna; of this sort there are sixteen exhortations concerning common concerns.

22. Nirraya; of this sort there are fourteen exhortations concerning hell.

23. Naga; of this sort there are fourteen exhortations in comparison of elephants.

24. Tanha; of this sort there are twenty-two exhortations concerning covetousness.

25. Bikkoo; of this sort there are twenty-three exhortations concerning Budhu priests.

26. Brahmanna; of this sort there are forty exhortations concerning brahmins.

Altogether there are 417 exhortations.

The several exhortations of the first sort are these, viz.:—The mind is the origin of all the different thoughts; and whatsoever sins a person does by means of his mind, they go together with him or her into his or her next life in hell, in the same manner as a wheel goes after an ox who draws it.

Whatsoever good or charity a person does by means of his mind, it goes in the manner as a shadow with that person, &c.

Of the second sort, viz.—He who does not delay of doing charity, has already obtained the everlasting glory. He who does delay in doing charity is already dead. He who does charity, though he is dead, he is like unto a man who is not dead. He who puts off doing charity though he is not dead, he is like unto a dead man, &c.

Of the third sort, viz.—The wandering mind, a wise man would make it straight in the manner that a carpenter makes straight an arrow, &c.

On the books called Sariputtra and Roopamatawa.

The first contains the art of constructing of Budhu's image, by taking the measure of the length, breadth, circumference, and size of each part, each limb or joint, from the head to the feet of the same; and the second contains the manners, forms, and the different colours of all and every distinct part or parts for constructing the different images of different deities, devils, and animals, &c.

The book called Amarapura-warna-nawa contains the story of the last Budhu's coming to Amarapura country, and how the Budhu's religion prevailed in that country.

This book is in the Pali language, and has no Cingalese explanation of it.

A

DETAILED ACCOUNT

OF

THE TRANSPORTATION

OF THE

BRANCH OF THE BOGAHA TREE

FROM

JAMBU-DWIPA TO BODI MANDELLA,

AT ANURADHE PURA,

BY ORDER OF KING PATISSA THE SECOND.

HAIL, BUDHU!

The King Patissa the Second having constructed ships, then sent for ninety-six kelles of maha-rahatoons, (those were Budhu priests who could walk on the sky); and, together with them, after a seven months' navigation, landed at the place called Bodimandella; when the king of that country, Sribodi-Rajah, came out of his palace, and, after having bade the said rahatoons to sit down, he asked the cause of their coming thither. Then the King Patissa the Second said that he came to take away the bodinwahansa (that is, a tree which the Budhists worship); whereupon Sribodi-Rajah replied and said, that he would not allow it. Then the priests cried out, saying, that they could not settle the dispute between the parties (meaning the two kings), and they adjured the bodinwahansa. The King Patissa the Second stretched forth one of his hands towards heaven, and the other towards the earth, and said, "Our bodinwahansa be ours; and our bodinwahansa witness us, if you have mercy upon our Cinhala (Ceylon)." Thereupon, the bodinwahansa roared like thunder without rain. The King Sribodi-Rajah, being affrighted, desired them to take away the bodinwahansa; then the priests said to the King Patissa the Second, no one could take the bodinwahansa away except a bickshou (a female hermit), of your Cinhala-Sakka-Coola, (that is, of the royal family called Sakka-Coola, in Ceylon,) who never felt the breath of a male. The priest having seen by their heavenly eyes such an one, desired to send messengers to call the priest Mihidoomaha-Teroonancy's younger sister, who had been performing her functions as a hermit, in a painted cave in the rock called Sayagriparwetta. Upon that, the two priests, namely, Malliyamaha and Mihidooma, went up to the said Sayagri-parwetta in less time than a spider's web, taking fire from the lower side, could blacken the upper side; and after having called the said sister of the priest, Mihidoo-maha desired her that she would not eat any food cooked on the hearth but fruits, and that she should change her dress thrice a-day after having washed herself in smelling-water. So saying, the priests went to heaven, when the gods Sākkraia, Brahma, &c., having constructed two seats called Watjrasennah, fourteen cubits high, making them sit upon them, offered to them Dassawidderatnah, (that is, the ten precious things, namely, pearl, precious stones, gold, silver, &c.) and began to hear their preaching. The priests desired the gods to offer as a gift to their Tonuroan, (that is, Budhu, his word, and his priests,) two heavenly clothes, and sixteen golden pots, which they accordingly got from them, and afterwards giving blessing to the gods, and taking with them sixteen heavenly women, came to the lake Anotatta-Willah, and having taken sixteen potsful of smelling-water from that lake, went their way back to Sayagri-parwetta, and caused the said female hermit to wash in sixteen pots of smelling water, after which she took in her hand the heavenly cloth brought by the priests to dress herself; and hardly had she taken off the cloth which she had already on, than she obtained the power of going on the sky; so she proceeded to go with the heavenly women, and the priests followed them.

When they came to Bodimandella they introduced themselves to the king; and having sent for the flowers of Dambagassa, (a tree, the leaves, flowers, &c. of which are said to be gold,) and the said flowers being gold were ground in mercury, and it being made liquid, it was given into the hands of the female hermit. The golden ladder being placed, she climbed the ladder, taking with her the gold coach, the golden cup, and the golden pencil; and she being so directed by the heaven and earth, did draw a line on the tree bodinwahansa, saying, " Bodinwahansa, come to our Cinhala." Then the tree fell asunder from the place where the line was drawn, as if it was cut with a golden saw, and went up to the sky, and came back and set itself in the golden coach. There also issued blood* from the two ends of the tree that was so cut. The female hermit having torn the heavenly cloth which she had on her, covered the two ends of the tree; then the blood stopped. Sribodi Rajah permitted the Mallawa princes to conduct the bodinwahansa, giving them three golden tiles to offer them to the bodinwahansa at any place where it would set itself, with further directions to offer Satroowan and Miniroowan flowers, (that is, seven precious things of which the flowers are made, namely, gold, silver, pearl, precious stones, &c.); and further desired the King Patissa the Second to keep peace with the said Mallawa princes.

Now, the bodinwahansa tree, in the space of seven days, came to Mahatotta, or Matura, thence to Samanalla-Sripada, and thence to Mai-

* The personification of the tree reminds the reader of Tasso's enchanted grove, and the northern legends.

hangana. But the people of Ceylon, not having been able to know where the bodinwahansa went thence, began to lament and cry, which cry was heard like thunder throughout the whole of Jambudwipa. Sribodi-Rajah having heard this cry, went up to the said mountain Maihangana, and begged the bodinwahansa to come forth: (since that time that mountain was called Hunnasgri-Canda). The bodinwahansa came forth, and thence proceeded to the place called Santaneya; when it came there gifts were offered to it. Thence it went to the mountain called Yabahoo, belonging to the priest Yama; thence to the village Nalligamma, where the bodinwahansa let fall a piece of bark; and from thence went to the mountain or rock at the place called Allegalla. There it tarried some time, and, by the power of the bodinwahansa, those who were in the cave of that rock were caused to come out, and they were made stones on the spot. The upasakka (a religious man) of that village seeing this, took a golden cupful of honey, and went and offered the same to bodinwahansa, begging it to come down. The bodinwahansa let fall a branch with leaves into that golden cup, and sunk itself thirty cubits deep into the earth, and stood stretching forth its branches; thence proceeded again and went to the mountain Demmettedenny; after having placed there a sandal-wood tree, it went to Calany; thence it went to Bopittiya, and after having let fall there a piece of bark, went to the wood Mahatal-himay: there having caused to be made a fortification of a hedge of Sal-trees, and in the middle of that fortification having placed a golden-coloured branch with leaves, it went to the wood called Nitipatma-Unnewanney, in the village of Maha-daiwa-gamma, where the bodinwahansa stood still in the golden-coach on the sky; so it stood seven weeks viewing the earth. Now, the King Patissa the Second having caused to be assembled gods and men, and ninety-six kelles of maha-rahatoons, or Budhu priests, nine kelles and nine lacses of men, seven kelles of wissi-maha-yodeas (giants or warriors), sent for the blacksmith Drowah, and, on the lucky hour Uttersala-Nakketta caused to be made the following instruments, viz. kettes, mammetties, axes, adzes, chisels, iron crows, and anvils; and begun to prepare a ground (such as is called in Cingalese Maluwa) for bodinwahansa, which was in breadth 100 cubits, in circumference 440 cubits, and 32 cubits high. There was placed in this Maluwa a golden pot of seven cubits, called Kallessa: after which, the bodin-wahansa proceeded to descend from the sky to come to the Maluwa, on the lucky hour of Rehenne-nekketta, on a Tuesday full moon, (according to the Cingalese reckoning of time, by the shadow), the sun to be at meridian, or height, in the month Assalla (July); but the bodinwahansa, looking at the golden pot above-mentioned, would not come down; upon that the golden pot sunk itself into he ground at the Maluwa, or the ground prepared for the bodinwahansa. Whereupon Sonattra-Teroonancy, by his heavenly eyes penetrating the earth at a look, went to the bottom of Mahameru; thence he brought Satroowan-welly (that is, seven precious kinds of sand), putting the same into one end of his cloth which he had on, and came as the water-fowl called Diyakawah, and splitting the earth, rose up from the Maluwa as the full moon; and after having scattered the sand in the Maluwa, cried out "Sadu!" and the gods called out so as to cause the earth to tremble, saying, "The virtue of the bodinwahansa will endure for 5000 years henceforth;" and they then gave this island the name Sri-lanka.

Then were granted to the Maluwas, by the King Patissa the Second, on account of their expertness shewn on behalf of him, the following lands: Sry-sakan, Sry-boomi, Pihitty-Ratta,

Maya-Ratta, Maddegam-Nuwerra, Jayaboomy, as far as to the step of marble stones of the city called Pandoohas. Prince Rama got the lands Trinanboomy and Yapa-Pattoona, or Jaffna, after which the king departed this life. Thereupon the lands, beginning from the city Pandoohas, became a dependency of Malakka; and the other lands, including the city of Anurahde-Pura, went to Heddy-Demallos (a Malabar nation). So it remained under them for 120 years. Afterwards, the King Dootoogameny, who had ten giants and a cadol elephant, captured 300 batteries and fortifications of metal, and the strong fort of Bomaluwa, (which is the place where the bodinwahansa-tree stands), which was eighteen cubits high, and made of metal; and after having destroyed the Heddy-Demallos, he subdued the Isle of Lanka, and reigned over the same.

Now, the king had asked the teroonancies, "Shall I have committed sin by having killed these Malabars?" the priests answered and said, "O king, you cannot be absolved from the sin of having killed four certain persons." Then the king asked the priests what was to be done to be absolved from it. The priests said, that he should cause to be built a cave called daggoba, placing in it the dawtoo of Loutoorah-Budhu. Thereupon the king began to clear and repair the cave called Ratnamali, which was in length and breadth 120 cubits, the four walls of it were caused to be painted, mats were spread on the floor, and images of Sakkraia and Brahma, gods, &c. of gold, valued at six lacses, were placed in it; at the east gate was placed a maikkadda-pahanna (a semi-circular step made of a precious stone), which was worth the three worlds, namely, the Dewa-Lōka (or heaven), Manoepe-Lōka (or the world), and the Naga-Lōka (or the cobra capiles' world). The image of Loutoorah-Budhu was made of pure gold; the Sri-maha-bodinwahansa-tree was made of gold; a seat called watjrasenna was made of blue sapphire; in the middle of the cave thereupon were placed the image of Loutoorah-Budhu, and his two diagasan (or the two Budhu priests) used to sit on the right and left-hand side of Budhu when he was alive; a statue of the King Dootoogameny, having the golden sword, as if he was praying to the Budhu. A box of seven cubits having been made of pearl, the Budhu priest Sonattra was sent to Naga-Lōka to bring the dawtoo or bones of Budhu; who went to Naga-Lōka and demanded from the cobra capiles the said bones of Budhu, but they refused. Thereupon the priests came away, saying, "Let our will be done:" upon which the belly of the great king of the cobra capiles, called Mutchalindah, became empty; (it is said that the said cobra capile had the box of bones of Budhu in his belly, and after the demand made by the priest it came away by itself.) So the cobra capiles came to the Maluwa, the place prepared by the king, and claimed the bones; then all the priests disputed against them, and, in the mean time, the Maluwa princes took away the box of dawtoo bones to Ramag-gramaya, where they deposited it, together with our pearl dawtoo-box, in a cave, and built a steeple over it, which being broken open on the sea-side, the box of pearl fell into the sea. The cobra capiles found it out; on that account the pearl-box, and the measures by which the dawtoo are measured, were given to the cobra capiles for their trouble of finding the same again, and the dawtoo were measured and received, being thirty paras: afterwards the cobra capiles offered as a gift the measure, and went away.

The dawtoo, or bones of Budhu, having been put into the new box, and the same being shut, it was carried on the heads of the Maluwa princes to the King Dootoogameny, and delivered to him. The king having called together the gods of two lōkas (or worlds), namely, Sakkraia, Brahma, &c., and a number of priests, amounting to the number of kelle-laksa-sowahas, and men also, and having dressed himself in gold like the King Wessamooni, the king over the devils, or like the rocks called Suddarsanah and Yugandara, went into the cave in a procession, accompanied with the sounds of the five sorts of music called Pantchatoorya-nada, like the sound of the sea, and placed the box of dawtoo, the bones of Budhu, upon the seat called watjra-sana. When the king came out he sent for smiths and carpenters, and caused the cave to be locked and shut, and it was likewise covered over, and walls built round the place. In the middle of these walls, the covering over of the cave was filled up with rape-seed oil and butter; and after having mingled the same by elephants during seven days, and paddled boats on it, he opened the drain, and the place was made clean. The king having asked the chief priest how to build the steeple, or the tower upon it, and tiles having been brought in a golden plate, and clay being prepared, he began to build the tower. Before the building of the tower was finished, the king foresaw his death approaching, and asked how or in what manner the top of the tower should be placed. Upon that, a top of cloth was made and placed on the tower, to be viewed by the king; and whilst he was viewing it there appeared to him the heavenly coach, brought to him to go from this world. He made it known to those who were about him, but they would not believe it. Upon that he ordered four wreaths of flowers to be brought, which he took into his hands and cast upon the coach, and they were suspended on it. Then the multitude cried as the king went away to heaven, or departed this life; the king's elephant, called Cadol, broke the chain with which he was tied up, and went away to Saddantawilla, a lake; Mallalloo, went to Malakka; and this lanka, or the island of Ceylon, was left to the prince Tissa.

Afterwards, a nation called Cakamukkoroo came and landed at this island: their king was called Nalla Modeley, who possessed the land on the other side of Cala-oya rivulet as far as Ma-oya rivulet; and he constructed different fortifications: the rest remained under Prince Tissa. This prince being unable to fight against Nalla Modeley, letters were sent to the country of Aiotty-Pattelam, and from thence were brought nine sorts of Malabars, namely, 500 men of the class called Powittewah, 700 men of Kewattewah, 300 men of Kalingawah, 150 men from Itcha-Ottah, 12,500 men of Nallandowah, 8000 men of Pallewah, 400 men of Mooddewallangan-padi-Tewerreya, 900 men of Weddhi-rissah, 500 men of Marrewarrah. These men were landed at the isle of Kuddira-Malla, and the King of Ceylon having gone thither, took an account of the men and great guns, and ordered that hire should be given to them from his treasury. Those men asked the king, " What will your majesty give us if we gain the battle ?" The king answered and said, " I will give you women of this country in marriage." After the Malabars had landed Cara rice, and heaped it up together, the place was thenceforth called Cara-Doowa. Now the men went to battle, and after seven days' battle took possession of the fort Nallewa-Cottoowah, after which they went to the king's palace, and addressed themselves to the king. He being much pleased by it, got ready food for them, and desired them to eat, and also asked them whether they would have women in marriage. They said that they did not want women in marriage, but they ate ; after which they again asked the king what he would give them. The king ordered them to fight against Nalla Modeley, and to take the land which he had the possession of. Thereupon they, having obtained orders from the king, prepared every thing that was necessary for the battle, and loaded 900 cannons on carts, besides bandies and horses for their journey. So the king went and met them, and gave them leave to go to battle. Thereupon they asked the king where they should erect a battery. He ordered them to erect a battery in the centre of the place called Calalgoruwa-Duwah, belonging to Triparmeswarah, a hermit. Accordingly they erected the battery on that place; after which they went on horses to meet Nalla Modeley, and encountered him at Galgommuwi. When Nalla Modeley approached their battery, they, the Malabars, fired at once all the 900 cannons; so the said Nalla Modeley and his men were slain. After which they went to the strong fort of Nalla Modeley, and destroyed the same. Thence they went and tarried at Tarragodda-gallah three months. On receiving a message from the king, they came up to him, leaving the following posts, namely,—the post of Pottoopittiya; the post of Soorrowitta; the post of Potana, at Calluwella; and met the king at the lake of Nuwerra or Candy. The king having received them with joy, gave them the possession of the lands called Anakatjanah-boomi and Caluratta, fixing limits for the same.

After the death of the king, there prevailed in this island a famine called Millalapah; then the Malabars, leaving this island, went away to their own country; and the other men and women of this island went into the woods or wilderness, eating leaves, bark of trees, white ants' nests, &c.

Afterwards there proceeded a king to this island called Buwanaika Bahu; and about that time the King Mallawah, of the country of Mallawa-Ratta, having died, leaving seven sons, that country was taken possession of by another king, who was a competitor of the late King Mallawah's: so the princes remained concealed in a vihari; and afterwards they thought to themselves, as they were unable either to fight against him or to pay him tribute, that they would come to Cinhala, or Ceylon, again; so they came away from the Budhu temple of Bodimandella, and went on board ship, and came and first landed at Madura-pura, thence Mailla-pura, thence at Ayotti-Pattenam. When they came there, they inquired the way to come to this island of Ceylon from seven different castes of Malabar chitties, and two or three families of them also desired to come along with them; so they sent for four carpenters, and built dhoonies and ships; and having taken each of them separate presents to give to the King of Ceylon, accompanied by their people, namely, the carpenter called Kotta-waduwah, who built the vessel called Hambana, for the King Semasinha, of the country Tellenga; the smith called Galwadduwah, who sawed crystal; the carpenter who made the spy-glass; Abarrena-badalah, the goldsmith; Cappuroe-hettia, Wettella-hettia, Pakku-hettia, Chunnambo-hettia, Handun-hettia, Wahoon-wallakarrua, Manternetti-lianna-pandittia, Sakkanadigurroe-whatalawirridou-ogan-panikkia, and Dellasawantani Chakkrewanni Sudda-halluwa, came and landed at Ceylon, and having given their different presents to the King of Ceylon, obtained the following titles, viz.: one of the said persons, called Nalantadewah, presented a silk cloth, and obtained the title Raja-wanniah; one person, Palak-koomara, a prince, presented a silk cloth, and obtained the title Sinha-wana; one person, Malleloe, presented a golden chair, and obtained the title Raja-gurroe-Modiansa; Prince Malla presented a golden cat, and obtained the title Mallawah-Bandara; Eriawe-pannikki-rata presented an elephant, and obtained the title Sinhappoe-Modiansa; and one person, Prince Samasinha, presented a silk cloth, and obtained the title Hetti-Bandara.

The country had been divided, and the following were fixed as land-marks, viz.:—one vihari (a tower); mioya (a rivulet); the hollow place at Dekkehawunotenna; the hollow place called Ellewallakadda; Kottekumbook-kalia; Palukandewewa-shallawehera (a tower so called); the stone pillar on which an axe is engraven, and planted on the end of Attikkulamaygalkanda, a rock; the rock on which is engraven a peacock; Maillawewa-Shellawehera (a tower so called); Galtenwehera, a tower at Tammannagodda; Kalla-oya, a rivulet; Panankani; Sriwarddana-nuwara; Dadduro-oya, a rivulet; Ratmallegallai-galwettya, a rocky bank; Degoddeturah-Canda, a mountain; Nana-Ella; Hewan-Ella; Pottoopettiya; Morregodda-inna; Goorrugamma-vihari; Niandewanna-vihari; Mapakalankoottiya; and Galmaddudekka-Vihari. Thus ended the land-marks of the four Wanni-Pattoos. The King Buwanaika Bahu viewed this division of the up-side land granted to them by him, so that it might not be alienated while the sun and moon endure.

Epologamma Hetti Bandara, Eriawa-panikki Modiansa, and Oddooweria Mallela Bandara, received grants, engraven on slabs, and ministered to the Prince Mallewa, and were honoured with the titles of Siama-sinha, Rajegorru, Bandara Modiyansa; and the villages Oodugampolla, Kurewella, Mahara, Yakedættaiwe, Wattella,

Banpana, Yattahaina, Calany, Madula-pittia, Toppou, Borregodda-watta, Malwana, Cattotta, Halpa, Ballegalla, Botella, Hettimolla, Kahambilia-pittia, of the Hina-corle, which were marked out and granted free from the following duties:—madiungan, palimarala, binpolottoo, gatepolla, kaddappo, tirrappoo, tuwakkoo-aya, etaya; and they were appointed as desaves and adigars, and granted a sannas engraven on a copper-plate, to remain as long as the sun and moon endure.

The two Budhu priests of a Budhu temple had conferred on them the titles of Budhu-Chittra teroonancy and Sairenankara teroonancy, by clothing them with the robes called Sangalla-patta and Siwooroe, and lived as glorious as the Sree-maha-bodinwahansa, who were commonly called Mahatottagammoe Terre and Weedagamma Terra.

Eriawa Pannikki-rata and Dippitigamma Liannah-weddah were commanded by Buwanaika Bahu, the King of Cottah, to come together with the four wannias of the four pattoes, and the pannikkias* thereof, to wit, the said Eriawa Pannikki-rata himself bringing with him fifty men; Galawewa Panikki-rata bringing with him twenty-two men; Doopatagamma Panikki-

* Keepers of elephants.

rata twelve; Kaikoonawa Sinhanada Panikki-rata twelve; Wilawe Gajasinha Panikki-rata sixteen; Warragammana Wanniaddi-Panikki-rata twenty; Golloogalla Irroogal-Newadootton Panikki-rata thirty-two; Aggattigammana Wanaweera Gaja Panikki-rata eighteen; Wendekaddoowa Winnakeswerra Gaja Panikki-rata twenty-two; Magalla Oloopokkoona Soondra seven; pingos of ropes and thongs, and doonookayawa polhiria also; wagapolloos or clubs for driving elephants, who were ordered to go with the elephants of the four cooroowes and their keepers to catch wild ones. The elephants and the keepers were at Coemboorupittiya; the four wannias, and the panikkias of the four pattoos, also went to the spot where the elephants were kept, and declared the king's order to them, and, together with them, went and stopped the elephants at Magalla, being on this side of the rivulet called Deddooroo Oya; thence they went and stopped at Atteregalla; thence at Galgommoowa; thence at Madinnorowa; thence they departed and went round the forest called Mahanaga-Sola Himaya, where, finding an elephant, they surrounded him by the tame ones, and got him tied by the panikkia named Laboonnoruwa. Afterwards they went and stopped at Kahalla, and having promised to give offerings to gods, the keeper of an elephant mounted upon the elephant, and began to proceed; so they went and stopped at the city of Mooddakondapolla, thence at Dambedenia, thence at Kalloogalla, thence at Sitawak, where the king Buwanaika Bahu, of Cottah, came out to the audience-hall, and ordered the elephants to be let loose, while people watched around beating tom-tom, and then that the four wannias should tie up the elephant, in order to make a trial of their dexterity. Whereupon the malleloes went into the midst of the elephants, tied up one of the fore legs of the elephant, and made their bow to the king, who gave presents, and the title of Airiawa Wanninayaka Sinhappoo Modiyansa. Oodduweriya Winnagoonna, without being the least terrified by the noise of the elephants round about, tied up the other leg, and bowed down before the king, and obtained the title of Ratna Mallewa Jerrugal Bandara. Pattelemekkrantisila Kirti-rajatoranga, without being in the least afriad, went amidst the elephants and tied another leg, and bowed down to the king, and obtained the title of Tree-Raja Wanniah. Palewiya-Sinhala Keerty obtained the title of Rajepaksa Comara Sinha Wanniah. Addiwiddinottik Waddatta Moddatta obtained the title of Rajapaksa Gonnaratna Ipologamma Irrogal Modiyansa. Afterwards they were appointed elephant-catchers by the King Buwanaika-Bahu; and the six pattoos or provinces granted to them by the king were divided, of which the following is an account:—

1st. The lake of Ponparappuwa is eight cubits deep, it has eighteen dams; the fields which are watered by it are sufficient to sow 250 ammonams of paddy.

2d. Kalletirrella has seven ollegam lands, which are sufficient to sow forty ammonams of paddy.

3d. The lake of Mahatabbowa is twelve cubits deep; the land watered by this lake is sufficient to sow 350 ammonams of paddy; the lands overflown by the lake-water are eighteen magam lands, which were sufficient to sow 250 ammonams of paddy, 108 dams and ollegam lands, besides thirty-two ruins of Budhu temples. This is the land of Ayana Bandara; it is free from every duty, and on the dam of this lake stands a jack-tree, with a beetle-creeper, a temple, a chank-shell on the hik-tree, and two Budhu temples at the end of the wana, or water-course; and on that side of the land which was overflown were seventy-two giants' wells.

4th. Peronkandallama is sufficient to sow

forty ammonams of paddy; it has seven dikes, dams, and lakes, and, at Orrugala, a tower called Nellonatkanno-weherra.

5th. The lake of Ottookkoollama is seven cubits deep; the land watered by it is sufficient to sow forty ammonams of paddy: there are in the same district a stone cave, two Budhu temples, two giants' wells, and two ollegams, which were sufficient to sow nine ammonams of paddy, which were overflown by the lake. The said land is a place where cattle are kept, and it belongs to two temples.

6th. Sohonkandellama is sufficient to sow forty ammonams of paddy; there are twelve ollegam lands, two Budhu temples, and eighteen towers at Toottanaruwa-agoonowel Kanda, inclusive of those at Galpiti-Kanda. The land lying between Baiwoema-Galtaimba and Pahala-Aibba is a gift to a Budhu temple.

Now follows an account of the province called Marrikara-pattoo.

The lake of Ramankandellema is five cubits deep; the land watered by it is sufficient to sow forty ammonams of paddy. In the part of it which was overflown by the lake were twelve ollegam lands, two Budhu temples, and two giants' wells.

Pieremankandellema is sufficient to sow twelve ammonams of paddy; there are eighteen dams and two giants' wells.

Tamarakkollama is sufficient to sow forty ammonams of paddy; there are eighteen ollegam lands, dams, and dikes, and five giants' wells.

Kattekadduwa is sufficient to sow twelve ammonams of paddy; there are four ollegam lands.

Karrewikkoollama is sufficient to sow seven ammonams of paddy; there are in that district five ollegam lands and dams.

Maddewakkoolama is sufficient to sow twenty-five ammonams of paddy: there are in the same district five ollegam lands; the lake thereof is five cubits deep.

Wattoopola is sufficient to sow thirty ammonams of paddy; its lake is six cubits deep; it has five ollegam lands, two giants' wells, one Budhu temple: its limit is the stone pillar on which is engraven an aupotta or umbrella.

Ooppala-watta is sufficient to sow forty-five ammonams of paddy; there are seven dams and dikes; the lake of it is six cubits deep, and there is one giant's well, and one Budhu temple. The ground hereof, sufficient to sow five ammonams of paddy, is a gift to the temple.

Mankollemma is sufficient to sow twenty-five ammonams of paddy; it has five ollegam lands; the lake of it is five cubits deep; it has also one giant's well, and one galmaddoe, a building constructed of stones.

Koobookkadewella is sufficient to sow seventy-five ammonams of paddy; its lake is eight cubits deep; it has one Budhu temple, one giant's well, and some ollegam lands.

Kokkoomankoollama is sufficient to sow thirty ammonams of paddy. In that part of it which was overflown were ollegam lands, which were sufficient to sow forty-five ammonams of paddy; its lake is six cubits deep, and it has one hall built of stones and one giant's well.

Bamoonnaria is sufficient to sow eight ammonams of paddy; it has five ollegam lands, and one tower called Gaitta-Vihari.

Tattawewa is sufficient to sow sixty ammonams of paddy; it has five ollegam lands, besides five stone pillars in the jungle, and one giant's well.

Paritchankoollema is sufficient to sow fifteen ammonams of paddy; its lake is five cubits deep; it has one Budhu temple, and one giant's well. In that part of it which was overflown there were five ollegam lands.

Waddiggamangawa is sufficient to sow twelve

ammonams of paddy; its lake is six cubits deep; it has one Budhu temple and one giant's well. In that part of it which was overflown were five ollegam lands.

Karrewittawewa has seven ollegam lands. In that part of it which was overflown were twelve ollegam lands, dams, and dikes; its lake is five cubits deep. The land watered by that lake is sufficient to sow 250 ammonams of paddy; there is likewise one giant's well, the limits of which are Wellangria and Deddoorooya.

Kaddoopittia is sufficient to sow 150 ammonams of paddy.

Madampay is sufficient to sow 650 ammonams of paddy.

Ana-Ollendawa is sufficient to sow seventy-five ammonams of paddy.

Nellikkoolamma is sufficient to sow twelve ammonams of paddy.

Wendekkadoowa is sufficient to sow twenty ammonams of paddy; it has five ollegam lands and dams. This province was granted by Buwanaika Bahu the king to Panditapattoo Koomarasinha-wannia, by engraving the grant on a slab, and fixing as limits the following places, viz. Tonigalla, Wellangriya, and Deddoorooya.

Galkandellama is sufficient to sow twelve ammonams of paddy, and it has three lakes.

Sitta-wellia is sufficient to sow 120 ammonams of paddy; it has seven ollawewoo lakes.

Sellankandellama is sufficient to sow seventy-five ammonams of paddy; there are in it twelve ollegam lands, dams, and dikes; one hall built of stones, one Budhu temple, and one giant's well.

Karrebawewa lake is six cubits deep; the land watered by it is sufficient to sow thirty ammonams of paddy; and in that part of it which was overflown were five ollegam lands: the limits for the same are Midellagaha-kalia and Kohombewemboowa.

Meddegamma is sufficient to sow thirty ammonams of paddy; its lake is five cubits deep; it has five ollawewoo lakes, three ollegam lands, one Budhu temple at the corner of the mount, and three ammonams of ground. From between the stone pillar at the upper end, and the two stone pillars at the lower end, is a gift to a Budhu temple.

Ollikkooly is sufficient to sow twelve ammonams of paddy; its lake is six cubits deep; it has one Budhu temple, one giant's well; and on that side of it which was overflown there were eighteen ollegam lands, dams, and dikes.

Parria-wellia is sufficient to sow thirty ammonams of paddy; its lake is six cubits deep; it has five dams, one giant's well, and one Budhu temple.

Pettigama is sufficient to sow twelve ammonams of paddy; its lake is five cubits deep. In that side of it which was overflown were fifteen ollegam lands and dams, and the market-street of Kuweni (a she-devil so called) has five halls built of stones, one tiled house, five willas or ponds, eight pattas or tanks. The end of Kanda-Soottou-Pattoo.

Mooriak-kollama Kirrela-maddoowa is sufficient to sow forty ammonams of paddy; the lake of it is five cubits deep; there are twelve ollegam lands, dams, and dikes, six stone pillars, and one Budhu temple. Of this land, the ground sufficient to sow eight ammonams of paddy is a gift to a Budhu temple.

Kottookatchiya is sufficient to sow 150 ammonams of paddy; its lake is nine cubits deep; it has one Budhu temple, and two giants' wells. On that side of it which was overflown by the lake were thirty-two ollegam lands. Of this, ten ammonams of ground is a gift to a Budhu temple.

Katchimaddowa is sufficient to sow thirty ammonams of paddy; its lake is six cubits deep;

and on that part of it which was overflown by the lake's water were twenty-two ollegam lands and dams. There is in this land the stone cave which was the store-house of Premeswerra Rajah, of Parma-Canda, besides one tower, two ponds, and two giants' wells.

Ooriagamma is sufficient to sow 250 ammonams of paddy; its lake is fifteen cubits deep; it has two Budhu temples, three galattoos (stone barns), seven ollegam lands, five giants' wells, and three ponds; and on that part of it which was overflown by the lake there were fifty-five ollegam lands, six magam lands, eighteen towers, and eighteen wells.

The land between the following marks, viz. the rock called Diwooroon-galla at Tammánna-pittiya; the stone pillar on which an image of a woman is engraven, standing at the upper end of Karrembawewa (a lake); the stone called Hunnoogalla, standing at the water-course of the lake called Nannerra; the mountain Maddoomolla; the rivulet Kalaoya; Dikkallewella; the mountain Yaberra-Kanda; Welparappoowe; and the mountain called Rinooga-Kanda,—was granted to Raja Wanni, by the King Wireparakkan-bahu, on his having presented elephants to the said king.

Bogommowa is sufficient to sow sixty-five

ammonams of paddy. This land is an offer to the temple of Monnassiram.

Dettenna is sufficient to sow seventy-five ammonams of paddy. There are within this district twelve ollegam-lands, one giant's well, one Budhu temple. The limit of this land is a stone pillar, whereon an awoopota (a parasol) is engraven. The lake belonging to this district is five cubits deep; there are likewise two halls built of stones. On the upper end of Timbiri-pokkoona lies the land of Wirepandy-tewerra; the limits of this are the five stone pillars at Ilella-welliwembowa: this land is free from all duties. There is a Budhu temple in this village.

Here follows an account of Magool-Corle.

Monnas Serrama: the field of it is sufficient to sow seventy-five ammonams of paddy; its lake is fifteen cubits deep. There are within this district five giants' wells, five Budhu temples, eighty-one ollegam lands, dams, and dikes. Twenty ammonams of ground hereof is a gift to the five Budhu temples.

Santigammana, belonging to Saika-Raja, King of Pategamay, is sufficient to sow 100 ammonams of paddy. There are in it seventy-two ollegam lands, dams, and magam lands; its lake is eleven cubits deep. There are likewise in it two Budhu temples; and on that part of it which was overflown by the lake are two stone pillars and six giants' wells. This is the king's property.

Soellogalla is sufficient to sow eighty ammonams of paddy; the lake of it is nine cubits deep; there are in it eighteen ollegam lands and dams. Beyond the stone called Diagilmagalla there are fifty-six large lakes and dams; and a part of it beyond the stone called Lahallebee-galla is an offer to the Budhu temple called Soollogolloo-Vihari. There are likewise within this district five ruins of Budhu temples and ten giants' wells.

Rakkoossah-wewa is sufficient to sow 150 ammonams of paddy; the lake of it is twelve cubits deep; there is one sluice, one Budhu temple, one giant's well; and the limit of it is the dam of the lake. On that part of it which is overflown by the lake were seventy-eight magam lands, ollegam lands, and dams.

Elloopitia is sufficient to sow sixty-five ammonams of paddy; the lake of it is six cubits deep. There are in this district one tower called Galpitta-weharra, and one giant's well. On that side of it which is overflown by the lake were eighteen ollegam lands and dams.

Kalala-goruwa is sufficient to sow 150 ammonams of paddy; its lake is ten cubits deep. There are in this district one sluice, two Budhu temples, near the two wanes or water-courses, and two wells; and on that part of it which is overflown by the lake there were thirty-two ollegam lands and six giants' wells.

Maddagam-pola is sufficient to sow thirty ammonams of paddy; its lake is nine cubits deep. There are in this district one sluice, five ollegam lands, one Budhu temple, one banna-mandoo or preaching-hall, and one well, the brim of which is built of brick. On that side of this district which is overflown by the lake there were eighteen ollegam lands and magam lands; and at Kaddoopittia seven towers.

Karroonjan-coollama is sufficient to sow twelve ammonams of paddy; its lake is five cubits deep. There are in this district one ruin of a temple and one giant's well; and on that side of this district which was overflown by the lake were five ollegam lands.

Warrawewa is sufficient to sow six ammonams of paddy; its lake is five cubits deep. There is one hall built upon stone pillars; and on that side of this land which is overflown by the lake were five ollegam lands, and one well hewn out of a stone.

Dewegalla is sufficient to sow twelve ammonams of paddy; its lake is five cubits deep. There are five dams, and one coral rock.

Solagribawa is sufficient to sow 170 ammonams of paddy; its lake is thirteen cubits deep. There are seven stones called Pahankaddagal.

The village beyond the upper end of Mahagribawa is a gift from Magambati-Rajah to the tower called Bayagri; so the same became the property of a Budhu temple.

Wirepokkoona is sufficient to sow twelve ammonams of paddy. There is one bannamandoo, or preaching-hall, constructed upon stone pillars. The lake of this place is five cubits deep: it has one sluice.

Galkaddawalla is sufficient to sow twelve ammonams of paddy; its lake is five cubits deep. There is in this district a stone cave. On that part of it which is overflown there were five lakes, and on the mount lies a Budhu temple.

Tammanapittia has a lake which is five cubits deep; the field belonging to the lake is sufficient to sow seven ammonams of paddy; it also has five ollawewoo lakes, one hall built of stones, and one giant's well.

Palookanda-wawa is sufficient to sow eight

ammonams of paddy; there are five ollawewoo lakes and two ollegam lands.

Motta-pattawa is sufficient to sow fifteen ammonams of paddy; its lake is six cubits deep. It has one Budhu temple, and one gutter at the end of the water-course, and five ollegam lands on that part of it which is overflown.

Molaiwa is sufficient to sow forty-five ammonams of paddy; its lake is six cubits deep. There are five ollegam lands, one tower on the stone upon the mount, and one giant's well.

Kohombagaha-wewa is sufficient to sow twelve ammonams of paddy; the lake of it is seven cubits deep. There are on this district five ollawewoo lakes, one bannamandoo, or preaching-hall, built on stone pillars, and one giant's well.

Diwoolwawa is sufficient to sow twelve ammonams of paddy; its lake is five cubits deep. There are in this district five ollegam lands, and two giants' wells.

Walinpittia is sufficient to sow thirty-eight ammonams of paddy. There are twelve ollegam lands on that part of it which was overflown by the lake, and two stone caves on the mount, one ruin of a Budhu temple, and one giant's well.

Kewoonwewa is sufficient to sow seven ammonams of paddy; its lake is four cubits deep: it has five ollawewoo lakes, one giant's well, one sluice, two gutters, one Budhu temple, and one hall built of stones, seven ollegams and dams, and one ruin of a temple.

Konagribawa is sufficient to sow fifty ammonams of paddy; its lake is six cubits deep, and has one gutter, eight dams and dikes, and seven ollegam lands. On that part which was overflown there was one Budhu temple, and one giant's well.

Ooddagribawa is sufficient to sow 150 ammonams of paddy; its lake is six cubits deep; it has one sluice, one stone gutter, one Budhu temple, one tower, two giants' wells; and on that side which is overflown by the lake's water seven ollegam-lands.

Kandoowilla is sufficient to sow 250 ammonams of paddy; its lake is seven cubits deep. There are in this district six sluices, five ollegam lands, two Budhu temples; and on the mount there is a giant's well. These lands are a gift to the tower Bayagri.

Halmilla-kaddewalla is sufficient to sow fifteen ammonams of paddy; its lake is five cubits deep. There are ruins of a Budhu temple, and one giant's well; and on that part of it which is overflown by the lake's water there were five ollegam lands, and dams.

Konwawa is sufficient to sow twelve ammonams of paddy; it lake is five cubits deep. There is one ruin of a Budhu temple; and on that part of it which is overflown by the lake there were five ollegam lands.

Galwawa is sufficient to sow thirty ammonams of paddy; its lake is eight cubits deep. The fields watered by this lake are sufficient to sow twelve ammonams of paddy.

The lake Mahagala is six cubits deep. The land belonging to this lake is sufficient to sow thirty ammonams of paddy. There is on this land one Budhu temple, and one giant's well; and on that side of this land which is overflown by the lake's water were five ollegam lands.

Poddikkattoo-hawa is sufficient to sow seventy-five ammonams of paddy; it has one sluice, two giants' wells, twelve ollegam lands, and one Budhu temple.

Koobook-haddewallay is sufficient to sow thirty ammonams of paddy; its lake is seven cubits deep. There is one Budhu temple, two giants' wells; and on that side of this land which is overflown by the lake's water were ten ollegam lands.

Patkolla-wawa is sufficient to sow thirty

ammonams of paddy; its lake is six cubits deep. There is one Budhu temple, and two giants' wells; and on that side of this land which is overflown by the lake, were thirteen ollegam lands.

Hoonoogalla-wawa is sufficient to sow seven ammonams of paddy; its lake is seven cubits deep. On that part of this land which was overflown there were seven ollegam lands, one Budhu temple, and one giant's well.

Piddooroo-wella is sufficient to sow thirty ammonams of paddy; its lake is seven cubits deep. On that side of it which is overflown were eighteen ollegam lands and dams, and one giant's well.

Rallapana-wawa is sufficient to sow thirty ammonams of paddy; and on that part of it which is overflown by water were twelve ollegam lands, dams, and dikes, and one giant's well.

Kettapahoowa is sufficient to sow forty ammonams of paddy; its lake is eight cubits deep; and on that part of it which is overflown by water were seven ollegam lands and dams, twelve stone pillars, one Budhu temple, and two giants' wells.

Hytokadda-wellay is sufficient to sow fifty ammonams of paddy; its lake is eight cubits deep; and on that part of it which is overflown were ten ollegam lands, dams, and two wells.

The lands lying between the following limits, namely, the mountain called Ulpottastrigaltemba, Nagalla, Attembooroogalla, Kumbookebba, and Ammonoopotanagaltemba, had been offered to the tower of Runa-magam by the King Tissa; so it is a gift to a Budhu temple.

The lake of Piella is eleven cubits deep: the ground watered by this lake is sufficient to sow thirty ammonams of paddy; the lands overflown by the lake's water were twenty-two ollegam lands and dams, five Budhu temples, two mandoos constructed upon rocks, and six wells called giants' wells.

The lake of Nallagalla is twelve cubits deep; the land watered by the lake is sufficient to sow **150** ammonams of paddy. The lands overflown by the lake's water, ollegam lands and dams, were forty-eight; Budhu temples, twelve; one pillima-house (that is a house in which the image of Budhu was kept); and twelve giants' wells. This land also belongs to the father of Rammarra.

The lake of Pepella-wewa-dippittia is five cubits deep; the land watered by the lake is sufficient to sow forty ammonams of paddy. The lands overflown by the lake's water were eighteen ollegam lands, three ruins of Budhu temples, and three giants' wells. The end of Ooddokaha-wanny-pattoo.

The lake of Maddegalla is eighteen cubits deep, and it has three water-courses. The ground watered by the lake is sufficient to sow seventy ammonams of paddy. Besides which, there are in this pattoo two Budhu temples, twelve giants' wells, two bannamandoos or preaching-halls, five lofts constructed upon marble pillars to lay paddy in, and a maligatenna, a place whereon a palace was formerly built. The lands overflown by the lake's water were, ollegam lands, magam lands, dams, and dikes, seventy-eight in number; eighteen ruins of towers, one tank, and ten pillimas or images of Budhu. The end of Maddegalloo Pattoo.

The lake of Siyambalangommuwa is fifteen cubits deep; it has two water-courses and one channel. The land watered by the lake is sufficient to sow 300 ammonams of paddy. There are in the same district two Budhu temples, two ruins of Budhu temples, two preaching-halls, two houses constructed on stone pillars for Budhu priests, three lofts in which to keep paddy, and three giants' wells. The lands overflown by the lake were fifty-eight; viz. ollegam lands, magam lands, and dams.

The lake of Palookanda is ten cubits deep:

it has one water-course. The land watered by the lake is sufficient to sow 150 ammonams of paddy; and contains one Budhu temple, one house for Budhu priests, one preaching-hall, and one giant's well. The places overflown by the lake's water were forty-one; viz. ollegam lands, magam lands, and dams; besides three caves, one image of Budhu made of earth, and seven ruins of towers.

The lake of Atterregalla is nine cubits deep. The land watered by the lake is sufficient to sow ninety-two ammonams of paddy; and contains one ruin of a tower, one house for Budhu priests, one preaching-hall, two lofts for keeping paddy, eighteen magam and ollegam lands and dams, and one Budhu temple, called Nakollagam-totta.

The lake of Maddinnorruwa is six cubits deep. The land watered by the lake is sufficient to sow fifty ammonams of paddy. There are one temple, one preaching-hall, one house for Budhu priests, one giant's well. The places overflown by the lake were thirteen ollegam lands and dams.

The lake of Kattin-noruwa is seven cubits deep. The ground watered by the lake is sufficient to sow fifty ammonams of paddy. There are one Budhu temple, called Binpokkoona, two ponds, one ola-house at the place called Laggunwala, and two giants' wells. The places overflown by the lake were twelve ollegam villages and dams.

The lake of Migas-wewa, belonging to Tricinhala-tapaswarra, a Cingalese hermit, is ten cubits deep. The land watered by the lake is sufficient to sow 250 ammonams of paddy. It contains two water-courses, two Budhu temples, two houses for Budhu priests, and two wells called giants' wells. The places overflown by the lake were eighteen ollegam lands and dams, and five towers called Gatteweheres.

The lake of Mahakalankoottia. The land watered by this lake is sufficient to sow 250 ammonams of paddy. It contains one tower, one preaching-hall, one house for the Budhu priests, and two wells called giants' wells. The places overflown by the lake were eighteen ollegam lands and dams.

The lake of Eriyawa is six cubits deep. The land watered by this lake is sufficient to sow thirty ammonams of paddy. There are one tower, and one well called giant's well. The places overflown by the lake were ten dams and ollegam lands.

The lake of Kaddingawa is five cubits deep. The ground watered by the lake is sufficient to sow thirty ammonams of paddy. The places overflown by the lake were eighteen ollegam and magam lands, dams, and dikes, one Budhu temple, one tower, two giants' wells. The land between Ihelladryabetnawa and the two stone pillars is an offering to the Budhu temple.

The lake of Likollapitia is six cubits deep. The land watered by this lake is sufficient to sow forty ammonams of paddy. The places overflown by the lake, ollegam lands, magam lands, dams, and dikes, were twelve. Between the two stone pillars standing on the lower side of the land, from the two stone pillars called Shella-gattan, and the stone pillars on which are engraven the letters called Nagarra, there are one Budhu temple, and one giant's well; and the land belonging to the same is an offering to the Budhu temple.

The lake of Attangana is seven cubits deep. The land watered by this lake is sufficient to sow fifty ammonams of paddy. On the other side of this lake there are altogether ollegam lands, magam lands, and dams, twenty-seven. Between the two stone pillars standing at Ihellabetnawa and the pillar standing at Patralabetnawa there are one Budhu temple, two giants' wells, one mandoo-house constructed of stones, one tower, and one dewalaboomia (that is, a place on which a temple has been built). A part of this land, sufficient to sow ten ammonams of paddy, is an offering to the Budhu temple.

The lake of Malpanawa is five cubits deep. The land watered by this lake is sufficient to sow fifty ammonams of paddy. The places overflown by the lake were, altogether, ollegam villages, dams, and dikes, seven. A portion of ground, sufficient to sow five ammonams of paddy, lying between the places called Ihelladryabetnawa and Pahalagalgoddella, is a gift to the Budhu temple; and on the end of the water-course of the lake stands a temple.

The lake of Ooddonawa is seven cubits deep. The ground watered by the lake is sufficient to sow sixty-five ammonams of paddy. Towards the end of the water-course of the lake there are one Budhu temple, one mandoo-house constructed of stones, one tower, and two giants' wells. The places overflown by the lake were twelve ollegam lands. Towards the side of the dam by the lake, there are, between the places called Ihellagallawa-galgodella and Diggalpotta, altogether, ollegam lands, dams, and dikes, 1000; whereof twelve ollegams are an offering to the Budhu temple. The lower end of Kellagammadiyabetnawa, and of the Monnikkoolemadiyabetnawa, lying beyond the marble pillar, forms the limit of Uddoonawa.

The lake of Abokkagamma is three cubits deep. The ground watered by the lake is sufficient to sow nine ammonams of paddy. The place called Ihella-ella is the limit of the same.

The lake Midellagaha-wewa is four cubits deep. The places overflown by the lake were seven: those were ollegam lands and dams. The ground watered by the lake is sufficient to sow twelve ammonams of paddy; besides which there are two giants' wells, eight ponds; towards the end of the watercourse of the lake, one Budhu temple and one tower. The land between Ihelladiyabetnawa, Yodekammalgoddella, God-depatta, and Goddepottahella, is a gift to the Budhu temple.

The lake of Muddattawa is seven cubits deep. The land watered by the lake is sufficient to sow fifteen ammonams of paddy. The lands overflown by the lake lying between Diyahitti-kanda and Pahalla-ella were seven ollegam lands and dams.

The lake of Dehannagamma is four cubits deep. The ground watered by the lake is sufficient to sow thirty ammonams of paddy, besides eighteen ollegam magam lands, dams, and dikes, and one Budhu temple at the end of the water-course of the lake. These lands are lying between Ihellabetnawa and Ikkiry-goddella.

The lake Karriyatty-Kollama is four cubits deep. The ground watered by the lake is sufficient to sow five ammonams of paddy. There are over the lake thirteen ollegam lands, dams, and dikes. The land between Ihellagal-goddella and Pahalagal-goddella was granted to the Prince Mallawa, who had obtained the title Mallawa-Bandara on his presenting the silk cloth called wannigawarrian.

The said Mallawa-bandara, together with another, Hetty-bandara, formerly called Moddattawa-chitty—who, having presented a four-square precious stone, had obtained the title called Muddattawa Hetty-bandara—were granted by the king Bowennaka-bahou the following lands; viz., the land between Pahalla-ella and Diwooroon-galla rock; the land between Diyabetnawa of Kellagamma and the pillar on which is engraven the letters called Nagarra, which is planted in the lake called Hoddeliyawa belonging to Donnoo-kayawa at Pulhiria; and the land between the four-angular pillar which is planted in Diyaba-wooma of Dunnukaiyawa, Gorrookanda at Unnala-diyabetnawa, and Yodekammala. Besides the lands of the said Moddattawa-chitty, the lake belonged to Mallawa prince, which lies beyond the place called Diyahitty-kanda, and is called Mettawalliya; this lake is six cubits deep. The ground watered by this lake is sufficient to sow fifty ammonams of paddy. The places overflown by the lake were eighteen ollegam lands and dams. There is a Budhu temple towards the end of the water-course of the lake, and two giants' wells. The ground, sufficient to sow seven ammonams of paddy, of this district, is a gift to the Budhu temple, which is situated between Ihelladiahittiya-diyabetnawa, and Diyabitty-kanda.

The lake of Unnala is seven cubits deep. The land watered by the lake is sufficient to sow sixty-five ammonams of paddy. The lands overflown by the lake were twenty-eight ollegam lands, magam lands, dams, and dikes. There are, over the lake, one Budhu temple, one tower, one mandoo-house constructed of stones, and two giants' wells. The ground between Ihelladiyabetnawa and the pond at Yodekammalgodda is a gift to the Budhu temple.

The lake of Hallabehena belonged to Mooddiwalanganpadey-tewerreya. The ground watered by this lake is sufficient to sow thirty ammonams of paddy. The lands overflown by the lake were thirteen ollegam lands, dams, and dikes, and one spot of ground on which a temple was constructed. The depth of the water at Ihelladeyabetnawa is five cubits.

The Regulation of the Pooja Days, in honour of the Budhu Guadma.

The public worship of Budhu amongst the Cingalese is fixed upon four days in every month, that is to say, on the days of the four phases of the moon, when they go to the temple, where they offer any thing they like, consisting of flowers, provisions, money, &c., before the image of Budhu, and promise, some persons to keep five, some eight, and some ten commandments, and on that day abstain from their evening meal. The great solemn time of their worship is the day of full moon in the month called Wasak (May), being that on which the Budhu was born and departed this life. The commandments above mentioned, are as follow:—1st, not killing; 2d, not stealing; 3d, avoiding fornication; 4th, not lying; 5th, not drinking of strong liquors; 6th, not eating of any victuals after the sun has passed the meridian; 7th, not looking at dancing, nor listening to singing and beating of drum; 8th, not using of flowers and other sweet-smelling things, also of jewels and other ornaments; 9th, not using of high seats, and other places covered with valuable cloths; and 10th, the non-reception of gold, silver, and money.

PARTICULARS

REFERRING TO

THE FIVE HUNDRED AND FIFTY TALES

FORMING THE CELEBRATED BUDHIST BOOK

TERMED

THE PANSIYAS PANAS JUTAKA;

OR,

INCARNATIONS OF THE BUDHU GUADMA:

WITH

TRANSLATIONS OF SEVERAL OF THE STORIES.

P S.—The entire work, in the original, is in the possession of the Royal Asiatic Society, presented by Sir Alexander Johnston. This valuable book is the more important for the Illustration of the Budhu History or Doctrines, as it appears that complete copies are extremely rare, and not to be met with even in the most celebrated Viharis, although there is not a single Vihari which has not some portions of a work deemed the most distinguished compendium of the Budhist Faith.

The Names of the Jutakas Guadma relating to the Budhu.

Apannaka
Wannupatha
Siriwanija
Chulla-setti
Tandudale
Dewa-darma
Katt-ha-hari
Gamane
Makha-diwa
Sukha-wihara
Lakshana
Nigroda-mraga
Khandina
Watha-mraga
Kharajiya
Tipallatthi-mraga
Maluta
Matakathatta
Ayachithab-hatta
Nalapana
Curungamerga
Cuccura
Bojahjahniya
Ajanie
Nirtheca
Mahilahmucca
Abinba
Nandiwisala
Kanha
Munika
Kulawaka
Nada
Sammodamana
Matsya
Wattaka
Lakuna
Tittira
Baka
Nanda
Cadirangahra
Loseca
Capotha
Weeluca
Macasa

Rohiny
Arahmeduse
Waruny
Weedabbe
Naccattha
Dummeda
Mahasielewa
Chullejaneca
Punnejany
Ele
Pantchayuda
Pantchanascanda
Wanerinda
Tayodarma
Beeriwahda
Sancadammeny
Asahtemanta
Andebuta
Thacca
Durachara
Anebiraty
Mudulaccane
Utchanga
Sahketha
Wisewantha
Cuddawla
Warena
Sielewenagarahja

Satchankira
Ruccadarma
Matcha
Asankiya
Mahasupina
Sillisejahteca
Mekerasseca
Rimesena
Surapana
Calecanny
Attassedwara
Kinpacca
Silewimansa
Mangala
Saramba
Cuheka
Accatatnea
Litta
Mahasara
Wiswasebojena
Lomehansa
Mahasudassena
Thelepattha
Namesiddy
Cutewanija
Parosehassa
Asateruha
Puneparosehassa

Pannica
Weery
Mithewinda
Durwelecanta
Udancheny
Salica
Baheya
Cundecapuwa
Singala
Mithaminthy
Sacuna
Dubbetcha
Thintira
Watteca
Acalerawy
Bandenemocca
Cussenaly
Dummeeda
Nagulisa
Ambeja
Cataheca
Asilaccana
Calanduca
Rilara
Aggidanta
Cosiya
Asampedawna
Pantchegarn

Sanrena
Jatesocha
Chandaba
Swarnehansa
Ranelu
Goda
Ubeyabrarta
Caca
Goda
Singala
Wirochena
Nangunta
Rahda
Pupperattha
Singawla
Eccapattha
Sanjiwa
Rahjowahda
Singawla
Sucara
Urrenga
Ganga
Almechettha
Gunna
Suhennu
Swarnemayoora
Winila
Indeguttha

Santha
Susima
Gitjah
Nacula
Uppesallhecca
Samiddy
Sacunaggy
Areca
Calleana
Daddera
Maccateca
Duthiyamaccateca
Adedupattahna
Calawbemutty
Ninduca
Catchepa
Santhedarma
Duddeda
Assaduisa
Sangawmawechera
Wawlodeca
Girridattha
Anebirathy
Dadiwahanna
Chatumatta
Sinhechamma.
Silawnisansa
Ruhecca
Siricalecanny
Chullepaduma
Manichora
Parwetthupattha
Walahecca
Mitthametha
Rawda
Grahpathy
Sawdusila
Bandenahgawra
Kelisila
Bandecawattha
Wira
Gangawnan
Curungamiga
Asseca
Sunsumawra
Caccara
Candegala
Somedantha
Udellabattha
Barru
Punnenady
Catjepa
Matcheca
Seggu
Cutewanija
Garrehitha

Darmaddoja
Casawa
Chullananda
Putabattha
Catthiyawanna
Cosiya
Gutapawny
Cawmeniya
Palawsa
Duthiyapalawsa
Upahanna
Wennuthuna
Wicannewa
Ahithawboo
Watjaneca
Baca
Sawketha
Eccapawny
Arithamawna
Mahapingala
Sabbedawta
Suneca
Gutthela
Winiwatcha
Moolepariyaya
Nelowahda
Pawdawnjely
Kinsugocawma

Sahli
Capy
Sancappa
Thilamutty
Manicanta
Cudaccutchisindewa
Siewa
Rajedepawna
Gawmenichanda
Mahamandawtoo
Kiritewatcha
Dutha
Padumaw
Madupawny
Chullepatobena
Mahapanawda
Curagga
Wawthasawindewa
Carcatteka
Arawmedusa
Sujawtha
Cawkevoluka
Udepawnedoosa
Weagga
Catchapa
Lola
Dulusirah
Curudarma

Roma
Mahisa
Sathapattra
Cutasawca
Abbeantra
Seyasa
Waddesookera
Siry
Manisukera
Sawloka
Lawbegaroo
Matchadwara
Nawnawchanda
Silewimansa
Baddegatta
Supattha
Cayewitchanda
Jambucawda
Antha
Samuddra
Cawmewilopena
Udumbera
Cumarepattha
Bacca
Chullecawlinga
Maha-aswarohenna
Silewimansa
Sujawtha

Palawsa
Jawesecuna
Jawa
Sayiha
Puchimanda
Cassepamandy
Iksawntiwawda
Lohecumby
Mansa
Sasa
Eccarawja
Daddera
Matherodana
Caneweera
Tittira
Dubba
Cutidusca
Daddeba
Brahmadattha
Chanmachawta
Goda
Caccawroo
Cawca
Annennsochiya
Cawlabahoo
Silewimansa
Ratalatty
Jambuca

Brahatchattha
Pita
Thusa
Baweroo
Wisayha
Wanara
Cunthany
Ambechora
Gajecomba
Kesewa
Ayekoota
Aratcha
Sandibeda
Sujawtha
Donasaka
Uranga
Gata
Karandika
Latookika
Choolladarmapala
Swarnamarga
Sussondiya
Warnaroba
Sielaparicka
Geeree
Abiguntika
Gumbieja
Sawlieja
Tawasara
Mittawinda
Palawsa
Diegakosala
Moowapota
Moosika
Chulladanoerda
Capota
Ahwary
Iwatakata
Dareemooka
Naroo
Awsanka
Migahlopa
Sirikalakanny
Belawla
Darmaddwaja
Caraputta
Nandiyamarga
Soochy
Toondila
Swarnakarkataka
Mahesa
Dajawehata
Puspaganda
Wegawta
Wattaka
Kawkaw.

Kookkoo
Manojà
Sootanoo
Bidja
Dabbapuppa
Dassannaka
Santoobatta
Attisana
Kapy
Bawka-brachma
Gandawra
Mahakapy
Cumbakahra
Dalhadarma
Somadatta
Sooseema
Cotisimbaly
Dodmakary
Jahgara
Cummasapindy
Pahrantapa
Catehany
Attasabda
Soolasah
Soomangala
Gangamala
Chatiya
Indriya

Awditiya
Diepy
Bejanda
Cosanbeja
Mahagirah
Suloosoowa
Hawritta
Rawjowahda
Padamanawaka
Lomakassapa
Sakwah
Haliddy
Samoogga
Pootimansa
Titwattoo
Chatooddwara
Krisna
Chattooposata
Poorna
Sanka
Choollabody
Kanhadipayana
Nigoda
Jackahla
Mahadarmapale
Roockooha
Mattakundaly
Belalakosiya

Chackawahka
Mahamangala
Gatta
Matooposaka
Joonha
Darma
Udayabadda
Pawnieya
Yoodadja
Dassaratta
Sanwara
Suppahra
Chullakoonala
Baddasawla
Samuddawahny
Kahma
Janasantawa
Mahakanha
Mahapadooma
Chittachitta
Amba
Pandana
Jawanahansa
Chullanarada
Doota
Kalingabody
Ackierty
Taekawry
Rooroomarga
Jarabamarga
Sawlekadawra
Chandakinnara
Maha-nekoosa
Uddawla
Bissa
Soorichy
Panehooposata
Mahamayoora
Tatchasookara
Mahawanija
Sawdina
Dassabrachmana
Bickaparampara
Matanga
Sanboota
Seewe
Serymanda
Rohantamarga
Hansa
Sattygumba
Ballatiya
Somanassa
Champaiya
Mahapalobana
Hattypawla
Ayogara

Panchapandita
Kinehanda
Kumba
Jayaddisa
Chatdanta
Sambawa
Mahakapy
Dassarackasa
Pandaranawga
Samboola
Gandatindoo
Tasakoona
Sarabanga
Allaboosah
Sankapahla
Chullasootasoma
Naling
Sonaka
Manicundela
Sankida
Koosa
Sonananda
Chullahansa
Mahahansa
Soodabojana
Koonala
Sootasoma
Moogapacka
Mahajanaka
Sawma
Nemy
Candahala
Mahanaraddakassepa
Booridatta
Wedoora
Ummagga
Wessantara.

EXPLANATION.

No. 1, *Apannaka Jutaka.*—A certain foolish merchant set out on a journey with 500 carts loaded with merchandise, and a proportionate number of attendants. On arriving in the midst of a vast sandy desert which he had to traverse, he was met and accosted by some demons in disguise, who, by their artifices, prevailed upon him to throw away his whole stock of water; in consequence of which imprudent act, both himself and his followers fell into the power of the demons and were devoured by them. A short time afterwards, a wise and experienced merchant travelling the same road, with an equal number of carts and people, was encountered by the same demons; but being aware of their designs, the nature of which his superior sagacity had enabled him to discover, he completely succeeded in frustrating their sanguinary purpose. After which, he took possession of the most valuable articles belonging to the foolish merchant, which he found in the desert, and proceeded with them on his journey.

No. 2, *Wannu patha Jutaka.*—A certain merchant, with a train of 500 carts, and a suitable number of persons in charge of them, was once travelling through a sandy desert of considerable extent, when there happened a deficiency of water, in consequence of which they all suffered great distress, having neither water to drink nor to wash themselves. Upon this the merchant directed them to dig below a tuft of green grass which he had observed, and, on their complying with his instructions, they discovered a plentiful stream of water that afforded an ample supply to all their wants.

No. 3, *Siriwanija Jutaka.*—A certain covetous merchant, who dealt in rings and bracelets made of a sort of glazed earth, in travelling about the country with his merchandise, came to a house where there was, unknown to the inhabitants, a golden plate worth 100,000 pieces of money. The persons to whom the house belonged had originally been possessed of great wealth, but all that remained of the family at this time was a poor old widow woman and her young daughter. The little girl went and offered the plate to the merchant in exchange for a few of the bracelets, but he told her that the plate was not worth a madata, and that he would give nothing for it: so saying, he went away, intending to return afterwards and to get the plate upon his own terms. By the time he was out of sight another merchant, who likewise dealt in the same kind of bracelets, came to the house, and the little girl repeated her former offer; upon which this honest merchant informed her and her mother of its real value, and giving them all the money he had in his possession, amounting to 1000 masuras, he took the plate away with him. When the covetous merchant returned and heard that his fellow-merchant had got possession of the plate, his affliction was so immoderate that it broke his heart, and he died upon the spot.

No. 4, *Chulla-setti Jutaka.*—A certain opulent sita (a man of high rank) seeing a dead rat lying in the street, said aloud, "That any man who should take up that rat and expose it for sale would become a sita like himself." A poor man who happened to hear this took up the rat, and with the money he obtained from the sale of it, laid the foundation of a fortune, which he afterwards realised, of 100,000 pieces of gold. After having acquired this sum he married the daughter, and succeeded to the dignity of the same sita.

No. 5, *Tandudale Jutaka.*—A certain foolish officer, whose duty it was to fix a value upon every thing, was tempted by a bribe to value the city of Baranais, and all that it contained, at a single measure of rice, in consequence of which he was discarded from his situation with disgrace, and in his room a wise minister was appointed, whose valuations were always fair and equitable.

No. 6, *Dewa-darma Jutaka.* — In this jutaka, Bodi Sat is stated to have delivered his two brothers from the clutches of a rakshasa, by solving, to the satisfaction of the latter, a question proposed by him relative to the nature of genuine piety.

No. 7, *Katt-ha-hari Jutaka.*—A certain king had a son by a woman whose employment consisted in cutting fire-wood, but this son he refused to acknowledge; whereupon the mother, coming into the king's presence, threw the child up into the air, saying, "If thou art not the king's son mayest thou fall down and perish." Instead, however, of falling down, the child remained buoyant in the air with his legs crossed under him, immediately above the city, and began to preach to the people below; the king was then satisfied, and no longer hesitated to own his son.

No. 8, *Gamane Jutaka.*—In this jutaka is related the manner in which a young prince, by taking Bodi Sat's advice, obtained the succession to a kingdom even during the life-time of his elder brothers.

No. 9, *Makha-diwa Jutaka.**—In this jutaka is related the story of a certain king who, on observing a gray hair in his head, renounced the world and became a priest, notwithstanding that he had still 84,000 years to live.

No. 10, *Sukka-Vihara Jutaka.*—In this jutaka is related the story of a certain king who, becoming weary of the cares of sovereignty, abdicated his throne, and retired to a solitary cell, where he passed his days in the exercise of religious duties, and his nights in undisturbed sleep.

No. 11, *Lakshana Jutaka.*—In this jutaka is related the destruction of 500 deer who wilfully

* In the Mahawanse, vol. I. p. 14, is the recital of the circumstance here alluded to relating to King Makka-dewa.

neglected to follow their father's advice, and the preservation of an equal number who did in obedience to his instructions.

No. 12, *Nigroda-mraga Jutaka.*—In this jutaka is related a noble instance of generosity on the part of a golden deer, the prince of a herd, in offering up his own life to save that of a female deer, big with young, who was upon the point of being killed for the king's table.

No. 13, *Khandina Jutaka.*—A stag, struck with admiration at the beauty of a hind, followed her blindly wherever she went, and was in consequence shot through with an arrow by a huntsman laying in wait for him. Bodi Sat, who was then a tree, observing the fate of the stag, took this occasion to inveigh against the mischiefs of sensuality, and made the whole forest resound with his remonstrances.

No. 14, *Watha-mraga Jutaka.*—In this jutaka is related the story of a stag who was attracted to the court of the king's palace, and caught by the lure of a small quantity of honey mixed with grass. The king, on observing this circumstance, immediately exclaimed against the evil consequences of a too free indulgence of the sensual appetites.

No. 15, *Kharajiya Jutaka.*—In this jutaka is related the untimely death of a stag who disobeyed the injunction of his father-in-law.

No. 16, *Tipallatthi-mraga Jutaka.*—In this jutaka is related the story of a stag who, by following the advice of his father-in-law, fortunately escaped from the snare laid for him by a huntsman.

No. 17, *Maluta Jutaka.*—In this jutaka is related the story of a lion and tiger, of whom the one maintained that the cold was greatest from the new to the full moon; and the other, that it was greatest from the full to the new moon. Whilst they were engaged in this altercation, Bodi Sat came up to them and settled the dispute, by pronouncing that the cold proceeded from wind; with which impartial decision both sides were pleased.

No. 18, *Matakathatta Jutaka.*—In this jutaka is related the story of a goat who, though surrounded by a hundred persons assembled for the purpose of shielding it from danger, was killed by the splinter of a rock broken off by lightning. This punishment the goat was doomed to suffer for having committed murder in a former state of existence, and therefore all the precautions taken for preserving its life were in vain. Upon this occasion Bodi Sat, then a tree-god, addressed himself to those who had witnessed the untimely fate of the goat, cautioning them against the heinous sin of murder, and representing to them the punishment by which it will infallibly be followed.

No. 19, *Ayachithab-hatta Jutaka.*—In this jutaka is related the story of a certain person who put to death a number of animals in order to make a sacrifice of their bones to a dewatawa, or deity, whom he wished by that means to propitiate. Bodi Sat, the Warksha Dewatawa, or tree-god, to whom this sacrifice was made, expressed his abhorrence of this cruel practice, and directed, in the presence of numerous persons collected together upon this occasion, that so barbarous a custom should be wholly discontinued for the future.

No. 20, *Nalapana Jutaka.*—In this jutaka is related an ingenious contrivance of Bodi Sat, then a monkey, by means of which himself, and his 80,000 companies of the same race, procured water to quench their thirst from a tank wherein a rakshasa or demon resided. This they effected by drinking the water through reeds previously made completely hollow by their breath. In memory of the event, the reeds surrounding this tank grew without joints during the period of one entire calpa.

No. 21, *Nandiwisala Jutaka.*—In this jutaka is related the story of a man who laid a wager of a thousand pieces of money, that his ox would of himself draw a hundred loaded carts. On the appointed day the carts were all ranged in a line one behind another, and the ox was harnessed to the foremost cart. The master, however, having spoken harshly to the ox, the latter would not stir a step, in consequence of which the master lost his wager. Not discouraged at his ill success, he laid another wager, of double the sum, that his ox would draw a hundred carts loaded with gravel and sand, and this he won by speaking kindly to the animal; for he had discovered the cause of his former failure, and took care to avoid committing the same error a second time.

No. 22, *Kanha Jutaka.*—In this jutaka is

related the story of an ox who, being rewarded by a merchant with a thousand massas for dragging five hundred carts out of a slough, carried that sum, which the merchant, at his request, had tied about his neck, and presented it to the old woman to whom he belonged, and by whom he had been fed and reared up.

No. 23, *Munika Jutaka.*—In this jutaka is related the story of two oxen, the younger of whom longed for some food which he saw carrying to a hog, and which was intended to fatten up the latter for an entertainment shortly to be given upon the marriage of their master's daughter. The elder ox cured his brother of this longing by representing to him the peril to which the hog was exposed from eating the rich food placed before him, and the safety which they enjoyed from feeding on nothing but plain grass.

No. 24, *Kulawaka Jutaka.*—In this jutaka is related an instance of great humanity on the part of the god Sakkraia, who, in endeavouring to make his escape from the Assuras, after an engagement with them in which he had been defeated, struck so much terror into the Garudas (through whose country his route lay) by the rattling of his chariot, as to cause some of them to precipitate themselves headlong into the sea. On observing their distress, he resolved to return and give himself up to the Assuras, upon the principle that it was not consistent with a merciful disposition to endanger the lives of the Garudas merely for the purpose of securing his own safety. The effect of this measure was, however, more fortunate than could have been expected, for the Assuras, seeing the chariot, thought the Sakkraias of all the other worlds were about to fall upon them, and, under this impression, retreated as fast as possible to their own regions.

No. 25, *Nada Jutaka.*—In this jutaka is related the story of the royal henza (swan), the king of the birds, who assembled all his subjects in an extensive plain, in order that his daughter might choose a husband from amongst them. She singled out the peacock, who, vain at the preference, immediately began to dance, and, spreading out his tail, displayed to the company those parts which ought never to be exposed to view; at which indecency his majesty was so much shocked that he instantly broke off the match.

No. 26, *Sammodamana Jutaka.*—In this jutaka is related the story of a snipe who extricated himself and his companions from the net in which they had been caught, by suggesting that each bird should apply his head to one of the meshes of the net, and that they should all lift it up at once, fly with it to a neighbouring bush, leave it there, and make their escape from under it. Some time afterwards, observing that many of his companions were quarrelling amongst themselves, and knowing that where discord prevails nothing will prosper, he withdrew himself from them, and, accompanied by those who were attached to him, went to another place. Ere long, the snipes whom he had quitted were caught again, but not being able to agree amongst one another as to the method of lifting up the net, they fell into the hands of the fowler, and perished.

No. 27, *Matsya Jutaka.*—In this jutaka is related the story of a fish who, whilst pursuing a female, was caught in a net, and dragged to the shore, where, regardless of pain and death, he did nothing but bewail his misfortune in being separated from his dear mistress. Bodi Sat, who was then purohita to the king, happened at this time to be walking by, and hearing the lamentations of the fish, whose language he understood,—“ If,” said he to himself, “ this poor fish should die in his present condition, he will assuredly be born again in hell; a fate which a compassionate being like myself ought to try to avert, if possible.” Going up, therefore, to the fisherman, he begged to have the fish, and after getting it, he put it with his own hands into the sea; thereby delivering it, at one and the same time, from two imminent dangers, that of death, and that of a renewed existence in a state of misery.

No. 28, *Wattaka Jutaka.*— In this jutaka is related the story of an unfledged snipe, who, one day, during the absence of his parents in quest of food, was hemmed in on every side by a fire which some persons had kindled, and which, like the all-consuming fire at the end of the calpa, threatened to destroy every thing that opposed its progress. In this desperate predicament, without wings to fly away, or feet strong enough to convey him out of the reach of the spreading flame, the defenceless bird had no resource left excepting that of an appeal to the Budhu. Such, however, was the sincerity with which this appeal was made, that, as the course of a mighty conflagration is suddenly arrested on its arrival at the borders of the wide-extended ocean, so the flames were not suffered to approach within a considerable distance of the spot where he was lying; and, in memory of the event, during the space of one entire calpa from that period, no impression could be made by fire on the area which had been thus miraculously rescued from its destructive effects.

No. 29, *Lakuna Jutaka.*—In this jutaka is related the destruction of certain birds, who, after having been warned by their king that the trees in which they had placed their nests would shortly take fire by the friction of the dry branches, foolishly neglected to adopt his advice, that they should remove to some other place previously to that disaster. In the same jutaka is recorded the preservation of certain other birds, who prudently attended to the recommendation of their king, and, by removing in time, were fortunate enough to escape the impending danger.

No. 30, *Tittira Jutaka.*—In this jutaka is related the story of an elephant, a monkey, and a partridge, who were all living amicably together near to a nuga-tree, when one day it occurred to them that, notwithstanding the friendly disposition which they bore to each other, there would be a greater degree of regularity in their society if they could ascertain which of them was the elder. The elephant set up his claim by stating, that when he was quite young there was room enough for the tree between his fore and hind legs; the monkey declared, that he had eaten some of the buds of the tree when it was scarcely raised above the ground; but the partridge obtained from both parties a ready acknowledgement of his superior pretensions to seniority and reverence, by telling them that the tree was produced from a seed which he had swallowed, and which he afterwards voided in the very spot where it then grew.

No. 31, *Baka Jutaka.**—An artful cormorant, addressing himself to some fish who were living in a very shallow tank, offered his services to convey them to another, in which, he assured them, there was abundance of water. The simple fish, seduced by this tempting offer, permitted the cormorant to take them out in succession; but, instead of conveying them to the promised tank, he had no sooner got them out

* This is also related in Pilpay's Collection of Oriental Tales.

of sight of their companions, than he fell to and devoured them. One day he happened to address himself to a crab, who resided in the same tank, and who readily accepted the offer, but proposed, as the most convenient mode of transporting him, that he should cling about the cormorant's neck. The cormorant consenting to this arrangement, they proceeded on their journey. After having gone some distance, the crab, looking round and discovering no appearance of a tank, suspected the intention of the cormorant, and, seizing him fast by the neck, threatened him with instant death unless he went back immediately to the tank they had quitted. The cormorant, not daring to refuse, returned accordingly with the crab, who, just as he was entering into the water, with his piercing claws nipped off the cormorant's neck, in the same manner as the stem of a lotus is cut in two by a pair of sharp scissors. Bodi Sat, then a tree-god, observing what had passed, proclaimed aloud the mischiefs of deceit, and the just punishment by which, in this case, it was followed.

Six Explanations of the foregoing Jutakas.

No. 1.—This story was related by Budhu for the purpose of reclaiming 500 of his disciples, who had quitted him, and placed themselves under the guidance of the anti-Budhist Dewadah, who, he tells them, was, in a former state of existence, the foolish merchant herein spoken of, and in whose service they were then unfortunately placed, whilst he himself was the wise merchant, and his present followers were at that time the servants employed in conducting the carts through the desert.

No. 2.—This story was related by Budhu for the purpose of encouraging certain priests to persevere in the ordinances of his religion, by shewing them the benefit they had derived in a former state of existence from acting in conformity to his directions.

No. 3.—In this story Budhu communicates to his priests the circumstances which gave rise to the enmity of Dewadah, who, in a former state of existence, was the covetous merchant therein alluded to.

No. 4.—A certain person having derived much benefit from following some advice given to him by Budhu, the priests were one day discoursing on the subject in the hall of the temple, when Budhu entered, and learning the nature of the conversation in which they had been engaged previously to his arrival, related this story, in order to shew that the occasion of which they had been speaking was not the only one upon which he had been serviceable to the person alluded to, but that he had likewise essentially befriended him in a former state of existence.

No. 5.—One day there was a great uproar in the eating-room of the temple. Budhu having sent to inquire the reason of it, the priest came and informed him that Dabba Mulla, whose office it was to distribute to each person his portion of rice, had managed the business so ill as to give great dissatisfaction; and that this was the cause of the disturbance. Budhu having ordered Dabba Mulla to be brought before him, dismissed him from his employment, relating, at at the same time, a similar disgrace which had befallen him, in consequence of his stupidity, in a former state of existence.

No. 13.—This story was communicated by Budhu on account of a priest who, captivated by the charms of a handsome woman he had accidentally seen, began to neglect his religious duties. Budhu cured him of his attachment by relating the disaster which had befallen him in a former state of existence from giving way to a similar passion.

Portions of the Pansya Pana Jutakas, not given in the List of Titles.

No. 1.—The introduction to this story resembles that which precedes the Wittakka Jutaka.

During the reign of Brachma-datta, king of Baranais, Budhu was an opulent sita, or banker, and resided in that city. When his son was of a proper age to go to school, he sent him thither, accompanied by the son of a female slave, who lived in the house. This lad, whose name was Kataha, and who had been born on the same day with his young master, being possessed of a good understanding, soon attained a considerable proficiency in various branches of learning, insomuch that, on his return from school, the sita appointed him to the superintendence of his household. Whilst engaged in exercising the duties of that office, the following reflections one day presented themselves to his mind:—"The situation to which I have been appointed," said he to himself, "is very precarious; if I commit any fault whatsoever, I may be dismissed, and reduced to great distress; I must therefore endeavour to hit upon some expedient by means of which the impending evil may be averted. The sita, my master, has a friend also a sita, who resides at some distance in the country, I will go to his house, and, telling him that I am the son of his friend, will solicit the hand of his daughter."

In pursuance of this project he forged a letter as from the sita his master, which ran as follows:—

"I have sent my son to you: as our families are of equal rank, you will not be surprised at my proposing an alliance between him and your daughter, with whom I shall, of course, expect that you will give a handsome dowry. Being very much occupied with important affairs, it has been out of my power to attend on you at this juncture, but I will soon follow."

Having written this letter, he packed up some perfumes and fine clothes to take with him, after which he mounted one of the sita's best horses, and proceeded on his journey. On arriving at the place of his destination, he went, without delay, to the house of his master's friend, whom he saluted with great respect. The old sita asked him from whence he came, whose son he was, and what was the object of his journey. To these questions he replied, that he was the son of the Baranais sita, whom he named, and that the purpose of his coming would be best explained in the letter which he had brought, and which he then delivered. The country sita having read the letter, immediately gave his daughter in marriage to Kataha, and with her a considerable portion.

On the day of the nuptials, the newly-married lady displayed to the view of her husband the viands, perfumes, and clothes, which had been sent to her upon the occasion. The moment Kataha saw them, " Is it possible," exclaimed he, " that any human being can eat such food as this? or make use of such perfumes as these? and who can wear clothes of this description? Such good-for-nothing presents bespeak the mean condition of the uncouth rustics who inhabit this remote village."

Whilst Kataha was thus giving vent to his peevish disposition, the Baranais sita was using his endeavours to discover the place to which his slave had absconded; and having at length ascertained that he had gone to the house of his country friend, determined to proceed thither immediately in quest of him. Kataha, as soon as he heard of his master's approach, communicated the intelligence to his father-in-law, recommending, at the same time, that every thing should be prepared for his father's reception and entertainment, and signifying his intention to go and meet his pretended parent. Accordingly, on being informed that the Baranais sita had arrived within a day's journey, he went out to meet him. On coming into the sita's presence, he saluted him very respectfully, and laid before him the gifts brought for that purpose, earnestly entreating at the same time that the sita would not ruin his good fortune. The sita, pleased with these tokens of his humility, promised not to betray him, and proceeded to the house of the country sita, who gave him a most cordial reception. A few days afterwards he sent for the newly-married lady, and desired her to comb his hair. Whilst she was employed in this office, he inquired how her husband behaved to her. To this question she replied, that she had nothing to complain of, except that whenever she performed any service for him, he invariably found fault with her, and abused her. On hearing this, the sita taught her a charm, which he assured her would effectually bind up her husband's mouth upon such occasions. And soon afterwards, taking leave of his country friend, he returned to Baranais.

It was not long before an opportunity occurred of trying the efficacy of the charm, for the Baranais sita's back was scarcely turned, when Kataha began to give himself still more airs than formerly, and one day, when his wife presented him with a plate of rice, he took that occasion to find fault with her and abuse her; upon which, advancing towards him, she, in a firm tone, repeated the magical words which had been taught her, and which were as follows:

Bahumpujo Wikatt'heya Angyang Jana Padang gato Anwaganatwa nadusiya bhunga Bhogi Katahaka.

This sentence being in Pali, the meaning of it was entirely unknown to Kataha's wife, but he himself understood it perfectly well, and from that period was very careful to avoid giving her any offence. The following is the interpretation of the miraculous sentence which produced this happy effect:

"Thou who art come hither from another country, hast thou forgotten thy mean condition? The sita has gone away for this time, but if he return he will cause thee to be severely punished, and take thee away with him, and so he hath desired me to tell thee."

Budhu was the sita of Baranais, and the priest Pintu, on whose account this jutaka was related, was then the slave Kataha.

No. 2.—During the period of Budhu's residence at Jeta Wana Arama, the priests assembled in the temple were one day speaking of another priest called Kaludayi, who, when any person came to request that he would preach upon some joyful occasion, never failed to deliver a discourse suited to a melancholy subject, and *vice versâ*. Budhu having entered and learnt the purport of their conversation, related to them some incidents that had occurred to the same priest in a former state of existence, from which it appeared that he was just as great a blockhead then as now. Budhu lived at that time in the city of Baranais, and was master of a school, the terms of which were, that the sons of wealthy persons should pay 1000 massas, and present the master with two pieces of cloth, as the price of their education, and that the sons of indigent persons should receive instruction, on the condition of their performing menial services for their tutor.

Kaludayi was one of the latter description of scholars. After a day spent in performing various services about his master's person, it occurred to the latter, that so long as his follower should be employed in servile occupations he would always remain an illiterate being. The benevolent tutor determined therefore to adopt a plan which he conceived might tend to Kaludayi's improvement. This plan was, to make Kaludayi, on his return from cutting fire-wood, relate what he had seen during his absence from home, and illustrate it by some apt comparison. The first day after this expedient had been resolved upon, Kaludayi being questioned as to what he had seen whilst abroad, replied, that he had seen a serpent, and that it was like the pole of a plough: as there was actually some resemblance between the two objects compared, the master conceived some hopes of his pupil. Being questioned again on the following day, he replied, that he had seen an elephant, and that it was like the pole of a plough. This comparison was likewise thought by the master to denote some symptoms of an intelligent mind, as it could not be denied that there was a resemblance between the pole of a plough and the trunk of an elephant. A similar question being put to him on the third day, he replied, that he had seen a sugar-cane, and that it was like the pole of a plough. Neither was the master dissatisfied with this answer, as, in some respects, the pole of a plough and a sugar-cane were not unlike. On the fourth day, being on his way to the forest, he passed by an alms-house and partook of some rice and milk which had been prepared for the poor. On his return home he mentioned the circumstance to his master, who made the usual inquiry. To this Kaludayi replied, that the rice he had eaten resembled the pole of a plough. Hereupon the master said to himself, that though there was certainly some resemblance between the objects seen by Kaludayi on the preceding days and the instrument to which he compared them, yet it is impossible to trace the smallest similitude between a dish of rice and the pole of a plough: to attempt the instruction of such a blockhead, will, therefore, be a fruitless task, and I must even let him continue in his present menial capacity, for which alone he seems qualified.

No. 3.—Once when there were no Budhus, neither his priests nor religion in the world, there was a king called Dahamsonda, in a kingdom of Jambu-dwipa, who, having a strange desire to be acquainted with Bana (what the Budhu had preached), sent for the ministers and the nobles of his court, and inquired of them whether they were acquainted with Bana, or knew any person who was acquainted with it, or in what part of the world they thought any of them could be found. They all answered with one voice, that they never heard any such thing, nor was it ever mentioned to them by their ancestors of any such thing ever having been in the world; but advised the king to send throughout the kingdom a tom-tòm beater to proclaim his desire, with an offer of a reward to any person who should gratify it. The king thereupon ordered one of his courtiers to put 1000 pieces of gold in a purse and place it upon an elephant, and then to cause the desire of the king to be proclaimed throughout the markets, towns, and all the public places, and that if he found any person who was acquainted with Bana, to make him a present of the purse, and to bring him to the king, after having him placed upon the elephant. But the courtier returned after having made fruitless inquiries through every part of the kingdom. The king's desire to become acquainted with Bana daily increased to such a height, that it made him resolve in his mind to travel in foreign countries till he met with a person; and accordingly the king took his leave from the court, and, after having passed over his dominions, entered into a wilderness. The god Sakkraia having seen this through his divine power, appeared before the king in the form of a monstrous devil, and asked him who he was, and where he was going to. The king acquainted him both with his name and the cause of his travel. The pretended devil then asked the king what he would give him if he should acquaint him with Bana. The king replied, that if he was in his palace he could give him any wealth which was in the world at present; but being in the wilderness, he had nothing to give him but his own flesh. "Well," said the devil, "I will be satisfied with it." And the king readily consented to it, in hope of learning Bana. The devil then said to the king, "Well, then, ascend that black rock (pointing out one which was in the front), and jump from it into my mouth, which I shall keep open, and as soon as you have left the rock and jumped, I will begin to acquaint you with Bana, which you may learn before you shall reach my mouth." The king readily agreed to it, and jumped from the summit of the rock; but before he reached the ground, the devil, changing to his natural shape of god, took up the king into his arms and carried him alive to the heaven. Afterwards, having taught him Bana, he replaced him on the throne of his native country.

The king in after-time became Budhu, and the god Sakkraia became Anurahde, one of his priests.

4.—A wicked man travelling through a wilderness met with a parrot, and the parrot addressed the man thus: "Friend, why do you go in this road; are you not aware that there is a tiger near the road in which you proceed, which feeds upon human flesh?" The man, without listening to what the parrot said, continued on his journey. The parrot thereupon called out to him again, and said,—"My good friend, if you are resolved to go through this road, take my last advice, and tell the tiger when he comes to attack you, that you are coming from his friend the parrot." The man thinking that the parrot was joking him, turned back with anger and killed it, and pursued the same road; but he did not go far before he was met by the tiger, with its mouth open, and running towards him apparently to devour him; but the man, who was terrified at the sight of the tiger, recollecting what the parrot had told him, spoke out thus: "O, tiger! do not kill the person that comes from the parrot your friend." The tiger stopped at once at the mention of the name of his friend, and asked him where and in what part of the wilderness his friend was, and upon what tree;" and by the answers given by the man, the tiger, convinced in his own mind that the man really came from his friend, introduced him to his father, who was an old and blind tiger, in order that he might be treated kindly; and while the man was conversing with the father, the son went in search of food to entertain him, and, on his return with provision, his father mentioned to him that he had reasons to suspect, in the conversation with the man, that he had killed the parrot his friend. The son immediately went to the place where his friend was, to ascertain the truth, after having given secret instructions to his father to take care that the man did not run away. The man, in the mean time, apprehending that they suspected him of having killed the parrot, tried every means to fly away from the place before the return of the young tiger; and finding at last that it was impossible for him to do so while the old tiger was there, he took up a large stone and threw it upon the head of the old tiger, which instantly killed him on the spot, and then took that opportunity to make his escape. The young tiger, that had gone to see the parrot, finding that it was killed, returned in rage to destroy the criminal; but finding that his father was also killed and the man gone, his rage increased, and he pursued him with full speed. The man, in the mean time, not doubting that the tiger, when he saw his father was killed, would pursue and overtake him, armed himself with a club, and lay concealed near the road to destroy the young tiger likewise; but no sooner did he see the tiger's fierce countenance, than he was so much terrified that it made him drop his club; and as he had neither the courage to defend himself, nor the power to run away, he prostrated himself before the tiger, and begged of him his life. The tiger answered, "Thou treacherous wretch, thou hast killed my friend and my father, without considering the good they have done to thee, and was concealed here with an intention to kill me likewise; yet I shall grant thee thy life: begone directly out of this wilderness, and never think of returning again;" and left him.

5.—In former days, a hare, a monkey, a coot, and a fox, became hermits, and lived in a wilderness together, after having sworn not to kill any living thing. The god Sakkraia having seen this through his divine power, thought to try their faith, and accordingly took upon him the form of a brahmin, and appearing before the monkey begged of him alms, who immediately brought to him a bunch of mangos, and presented it to him. The pretended brahmin, having left the monkey, went to the coot and made the same request, who presented him a row of fish which he had just found on the bank of a river, evidently forgotten by a fisherman. The brahmin then went to the fox, who immediately went in search of food, and soon returned with a pot of milk and a dried liguan, which he had found in a plain, where, apparently, they had been left by a herdsman. The brahmin at last went to the hare and begged alms of him: the hare said, "Friend, I eat nothing but grass, which I think is of no use to you." Then the pretended brahmin replied, "Why, friend, if you are a true hermit, you can give me your own flesh in hope of future happiness." The hare directly consented to it, and said to the supposed brahmin, "I have granted your request, and you may do whatever you please with me." The brahmin then replied, "Since you are willing to grant my request, I will kindle a fire at the foot of that rock, from which you may jump into the fire, which will save me the trouble of killing you and dressing your flesh." The hare readily agreed to it, and jumped from the top of the rock into the fire which the supposed brahmin had kindled; but before he reached the fire, it was extinguished; and the brahmin appearing in his natural shape of the god Sakkraia, took the hare in his arms and immediately drew its figure in the moon, in order that every living thing of every part of the world might see it.

No. 6.—A brahmin had a field, and was in the habit of visiting it daily. In these visits he never failed to take into his hands, as soon as he got there, a crab of golden colour, which was in a tank within the limits of the field, and to leave it again in it after his walk in the field, and before he quitted it. A crow from a neighbouring tree observing the friendship between the brahmin and the crab, envied it, and went to a snake which was residing in a hole at the foot of the tree, and addressed himself to the snake thus: "Friend, my wife, who is about to lay her eggs, has a strong longing for the eyes of the brahmin who visits this field every day, to eat them up, after pulling them out; and if she fails in this she will undoubtedly perish,—if you will assist her in attaining this, she will not fail to reward you with her eggs. You are only to lie concealed to-morrow morning early, in one of the roads in the field in which the brahmin passes, and sting him as soon as he reaches you, and leave the rest to me." This the snake agreed to do, and concealed himself according to his promise. The brahmin, who knew nothing about this conspiracy, came in the morning into the field, and after having taken his friend the crab from the tank into his hands, continued his walk in the field as customary. The snake, which was anxious to comply with his promise with the crow, stung him as soon as he came near; when the brahmin fell senseless to the ground. The crow, who had been impatiently watching for the opportunity, came flying immediately, and perched upon the body, to satiate the desire of eating up the eyes. The crab, which was in the hands of the motionless brahmin, perceiving their combination, laid hold with one of its tongs by the neck of the snake, and with the other by the neck of the crow, and threatened to kill them if they did not take off the poison and cure his friend. The snake, being very much terrified at the treatment of the crab, begged him to allow its mouth to be applied unto the wound; which being granted, it soon extracted the whole poison from the body of the brahmin, who, by the relief he had received, got up immediately, as if nothing had happened to him. The crab, which was still holding the necks of the two, said that it would be improper to suffer two such wicked creatures to live any longer; so he pressed the necks of them both with his two tongs and killed them instantly.

The brahmin was afterwards born Budhu, the crab was born one of his priests, the snake Wasewarty,* and the crow Dewa-dattaya, his enemies.

* This character appears throughout the jutakas, as in the whole history of Budhism, as the rebel Assura, whose hostile appearance at the birth of Guadma is constantly adverted to. See Mahawanse, p. 161. And for references to his unceasing hostility, vide "Asiatic Researches," vol. vi. p. 207; also many parts in the "Doctrines of Budhism."

The manner of making a Samenera or Ganoonnancy.

A person who wishes to be made a ganoonnancy, or a priest, is, in the first place, to obtain leave from his parents for that purpose, and then to go to a teroonancy or high-priest, and say to him "Bura (Lord), I beg you will make me a samenera or ganoonnancy, and give me a habit of a priest." And after his having repeated this three different times before the priest, the priest will teach him the ten principal commandments of Budhu, which he who is going to be made a priest is to repeat after him; viz.: Not to kill any living thing; not to steal; not to have any carnal pleasures; not to lie; not to drink any spirits or strong drink; not to eat after the appointed time, which is before the sun has reached the meridian; not to see or hear any pleasures, as dancing, singing, and music, &c.; not to wear any flowers, nor to anoint his body with any thing that will give any good smell; not to sit upon a seat which is higher than a cubit, or covered with any valuable cloths; and not to receive nor to touch any gold, silver, or money: and then he will receive the habit of a priest, from which time he is to obey and observe the ten commandments, and likewise learn the religious books.

How to become a Teroonancy or High-priest.

A ganoonnancy, after having learned by heart the following books, viz. Pilikulbawanawa, Satara-sanwara-sileya, Satara-kamata-han, Dina-chariawa, Herana-sika, Sekiyawa, Dampiyawa, and Piruwana-satarabanawara, is to go to Candy, and there he is to be examined by the first and second chief-priests, and a great number of other learned priests, who will assemble at the large hall of the priests for that purpose; and after having examined him, by putting many questions, they inform the king of the same; after which the first and second chief-priests, and a number of other high-priests (this number cannot be less than twenty), will assemble again, and there, after having some holy words pronounced (which is a kind of blessing) by two of the priests, confer upon him the title of teroonancy, and appoint him a high-priest. This appointment takes place either with great pomp, or without it, as the opportunity affords; and from which time he, the priest, is to obey and observe

8,820,000,000,000,000,000,005,000,036 (eight thousand eight hundred and twenty quadrillions, five millions, and thirty-six) commandments. A samenera or ganoonnancy who is younger than twenty years cannot be appointed a teroonancy or high-priest.

Livelihood of the high and subordinate Priests called Teroonancys and Samenera Oenancys.

The religious people used to build houses and place the high-priests therein, from the full-moon day of the month of July until the full-moon day of the month of October, and, during the space of that time, provide them victuals, and furnish them with all necessaries, such as bedsteads, spreading cloths, pillows, lamps, spitting-pots, cups, pots, &c. &c. After the expiration of these three months, they offer three yellow gowns, or attepirikere, according to the ability of the people. An attepirikere consists of three yellow gowns, one piece of cloth to sift water, one piece of cloth called pattia, one needle, one razor, and one pattra, used by the priests for eating the victuals in; and some people make an offering called kattinay, which consists of one yellow gown, one garden, one paddy field, one slave, cattle, one house, one bed, addices, axes, chopping knives, mammotties, chisels, saws, &c., to the value of more than three or four hundred rix-dollars. As the subordinate priests, called Samenera Oenancys, live with the high-priests, they support themselves by what the high-priests receive, and in the other months they are supported by the produce of the lands belonging to temples. The priests who have no such temples or lands, support themselves by begging alms, which, however, they do not ask for as the beggars, but they are only to wait in front of the house, and should any thing be offered, they ought to receive it, and if not, they go away, after having waited for a short while.

When slaves are offered, the priests emancipate them, or appoint them as priests.

List of different Siwoores or Priests' Garments.

Five cubits of cloth for the under garment.

Seven cubits of cloth for another siwoore, worn above ditto.

Six cubits of cloth, of one span broad, for a band.

Twenty-four cubits of cloth, of five spans broad, for the maha-siwoore.

Four cubits of cloth, of one cubit broad, for a band.

Twenty - four cubits of cloth for another maha-siwoore.

Sixty cubits of cloth will be sufficient for making the garments of the whole of the said siwoores.

One yard of cloth for a fan, which is made of the following kinds of cloth, viz. embroidered cloth, satin, velvet, or superfine scarlet cloth.

Query—is it lawful for the Budhist Priests to be sworn to their testimony?

Although I knew that religion does enjoin no oath to be exacted of priests, yet for a better understanding of it, I referred myself to various books, which prevented my sending an earlier reply. I could find no passage of a priest having been compelled to take an oath, or of having himself done it, as priests are forbidden to lie; so that a virtuous priest would never lie, but only those of degenerate principles; which morality and immorality in priests may be discovered by those who are well versed in the religion; but if the priest offending in the like manner be an artful one, and his immoralities are such as not to be easily discovered, on account of his cunningness, the sincere professor of the religion may punish the priest so lying, according as religion enjoins, by disclosing his purity or impurity. Endeavouring by all means to come at the truth, it is expedient to proceed in the investigation.

The following books, namely, Sāmantapawsadicawa, Adicaranawinishayacanda, Sarartadiepania, Wimatiwindania, and in the judgments of the books Winayalancaraya and Winayasangrahaya, contain as follows on this subject:—

The Budhu priests are always bound to speak the truth, which is one of the ten commandments of Budhu; as they ought to keep the ten commandments. It does not appear, in any of the books of the Budhu law, that priests should take their oaths to speak the truth; in case of any doubt of their statements, they should say what they have stated is true, for avoiding such doubts.

According to the rules of the Budhist religion, the priests are to avow twice a-day that they would conform themselves to their commandments called Apat; and by that means they are bound not to speak a lie,—the Budhus never deny the saying of the priest: but it does not appear in any book of that religion that priests are to be sworn.

The proper method of preventing Budhists from forswearing, would be to have a building constructed in the neighbourhood of the court-house, under the name of Boodalle (house of Budhu), and Dewalle (house of gods), a part of which should consist of an image of Budhu, and a Bana-potta (a book containing doctrines of Budhu), and the other part to consist of the images of several deities adored by them, and to intrust the same to the care of a religious priest and a capoorawla, for the celebration of the different ceremonies which are performed in other temples and pagodas, so that it may be more binding on the minds of the Budhists, and the oath of a Budhist should be taken at the said building.

Amongst Budhists there are some who believe that perjuries will be punished in the world to come, whilst others are of a different opinion, namely, that perjuries are punished by the deities in this world only; and the finding out of these two different sorts of believers being impossible, we think it proper that the person whose oath is required, after having washed himself, should be sent to the abovesaid building, and there the priest should explain to him the Pansil, or the five commandments of Budhu, and then swear him on the Bana-potta, and on the image of Budhu, and afterwards that the capua should also swear him in like manner on the images of gods.

As there are some persons who have little reflection of the punishment which will come upon them in this life, or in the next, for perjury, it would be proper that such a person (after his character and conduct are ascertained by inquiry) should be ordered to take his oath at the said building, on the head of a child of him or her, according to the customary way.

NOTE.—The important amelioration and improvement effected in the civil code of Ceylon, by Sir Alexander Johnston, rendered it highly important to ascertain a legal mode of obtaining the testimony of Budhist priests; and the foregoing detail not being satisfactory, the following were issued, which elicited the desired information.

It is ordered that each magistrate do report to the court what form of oath he conceives to be the most binding upon the Budhist priests in his district. What form upon the other natives professing the Budhist religion, whether that of swearing them upon the halampe, or in the temples, or that upon the head of their children or next of kin; adding whatever information the said magistrate may be able to procure from the best-informed people in his district, specifying at the same time the names and situation of the different people from whom he obtained information on the subject.

It is also ordered, that the magistrate do report what number of Budhist temples, or dewalles, or other places of worship, there may be in his district, specifying also the number of Mohammedan temples and schools, and the number of Christian churches and schools; and he will also add whether many or few of the people in his district are taught to read and to write, specifying whether the greatest number are taught to read and write by the Budhist priests at the Budhist temples, or at the Christian schools by the schoolmaster.

Ceremony of Marriage as practised in Ceylon.

The manner of marrying, according to the Cingalese custom, is, when a bridegroom comes, together with his relations, to the house of the bride's parents, for the purpose of marrying, there shall be spread a white cloth upon a plank called Magoolporoewe, and upon that white cloth there shall be scattered a small quantity of fresh rice, whereupon the bridegroom and the bride shall be put or carried upon the said plank by the uncle of the bride, who shall be on her mother's side—if there are none, by any other nearest relation—and afterwards there shall be delivered by the bridegroom to the bride a gold chain, a cloth, and a woman's jacket, besides which there shall be changed two rings between them; at the same time, the bridegroom gives a white catchy cloth to the mother of the bride, according to his capacity; after which ceremony, and while the bridegroom on the right and the bride on the left are standing upon the said plank, by the uncle of the bride, or by any of her nearest relations, as above stated, shall be tied the two thumbs, one of the bride and one of the bridegroom, by a thread, and under the knot of the said thumbs there shall be holden a plate, and some milk or water poured upon the said knot, and then shall the bride be delivered to the bridegroom. In some places, the two little fingers of the bride and bridegroom are tied, and the said ceremony performed; and, in some places, a chain shall be put by the bridegroom on the bride's neck, a cloth be dressed, and then rings be changed. In some places the marriage is performed without these last-mentioned ceremonies. This manner of marrying of the people who are not Christians was admitted in the time of the Dutch government, on which account the rights of inheriting property are according to the Dutch law.

Names of the Chief Viharis, or Budhu Temples, existing in Ceylon.

Nammobooddaye	Sallewe
Saggamme	Arrame
Pasgamme	Maddiliye
Arrattene	Dippittiye
Maadan-walle	Bampaney
Wilwalle	Kaariyegamme
Kadde-dorre	Gal-lelle
Morre-paaye	Aloot-nowere
Dimboole	Parrane-nowere
Poosool-pittiye	Maawelle

Niyangan-payestaneye
Walwasegodde
Kappagodde
Paddidorre
Ottoo-rale
Abooloogalle
Dannegire-galle
Waagere-galle
Lenne-galle
Allewattoore
Wattoore
Muakorawe
Kawoodoo-gamme
Bissowalle
Daddigamme
Arandorre
Dorewake
Maddebade-wite
Totte-geddere
Madooroo-pittiye
Attene-galle
Ooro-welle
Godde-geddere
Dorenagodde
Yatte-watte
Raagamme
Meegammoowe
Dambe-deniye
Bellegale

Maakaddewarre
Higoole
Bammoonoogamme
Wattaramme
Wattoo-deniye
Poohoriye
Galbadde-gamme
Koloore
Okde-palle
Odde-palle
Algamme
Navekolle-gammoowe
Atkade-vihari
Koorona-galle
Kooroowenniya-galle
Aada-galle
Ebba-galle
Yakdessa-galle
Naate-gamme
San-welle
Kadikawe
Malle-ganney
Kaballa-lenne
Niyede-wanne
Nagalle-vihari
Rasweroowe
Talangammoowe
Perriye-kadoowe
Dewe-giri-vihari

Nawegammoowe
Otooropawo-vihari
Bojas-lenne
Yaaw-lenne
Jayekadoo-lenne
Sagaa-lenne
Kombooro-lenne
Redec-lenne
Rammade-galle
Delwitte
Wilgamme
Asgiriye
Roseegamme
Ambocke
Milele-waane
Bamba-vihari
Rangire-duboolle
Seegiriye
Kalewe
Ballallawe
Anurahde-poreyche Sree-maha-bodinwahanse
Lowamaha-praasadastane
Mirese-watte-vihari
Abbeyegire-vihari
Jeetewanne-vihari
Denne-nakeye
Sangamoo-vihari
Bagre-nakeye
Ratnemaale-chiyetteyeye
Tooparamme-chiyettiyeye
Mihintalle
Attesette-lenne
Neetoopatpaane
Sooroolomaa-moniyawe
Moonnissarame
Attale
Makkame
Mannareme
Maan-totteme
Pomparappoowe
Malwille
Demmene-pattelemehi-Naage-koville
Kadaroogode-vihari
Tellipalle
Mallagamme
Memangame-vihari
Tannedewe-enne.
Agne-dewe-enne
Nage-dewe-enne
Poowagoo-dewe-enne
Kaare-dewe-enne
Molliyawalle

Terikona-malleye
Wilgam-vihari
Tissemaha-vihari
Elandegodde
Kadoorookotteyehe-Attoobaddeye
Lankaa-telekeye
Gaddela-deniye
Wijeyatpaaye
Abbeyegire-vihari
Jetwanne-vihari
Kapil-vihari
Esipattena-raameye
Kossina-raameye
Oorwa-raameye
Daksinna-raameye
Paschimma-raameye
Oottaraa-raameye
*Salloominne-saye
*Silloominne-saye
Demelemaha-saye
Polonnaroo-vihari
Solonnaroo-vihari
Dananjaye-vihari
Kakooloowa-vihari
Dembolagal-vihari
Naka-vihari
Nuwogona-vihari
Soronna-totte
Badooloo-vihari
Yoodeganna-pittiye
Roohoonobadde
Katteregamme
Oggal-alootnowere
Tambegammoowe
Moolgeriye
Owagere-vihari
Dewenowerehe-dewe-raje-baweneye
Otpelimegeye
Sittipelimegeye
Galganney
*Welligamme-aggre-bode-vihari
*Paregodde-vihari
*Tottegammoo-vihari
*Galepaate-vihari
*Bodimaloo-vihari
*Wannwaase-vihari
*Ben-vihari
Kalototte
Bentotte

* Those marked with a star are in the Galle districts.

Sorone
Weedaagamme
Kattalla-walle
Rabookkane
Paanedorey-dewaaleye
Bellan-wille
Pappiliyaane
Naavinne
Wijeya-raameye
Sobaddra-raameye
Jayewardene-kotteyehe Pilleme-geye
Sammoke-dewaaleye
Kitsiremewan-kalleniye
Rajemaha-kalleniye
Wibeesane-dewalaye
Walliwitte
Bolla-galle
Sewa-gamme
Desapatte-noogaye
Kaddoo-dewole
Bomeriye
Sanwelle
Kehelbattoowe
Attooroogere-vihari
Dennegammoowe
Delgammoowe
Battoogeddere
Denewake
Saparegammoowe
Gelee-maleye
Samantekoote-paroo-wateye
Dewagahawe
Ballahille
Sidegalle
Kalloogammoowe
Gangaateleke-vihari
Koballolloowe
Alloo-deniye
Illoopan-deniye
Seen-deniye
Niggammene
Atteregamme
Nadde-welle
Santaanagodde
Wegeriye
Ambecke
Lankatelekeye
Wattedaa-geye
Gaddela-deniye
Delliwille
Gagool-deniye
Oroola-watte
Kattebogodde
Ranmoon-godde

Deldeniye
Manik-dewele
Moneregodde
Kalloogalle
Walgampaaye
Dantotte-watoore
Siliballagodde
Dodanwelle
Deye-kelina-welle
Sooriyegodde
Kobbakadoowe
Ganoroowe
Kooloogammane
Atteregamme
Madde-wele
Gallalle
Dollepielle
Allewattoogodde
Kohone
Tebbatowawe
Abille-vihari
Aaloke-vihari
Koroowa-bogambewe
Kadoo-wele
Doono-wele
Ammoono-gamme
Abellenitte-wele
Sree-malwatte
Senkade-gale
Aloot-vihari
Parene-vihari
Naage-wimaaneye
Oposatta-raameye
Sree-dagistraw-daledaa-Mandireye.

Translation of a Budhist Tract on the merits of performing Budhu's precepts.

Question.— In case the dead can inherit the six habitations of the blessed, each by one particular good act, it then rests only upon six particular pious acts; are the other charitable acts then to be accomplished in vain?

Answer.—No rules of that kind appear in the precepts of the religion.

The precepts of the religion that treat on this subject are, a person having renounced the ten sins, and living as becomes the ten good acts, preserving in every respect the five moral objects, who also dies in full possession of the same, with a desire at his departure to be born in any of the said blessed habitations, he will accordingly inherit it.

The departure of a person suddenly from the present world will cause his future situation according to the manner of his behaviour in it, either in a blessed habitation or a miserable one.

The good acts are, the preservation of three faiths, eight pious acts, (the five moral objects inclusive), and farther, ten good acts, the above eight included.

This life is applicable to an individual not in the priesthood; and if it be a priest of the inferior class of the denomination of Samanera, or Ganoon-nancy, he must live to the same dignity, or becoming the above principles, with the additional preservation of forty different good rules. The priests of the superior class, who are denominated Oepasampata, or Teroonancy, are to live a pious life to its utmost extent, independent of the above-mentioned principles.

Tract on the Castes in Ceylon.

There are four high castes, namely, Royal, Braminy, Real Chitty, and Vellala, or, as the Cingalese expresses, Raja, Bammunu, Wellanda, and Gowy.

There are eighteen other inferior castes, denominated, in general terms, Naggar-akkarayo. The word naggarra means the city within which, and in such other divisions inhabited by any of the said four castes, they cannot reside; and, as they are subjects of them, they are known by the general appellation of Naggar-akkarayo.

The denominations which are applicable to each of the said castes, and the duties they are liable to, are as follow:—

1st, Peesakaraye, namely, Hallagama or Chalia, subject to the government duty of carrying palanquins, as also to peel cinnamon.

2d, Carrawoo, namely, fishers.

3d, Darawoo, namely chandos, liable to the government duty of training elephants.

4th, Nawandanna, consisting of goldsmiths, blacksmiths, and carpenters.

5th, Baddahallaya, namely, potters.

6th, Raddawu, namely, washers.

7th, Pannikky, namely, barbers.

8th, Sommaru, being leather-workmen and shoemakers.

9th, Hakkuroo, namely, jaggariers.

10th, Hunnoo, namely, chunam-burners.

11th, Berrawayo, being tom-tom beaters.

12th, Ollie, liable to the duty of procuring coal.

13th, Kinnaru, liable to the duty of making bamboo baskets, rush mats, &c.

14th, Padduwoo, subject to the duty of erecting walls of houses.

15th, Gahalagambadayoo, subject to the duty of disposing or removing out of the city which is called Nuwara the corpses, and carcases of elephants and other dead animals.

16th, Palie, liable to perform the duty of washers to the lowest castes.

17th, Hinnawoo, being the washers of the chalias.

18th, Roddy, subject to the duty of making ropes of leather, for tying elephants and other animals.

Of these eighteen castes, the 15th and 16th abovesaid are not in this part of the island.

A short Description of the different Castes on the Island of Ceylon.

Question.—Into how many different castes are the natives of this island divided?

Answer.—Exclusive of the Malabars, there were originally only four castes; but, in process of time, the fourth of these castes was subdivided into twenty-four different castes, making altogether twenty-seven castes.

What are the names of those castes?

The four original castes were the Kshatria or Rajapoot caste, the Bramiu caste, the Wysya or merchant caste, and the Kshudra or low caste.

Into what castes was the said lŏw caste divided?

The said Kshudra, or low caste, was divided into the four-and-twenty following castes, viz.:—

1. The Goigâma or Vellala caste, which is distinguished by the following names, viz.:—Khetta Jiewakayo, Kassakayo, Goyankaranno, Goigama Etto, Goi Bamuno, Goi Kulayo, Sanduruwo or Handuruwo, or, vulgarly, Wellalas,—which word comes from the Malabar.

2. The Halawgama, or Chalia caste, which is

distinguished by the following names: Paisakara, Brahmanayo, Tantavayo, Paisacawrayo, Paihairo or Paihaira-kulayo, Salagamayo .or Halagamayo, Mahabaddey-Etto, or, vulgarly, Chalias.

3. The Nawandanno, or goldsmiths, which is distinguished by the following names; viz. Cammakarayo, Suwannakarayo, Ayokarayo, Achariyo, Gooroowarayo, Nawankaranno, Nawandanno, Lokuruwo, and Kamburo.

4. The Waduwo, or carpenters, are distinguished by the following names; viz. Tachakayo and Waduwo.

5. The Mananno, or tailors, are distinguished by the following names; viz. Tunnawayo, Sochikayo, Sannawliyo, and Mahanno.

6. The Radawo, or washers, are distinguished by the following names; viz. Ninne Jakaya, Rajakayo, Radau, Paihaira Haliyo, Paidiyo, and Hainayo.

7. The Panikkayo, or barbers, are distinguished by the following names; viz. Cappakayo, Nahapikayo, Karranawiyo, Panikkiyo, and Embettayo.

8. The Sanmahanno, or shoemakers, are distinguished by the following names; viz. Chammarakarayo, Rattakarayo, Sommarayo, and Samwaduwo.

9. The Chandos are distinguished by the names of Soudikayo, Maggawikayo, Surawbeejayo, Maddino, Surawo, and Durawo.

10. The Potters are called by the names of Coombakarayo, Culawlayo, Pandittayo, Bada-Sellayo, and Cumballu or Cumbalo.

11. The Fishers are called by the names of Wagurikayo, Jawlikayo, Kay-wattayo, Kaywulo, and Carawo.

12. Shooters, or hunters, are called by the names of Weddo, Wanacharakayo.

13. The Drummers, or tom-tom beaters, are called by the following names; viz. Atodya-wadakayo, Bhera-wadakayo, Berawayo, and Ganitayo.

14. The Jagerers are distinguished by the following names; viz. Hangarammoo, Sakuro or Pakuro, and Candey Etto.

15. The Lime-burners are distinguished by the following names; viz. Chunna-karayo and Sunno or Hunno.

16. Grass-cutters or branch-cutters for the elephants are distinguished by the following names; viz. Pannayo and Jana Capanno.

17. Iron-burners, or makers of iron from stone, are called Yamanayo.

18. The Scavengers are called by the follow-

ing names; viz. Pookkoosayo, Pooplia, Chaddakayo, and Gahalayo.

19. Basket-makers are called by the following names; viz. Cooloopotto, Sinnawo, Hadayo, and Welwaduwo.

20. Palankeen-bearers are distinguished by the following names; viz. Paddo, Paduwo, and Batgama Etto.

21. Flower-gardeners are called Mawlacawrayo and Malcaruwo.

22. Maskers, or masked dancers, are called Uhuliyo and Oliyo.

23. Mat-weavers are called Pannakarayo, Cattakarayo, Tinakarayo, Kinnaru, and Hainawalayo.

24. Rodias, or barbarians, are called Rogadikayo, Adarmishtayo, Wasalayo, and Rodiyo.

Some of these castes or classes of people have existed for the space of 2360 years, and others for only the space of 2120 years.

Explanation of the above Names of the different Castes.

1. The Kshatria. The meaning of this word is landlord or landowner.

In the early ages of the world all men were equal, in consequence of which many contentions arose among them; and, in order to prevent or appease their strifes, they elected a chief to govern them. To this chief they all submitted, and for his support they gave the one-tenth of all the produce of their lands; and hence came the name of Kshatria or landlord.

As this landlord endeavoured by all means to satisfy the people, they gave him the name of rajah, which word is derived from the word *ranjite*, to satisfy, and hence came the word rajah, which is considered as equivalent to king; and as it was one of the Kshatria caste who became the first king of Ceylon, his name was changed from Kshatria to Rajah: and the kings of this island are called by the Cingalese Rajjuruwo.

2. Bramiu or Brachman caste. The meaning of the word is to put away sin; and hence in the said first ages of the world, such people as refrained from sin were called Brahmanayo, or Bramins; and as some of these men found their way to this island, and continued to reside herein, their name has been, by the Cingalese, changed from Brahmanayo to Bamino, which is, however, of precisely the same meaning.

3. The Wysya caste. The meaning of this word is to give and take, buy and sell, make merchandise, &c.; and hence, in the beginning, people who made merchandise were called Wysyayo, and had three different modes of employment. The first was dealing or merchandising, the second was that of feeding cattle, and the third was tilling the ground. Some of this description of people having come and dwelt in this island, their name has been, by the Cingalese, changed from Wysyayo to Welindo (merchant).

In those days all who did not belong to the above description of people were called Kshudrayo, that is, low people, and were divided into several classes; and especially in Ceylon were divided as follows:—

1. The Vellalas, because they lived by agriculture, were called Kettau Jiewakayo: the word signifies livers by the field.

Because they ploughed the land, they were called Kassakayo-ploughers; because they sowed or cultivated rice, they were called Goyankaranno, sowers or cultivators of rice.

Because they cultivated other grains, herbs, and vegetables, they were called Goiyo, or Goigama Etto, cultivators.

Because they were not guilty of destroying the creatures, but lived by agriculture alone, they were called Goi Bamuno, cultivating bramins.

Because they descended from ancestors who were cultivators of the soil, they were called Goikulayo, *i. e.* of the cultivating caste.

In the cultivation of their lands they were subject to the scoffs and abuse of their ill-disposed neighbours; and because they bore such insults with patience, and did not retort, they were called Sanduruwo, *i. e.* the Pacific, or Sons of Peace.

Sanduruwo and Handuruwo are the same.

2. The people called Chalias.

Because they were weavers of gold and silver thread, and refrained from every vicious practice, they were called Paisakara Brahmanayo, *i.e.* gold and silver-weaving bramins.

Because they stretched and ordered their warp, and wove it with weft, they were called Tantavayo, that is, yarn-stretching weavers.

Because they wove gold and silver thread they were called Paisacawrayo, *i.e.* weavers of gold and silver thread: the same word changed into Cingalese, makes Paihairo.

Because they were descended from the weaver

caste they were called Salagamayo, *i. e.* of the weaver caste.

The King of Dambadenia, in the Seven Corles, called Wathimi Buwanaika Rajah, in order to establish a cloth manufactory, caused a third colony of weavers to be sent from Jambudwipa (the continent), and appropriated to their use the place called Chilaw, and there they constructed spacious apartments, or halls, for the use of their manufactories, and hence they were called by the name of Salagamayo, that is, people who inhabit the large hall-village; hence the word Chalia caste now commonly used; and from this also came the name of the place Salawa, but now commonly called Chilaw.

In the time of the Portuguese, the said people were taken to serve as cinnamon-peelers; and as the cinnamon at that time was the principal source of revenue, it was called the great rent, which, in Cingalese, signifies Mahabadde, and hence the name of Mahabaddey-Etto, that is, people of the cinnamon department, was given to them.

3. The Goldsmiths.

Because they work in copper, brass, and silver, they are called Cammakarayo, which word signifies workers in metals, and because they work in gold, they are called Suwanna-karayo, which word signifies workers in gold.

Because they work in iron they are called Ayokarayo, which word signifies workers in iron. As these people were found useful to society, they were complimented with the name of Achariyo, which word signifies masters, and is expressed in Cingalese by the word Gooroo-warayo, masters.

Because they are in the habit of making old things new, they are called Nawankaranno, which word signifies makers of new; and because they know how to make things new, they are called Nawandanno, that is, knowers of the art of making new things out of old.

Because they melt their metal and form a vessel, they are called Lokuruwo, that is, founders or makers of vessels with melted metal. They are sometimes called Cammaro, which word is a corruption of Camburo, which is a term of reproach given to them because they take employment from high and low. Kamburanawa signifies to become subject or slave.

4. The Carpenters.

Because they smooth and carve wood they are called Tachakayo, which word signifies smoother or planer.

Because by their workmanship they enhance the value of timber they are called Waduwo, that is, enhancers of value.

N.B. The carpenters are in some places considered by many as belonging to the goldsmith caste, but this is not authorised by any book.

5. The Tailors.

Because they sew pieces of cloth together, they are called Tunnawayo, which word signifies weavers, or sewers of pieces; because they work with a needle, they are called Sochikayo, that is, workers with the needle; because they make armour or covering for the body with cloth, they are called Sannawliyo, that is, makers of cloth armour; and because they sew, they are called Mahanno, that is, sewers.

6. The Washers.

Because they restore to its former state what has been defiled, they are called Ninney Jakaya, that is, restorers.

Because they remove the dust from the garment they wash, they are called Rajakayo, that is, removers of dust, and is expressed by the Cingalese word Radau.

Because they make foul clothes clean, they

are called Paihara Haliyo, that is, cloth-cleaners.

Because they take payment for their work, they are called Paidiyo, that is, takers of payment.

Because they wash the foul linen of little children, and thereby are supposed to obtain the affection of the child for whom they wash, they are called Hainayo, which is a corruption of Snaihayo, beloved persons.

7. The Barbers.

Because they cut the hair of the head and beard, they are called Cappakayo, that is, cutters.

Because they, by cutting the hair of the head and beard, create comfort to the mind, they are called Nahapikayo, that is, comforters.

Because they use a razor, they are called Karranawiyo, that is, razor-users, or workers with the razor: because they cut the foliage of the head and beard, they are called Pannikkiyo, that is, leaf or foliage-cutters.

Because, as ministers of the cabinet, they approach the person of the king, they are called Embettayo, that is, near approachers, or livers near.

8. The Shoemakers.

Because they dress skins, they are called Chammakarayo, that is, skin-dressers, or workers in skin; because they make harness for chariots (or carriages), they are called Rattakarayo, that is, carriage-makers, which is expressed in Cingalese by the word Sommarayo; and because they do to skins what carpenters do to timbers, they are called Samwaduwo, that is, skin-carpenters.

9. The Chando caste.

Because they extract toddy from the trees, which makes all hearts glad; and because the man who first made the discovery of this art was called Soudamakaya, they are called Soudikayo, that is, producers of lust.

Because they sell toddy, which intoxicates, they are called Maggawikayo, that is, venders of intoxication.

Because they furnish toddy for the bakers, they are called Surawbeejayo, that is, toddy-makers, or producers of good taste.

Because they prune the trees, they are called Madinno, that is, pruners.

Because they furnish men with toddy, which inspires generous sentiments, they are called Surawo, that is, givers of pleasant taste.

Because evil is often the consequence of intoxication from toddy, they are called Durawo, that is, producers, or givers of the evil-producing taste.

10. The Potters.

The first two potters were called the one Coombeya and the other Culala, and therefore the potters are called Coombakarayo and Culawlayo, after the said two men.

Because they make their wares according to their own fancy, without any previous form, they are called Pandittayo, that is, wise men.

Because they burn their wares in places or halls close to their dwelling-houses, they are called Bada Sellayo, that is, possessors of near halls.

The name Cumballu, by which they are sometimes called, is derived from Koombakarayo.

11. The Fishers.

Because they are in the habit of wading and working in the water, they are called Wagurikayo, that is, workers or dealers in the water.

Because they make use of nets, they are called Jawlikayo, that is, workers with nets.

Because in fishing they surround the water, they are called Kay-wattayo, that is, surrounders of water.

The name Kaywulo, by which they are sometimes called, is derived from Kaywattayo; because they have their dwellings along the shore, they are called Carawo, that is, shore-people, or dwellers on the shore.

12. The Shooters.

In order to escape from oppression, or from being tormented, having taken refuge in the jungle, where they live by killing the creatures, they are called Weddo, that is, tormentors; and as they pass their time in the jungle or wilderness, they are called Wanacharakayo, that is, wild men, or men of the desert.

13. The Berawayas, drummers or tom-tommers, having been first appointed to do this duty by the minister called Atodya, who himself made and played on the first timbrel or drum with one head, which also was called by his name, they are called Atodya-wadakayo, that is, tormentors or beaters of the Atodya, or drum with one head; and because they beat the baira, or tom-tom, they are called Berawayas, or Berawayo, that is, tom-tom beaters; and because they are astro-

logers or calculators of the motions of the planets, they are called Ganitayo, that is, counters or calculators.

14. The Jagerers.

Because they make cakes of sugar or jagery as hard as stone, they are called Sakuro, or Pakuro, that is, stone-makers.

Because they defend or take care of the gardens of the priesthood, and because they take their own sisters as wives, they are called Sangarammu, which word has a double meaning: it signifies, in the first place, defenders of the gardens of the priesthood; and, in the second place, cohabitors with sisters, or with own blood.

And because they live on the mountains, they are called Candey Etto, that is, Candians or mountaineers.

15. The Lime-burners.

Because they burn and reduce to powder stones and trees, they are called Chunna-karayo, that is, reducers to powder; and the same thing is expressed by Sunno or Hunno, by which names the said people are called.

16. Grass or Branch-cutters.

Because they cut down branches and leaves

from the trees to feed the elephants, they are called Pannayo, that is, leaf-gatherers, leaf-cutters, or leaf-strippers; and because they cut grass for horses, they are called Jana Capanno, that is, grass-cutters.

17. Iron-makers.

Because they understand how to burn iron, they are called Yamanayo, that is, iron-creators or iron-makers.

18. The Scavengers.

Because they gather the dirt of a city, they are called Pookkoosayo, that is, removers of the city dirt.

Because they carry away the faded flowers from the altars of the gods, they are called Pupphachaddakayo, that is, casters away of flowers.

Because they throw away the dirt, they are called Kasalayo, that is, throwers away of dirt.

But the Cingalese, changing the *k* into *g*, and the permutable *s* into *h*, generally call them Gahalayo.

19. The Basket-makers.

Because they make winnowers with the peeling of bamboo-cane and reed, they are called Cooloopotto, that is, peeling winnower-makers.

Because they weave or plait their materials, they are called Hadayo, that is, plaiters.

Because they work with or make articles with rods, they are called Welwaduwo, that is, rod-carpenters.

Because they cut and bring home their materials, they are called Sinnawo, that is, cutters.

20. The Paduwas or Palankeen-bearers.

Because they reap the fields of grain for a certain proportion thereof, which proportion, amounting to one-fifth of the whole, is called Walahana, that is, hire, they are called Baddo, of which word the *b* being changed to *p*, makes it Paddo; and hence comes Paduwo, that is, rice-makers.

Because the villages which are possessed by the king, and which produce a great deal of rice, are given to be cultivated by these people, they are called Batgammu, or Batgamayo, or Batgama Etto, that is, rice-village people.

N.B. Bat signifies boiled rice, not raw.

21. The Flower-gardeners.

Because they cultivate, string, and make garlands, or chains of flowers, they are called

Mawlacawrayo, that is, chain-makers. The same word has been turned into Malcaruwo, which implies chain-makers, and also flower-makers.

22. Maskers, or Masked Dancers.

Because they appear with masked faces; make gestures, &c., they are called Uhuliyo; and, by permutation of characters, the same word is turned into Oliyo, that is, disguised actors or comedians.

23. Mat-weavers.

Because they weave a kind of leaves, they are called Pannakarayo, that is, leaf-workers.

Because they beat some kinds of trees till they become of a woolly substance, which substance they take and make into mats, they are called Cattakarayo, that is, workers in hard matter, or in wood.

Because they make some kinds of grass into mats, they are called Tinakarayo, that is, workers in grass; and by changing the *ti* into *ki*, and doubling the *n*, and suppressing the *k*, and by changing the *ra* into *ru*, the Cingalese call them Kinnaru, which signifies the same thing—workers in grass.

Because they make some mats with fringed

selvedges, they are called Hainawalayo, that is, fringe-makers.

24. The Rodias.

Because they, being lepers, were driven into the wilderness, where they remained separate from society, they were called Rogadikayo, that is, incurable sick men.

Because they were addicted to bestiality, they were called Adarmishtayo, that is, unrighteous men.

Because they are inferior, and subject to all people, they are called Wasalo or Wasalayo, that is, subject to all.

The name Rodia is a corruption of Rogadikyo.—N.B. The delivering any person to the Rodias is reckoned the greatest degradation. In former days, when the king happened to be displeased with any of his concubines, this was the punishment inflicted on the offender:—A Rodia being called, he was told to take the offender in charge, which he did by taking the betel from his own and putting it into her mouth; after which she was obliged to remain among the Rodias till death.

That the above-mentioned difference of caste has obtained in the island of Ceylon, from the preceding dates, appears in different books. But with regard to the Vellalas, it is to be observed, that since the time of Parakrama Bahu Rajah, who reigned about 800 years ago, they have assumed the title of high caste.

As one of the employments of the merchant caste was to till the ground, they claimed affinity with them, and, instead of three, they now enumerate four noble castes; viz. the Rajah caste, the Brahman caste, the Merchant caste, and the Vellala or Goigama caste, and all the rest they call Kshudra or low; which assumption, however, is not countenanced by any written authority whatever, but, on the contrary, is represented in the books as inconsistent and improper.

Time and circumstances have introduced some alterations with regard to rank and precedency among the natives of Ceylon, though divided according to the above classification by the most ancient writings.

According to the present bias which rests on the minds of the natives, the different castes rank as follows:—

1. The vellala, or goigama.
2. The halagama, or cinnamon-peelers.
3. The fishers.
4. The chandos.
5. The shooters.

6. The goldsmiths.
7. The carpenters.
8. The tailors.
9. The potters.
10. The washers.
11. The barbers.
12. The shoemakers.
13. The lime-burners.
14. The basket-makers.
15. The jagerers.
16. The berawayas, or drummers.
17. The maskers, or actors.
18. The grass-cutters.
19. The iron-makers.
20. The palankeen-bearers.
21. The flower gardeners.
22. The scavengers.
23. The mat-weavers.
24. The rodias; which, added to the three noble castes, make in all twenty-seven castes.

Among these castes, the Vellalas and the Chalias contend who are the most honourable, but though the first say we are high, and the second say we are high, it must be acknowledged, that, according to the usage which obtains in Ceylon, the Vellalas is the higher of the two.

But it is not only between the Vellala and the Chalia castes that there is a contest for honour; the Fishers and Chandos are equally jealous of one another; and from thence down to the Rodia, there is a constant strife among the Cingalese for honour.

Some account of the world, of mankind, of the generations of man, of the division of castes, and particularly of the Pesa Cowra Brahmania, now called the Mahabadda, or Chalia caste, as taken from the books of the ancient magi, or wise men, and the whole histories of the Budhists.

As appears in the book called Derga Nekha, in the book called Angotra Nekha Jutaka Atuwawa, as stated by Budhu himself, and in the book called Sawrasangraya, it appears, as said by the rahatoons (deified men), that this world having been annihilated was again formed, not made; but when the same was void, like the space within the rim of a timbrel, or a dark house, in which state there were a kela of lacses of unformed worlds, while darkness so pervaded all, it came to pass, that like as trees in their season put forth their flowers and yield their fruits without abortion, so in due time Brahma descended from the Brahma-Lōka, or highest heaven, which decayeth not, nor is subject to decay, and with the light of his own body illumined the dark abyss which now constitutes this world, and walking in the heavens, joyed in the possession of his glory.

In the book called Sumangala Wilasina Atuwawa, and in Tikawa, or explanation of the said book, it is written, that in the aforesaid manner, one Brahma, and then another, from time to time descended and dwelt in the heavens, and from the self-inherent virtue of the said Brahmas, this world below became sweet as the honey of the honey-bee.

It having so happened, it came then to pass, that one of the Brahmas, beholding the earth, said to himself, what thing is this? and with one of his fingers having touched the earth, put it to the tip of his tongue, and perceived the same to be deliciously sweet; from which time all the Brahmas ate of the sweet earth for the space of 60,000 years. In the meantime, having coveted in their hearts the enjoyment of this world, they began to say one to another, this part is mine and that is thine; and so fixing boundaries to their respective shares, divided the earth between them. On account of the Brahmas having been guilty of this covetousness, the earth lost its sweetness, and then it came to pass that the earth brought forth a production called Parpataka, a kind of mushroom; and these mushrooms the Brahmas ate for the space of 15,000 years; and having again coveted distinct shares of the earth so producing mushrooms, and having, as in the former case, appointed limits to their respective shares, the earth ceased to yield any more mushrooms.

After this the earth produced a kind of creeping plant called Badralataw, and this plant the Brahmas enjoyed for the space of 35,000 years, and then, in the same manner as before, the earth ceased to produce the said plant.

The earth next produced a kind of tree called Calpa Warkshia, which trees the Brahmas enjoyed for 2,200,000 years, and then, in the same manner as before, the earth ceased to produce calpa-trees.

The earth then produced a kind of grain-rice which was void of all husk; and this grain the Brahmas enjoyed for the space of 35,000 years, and then, as before, the earth ceased to yield the said grain.

The earth then produced another kind of rice-grain, also without any husk; and this the

Brahmas enjoyed for 60,000 years, and then, in consequence of the covetousness of the Brahmas, the earth ceased to yield the said grain again. It is written in the abovesaid books, and in the books of ancients, called Janamansa and Soottoottara, &c., that because of the sons of the Brahmas having greatly increased, and because of their having used substantial food, the light which once shone in their bodies was extinguished, and also the different qualities of matter began to grow in them, and their lustful desires began likewise to increase, and then there began to appear a race of women, men, and hermaphrodites, and lusting the one after the other prevailed.

It then came to pass, that some Brahmas who were more virtuously inclined, disapproved of the sexual depravity, and separating themselves from the rest, repaired into the wilderness, and from them proceeded what is now called the Brahma or Bramin caste, which caste was, in process of time, divided again into three castes; and on account of their having originally descended from the heaven called Brahma-Lōka, and having preserved their purity, they are still called the Brahma, or Bramiu cast.

The three castes into which the said Brahmas were divided are called—

1st. Soama Brahmas.

2d. Waida Brahmas.

3d. Paisakawra Brahmas.

The Soama Brahmas, are so called from their excellence in wisdom and knowledge, and on account of their virtuous lives, through which they meet with the favour and esteem of kings and great men, who choose them for their instructors.

The Waida Brâhmas are those who devote themselves to the study of the mysteries of their religion, which consist in sympathies and charms, and by virtue of which they perform charitable cures in the bodies of the distressed.

The Paisakawra Brahmas are those who wear cloths of gold and silk, and costly garments. These Brahmas having descended from heaven, having from the light of their own bodies illumined the obscure, and having depraved themselves to such a degree that from gods they became men, found themselves at last involved in darkness, and then they all, with one mind, began to deplore their fallen state, and desired light as a blessing, upon which the sun came into existence.

On the same day that the sun began to shine, a virtuous Brahma was born, who was therefore called the Son of the Sun; and the sun having shined thirty (Indian) hours, did set, and then it became again dark. Whereupon the Brahmas, with one accord, desired to have another light, and then was born or came into existence the meek and gentle moon.

In this manner the Brahmas were once glorious and happy, and fell from that glory; and again, through their virtuous actions, obtained many blessings, and by their industry in cultivating the ground, &c., acquired great riches. But then it came to pass, that they began to covet and steal the goods of one another, in consequence of which, quarrels and discord took place; on which account some of the wise men amongst them assembled together, and took counsel how they might prevent the said evils; and having drawn many people together, represented that it was because they had no appointed chief to govern them that the said troubles happened to them, which they were obliged to suffer.

A resolution was accordingly made to elect a chief, who should reign over them, and protect the good and punish the wicked; and, accordingly, as the abovesaid Son of the Sun was reputed virtuous above all the rest, they elected him to be their king, assuring him, that whoever would not obey his laws they themselves would punish and correct; and, therefore, from that day he was called Maha Sammata Rajaroowo, that is, by the general voice of the people elected king.

From the time that the Brahmas descended to this lower world, until the day that the Son of the Sun was elected king, was forty-three hundred and twenty thousand years.

In the above-mentioned book (and as was said by the rahatoons in the book called Maha Puja Walia, and in the book called Choola Nerdese and Maha Nerdesa) we find it came to pass, that in process of time the royal caste of Rajah Wangsa was divided into five parts; and it also happened, that those who maintained themselves by merchandising were called merchants, and they were likewise divided into two classes. Exclusive of those already mentioned, all the rest of the world were considered low, and called low-caste people.

Of these four castes, namely, the Brahmas'; secondly, the King's caste; thirdly, the Merchants' caste; and fourthly, the low caste, it sometimes happened that the Brahmas were considered the highest caste, and sometimes that the King's caste was considered highest.

Accordingly, it appears in the book called Dampaya, as having been said by Budhu, and in the book called Atuwawa, as having been said by the Atuwachary (the authors of the said book), as follows : —

That in the quarter of the world called Jambu-dwipa, one of the Paisakawra, or weaver Brahmas, named Huma Sena, was made a king; and in the book called Dhirga Nicaw Tiecawa, it appears as having been said by the rahatoons, that another of the Paisakawra Brahmas, named Jaishta, was also made a king; and in the books called Wangsa, Dupikaya, Soottoollaria, and Sooroo Namakia, as having been said by the ancients, that the castes rank next to each other in the following manner; viz. first, the Rajah Brahmas; secondly, the Paisakawra Brahmas; thirdly, the Merchants; fourthly, the Grahapatias, or husbandmen; and so on, from one to another. And accordingly, in the countries called Makanda Rata, Maha Patuna Rata, Cawsia Ràta, Grandhawra Rata, Sooloopata Rata, all belonging to the aforesaid quarter of the world, called Jambu-dwipa, there were no fewer than thirty-five of the Paisakawra Brahmas made king; and that in the country called Sagala Nuwara, also belonging to the same quarter of the world, there was a man of the Merchant caste, called Melindoo, made a king; and again, that in the country called

Caoroo Rata, there was another man of the Merchant caste, called Maha Damila, who was made king, and reigned in the city called Indepat Nuwara; and in many other books it appears, that of the aforesaid two castes, many were promoted to the first dignities in many places. With regard to the common castes, it appears in the book that some individuals have been promoted to courtly stations, but it nowhere appears that any one ever was made a king from the abovesaid two castes.

Having thus said something which, according to the ancient books, took place in Jambu-dwipa, we turn to speak of what took place in Ceylon. This Ceylon, as appears in many books, belongs to Jambu-dwipa, which is one quarter of the world, and contains 100 yoduns, (one yodun is equal to sixteen miles), and was, for a great length of time, a mere wilderness, and an abode of devils. While in this state, it came to pass that a king called Sinhabau Rajah, of Wagoo Rata, in Jambu-dwipa, had a son whose name was Wijaya, who began to oppress and torment the people of that country; which behaviour came at last to the ears of his father, who then called to mind that it was written in the book called Angotra

Sanjaya, as having been prophesied by Budhu, that this prince, his son, was to become king of Ceylon; he thereupon called his son, and, together with 700 giants, which were born on the same day with the prince himself, put him on board ship, and sent him to Ceylon, which at that time bore the name of Srilaka. Whilst yet in the midst of the sea, the prince lifted up his eyes and beheld the mountain Samanta Coota, that is, Adam's Peak, and concluded in his mind that this was an island which properly belonged to him and his followers; and, having made the shore of Ceylon, this prince and his giants landed at a haven called Tammene Totta (said to be near Manaar), and there took up his abode. From hence this prince sent presents to the country called Pawndy Rata; whence, in return for his presents, he obtained a princess to wife, with 700 women, and servants of the five sorts, in her train. This princess he crowned as his queen, and made her the first of his consorts; and the 700 women who came in her train he gave as wives to the 700 giants who attended and came with him from Jambu-dwipa. While reigning as king in this country, he sent many ambassadors and presents to the King of Pawndy Rata, in Jambu-dwipa; and having brought over many brahmas to this country, he conferred on them many honours; supplied them with elephants, horses, chariots, umbrellas, canopies, gold, pearls, precious stones, and other kind of precious treasure, and also abundance of lands; besides which, he raised them to great power in the country: and thus commanding universal respect, those brahmas made their abode in this island. The said king, when he had reigned thirty-eight years, went to the other world.

Since that time till this day the descendants of the said king sat on the throne of Ceylon, as appears in the books called Bodi-wansa, Maha-wansa, and Raja-waly.

It further appears by the said books, and also by the books called Jana-wansa, made by the rahatoons and the ancient people, that the second king of Ceylon was Deweny Paetissa Rajah; and that in his time the King of Jambu-dwipa and Darma Sōka Rajah sent as a present to the King of Ceylon the bo-tree; and to 100 of the Paisa brahmas, with a chief man over them, whom he sent at the same time, he gave presents of pearls and precious stones, elephants and horses, &c. And when they arrived at Ceylon, the said King of Ceylon receiving them with great joy, bestowed upon them twice as much as the King of Jambu-dwipa had done, and many villages and fields, and great honours, and made them manufacture fine cloths.

It appears also in the books called Sacranawatawra, and Raja Ratnacari written by the ancients, that a king of Ceylon, called Wijaya Prawkrama Bahu, who held his court at the city of Dambadeny, sent presents of precious stones to the country called Soly Rata, and caused several expert Paisa brahmas to come from thence to Ceylon, and conferred on them lands, and male and female slaves, elephants and horses, pearls and precious stones, and different kinds of treasure, and great honours; and then taking up their abode in this country, were treated with great respect by the husbandmen of Graha Patty Brahma, that is, the Vellalas.

The second Paisa brahmas who were brought for the first time during the reign of Wijaya Rajah, and those who came for the second time under the reign of Deweny Paetissa Rajah, having in process of time lost their expertness at weaving, betook themselves to the cultivation of their lands, in order to find a maintenance, and lived by that means.

The Paisa brahmas who for the third time came with the king called Wijaya Prawkrama

Bahu Rajah, are the people now called Chalias, of the Mahabadda. These Paisa brahmas, at their arrival on this island, obtained villages from the king, where they erected their working-shops, or mandoos, for their looms, which shops were called Sawlawa (signifying hall or salle); from which circumstances it came to pass that the name of Paisakawrra Brahma fell into disuse, and, instead thereof, the name of Sawlawgama was usually adopted.

It came to pass, after these Paisa brahmas had continued for a great length of time to manufacture their cloths, that, from the smallness of the island, and the dearth of gold thread and silk, the said branch began to decline, and very few cloths were manufactured; and at last, in the time of the king called Buwanaika Bahu Rajah, the King of Portugal established himself on this island, and made forts; and after the said Portuguese began to govern, they thought proper to make the cinnamon an article of revenue, and then it happened that the said Paisa brahmas, or people of Hawlagamie, were appointed to that service; and accordingly the said branch of government service began to be carried on by the said people.

Now it is to be observed, that any article set apart for the use of the king, or his stores, or from which any revenue is derived, is called in Cingalese Badda; and as the cinnamon of this island was soon found to be the chief article of the revenue, and more profitable than any other branch of revenue whatsoever, the same was distinguished by the name of Mahabadda, or chief revenue, and the people employed in that department are called the people of Mahabadda to this day. And hence it follows, that although the said Paisa brahmas, or Chalias, amongst the numerous tribes that are in Ceylon are but few in number, yet they are by no means a low people,—

1st, Because, according to the doctrine of Budhu, when the king of the gods, Sakkraia, who brings much good to the world, chooses to take upon himself the form of a man, it is in the form of a Paisakawra Brahma that he chooses to appear; which Budhu himself declares in the books called Coodhaka Nikawya, and in the books called Jutaka.

2ndly, Because, in many other books of the Budhist religion, the said people are spoken of as a noble and renowned caste; and because that in Jambu-dwipa many of the said caste have obtained the dignity of kings; and because also that in Jambu-dwipa many of the said caste were promoted to the highest and principal stations; and because it is written in the books called Soottootara Suranamaka and Wansa Dipicaya, that many of the said caste succeeded each other as kings of their respective countries; and because the Budhus and the Chakrawarty Rajas always proceed from this caste, and no other. Because it is written in the said book called Sooranamaka, that the first caste is the Sastria Brahmas, the second is the Paisa Brahmas, and the third is the Wysya, and the fourth the Grahapatties, or Vellalas; and because it is written in the Malabar books of their ancient kings and histories, that the said caste is noble and dignified; and also because that, even in this country, till a short time ago, the said caste, or, as they are now called, Chalias, were privileged in such a manner that they were not obliged to pay any tax or duty whatsoever, either upon their merchandise, their landed property, or any thing else whatsoever; and because they, the said Chalias or Paisa brahmas, were in like manner exempted from paying any toll or ferry-money at any gravetts or ferry to which they might come; and because the said people, however poor they may be, will not serve any other people than the government, or those who govern; and, lastly, because the people of this caste in particular will hold no intimacy with any but themselves, in order thereby to preserve their honour unsullied; also to their ruler they are faithful and constant, and are continually employed by, and are the most faithful servants of, government.

E END.

.R SQUARE.

Lightning Source UK Ltd.
Milton Keynes UK
UKHW012109271218
334533UK00006B/613/P

9 781330 604281